Tweets from the Campaign Trail

Bonner Beiträge zur Medienwissenschaft

Edited by Caja Thimm

Volume 11

PL ACADEMIC RESEARCH

Alex Frame / Arnaud Mercier / Gilles Brachotte / Caja Thimm (eds.)

Tweets from the Campaign Trail

Researching Candidates' Use of Twitter During the European Parliamentary Elections

PL ACADEMIC RESEARCH

Bibliographic Information published by the Deutsche Nationalbibliothek
The Deutsche Nationalbibliothek lists this publication in the Deutsche Nationalbibliografie; detailed bibliographic data is available in the internet at http://dnb.d-nb.de.

Library of Congress Cataloging-in-Publication Data
Names: Frame, Alex, 1976- editor.
Title: Tweets from the campaign trail: researching candidates' use of Twitter during the European parliamentary elections / Alex Frame, Arnaud Mercier, Gilles Brachotte, Caja Thimm (eds.).
Description: Frankfurt am Main : Peter Lang, 2016. | Series: Bonner Beiträge zur Medienwissenschaft ; Volume 11
Identifiers: LCCN 2016043861| ISBN 9783631670095 | ISBN 9783653061680 (E-Book) | ISBN 9783631697405 (EPUB) | ISBN 9783631697412 (MOBI)
Subjects: LCSH: European Parliament--Elections--2014. | Twitter--Political aspects--European Union countries. | Social media--Political aspects--European Union countries. | Communication in politics--Technological innovations--European Union countries.
Classification: LCC JN36 .T94 2016 | DDC 324.94/05612--dc23 LC record available at https://lccn.loc.gov/201604386

Umschlaggestaltung: Nina Adams
Gefördert durch das DFG-Schwerpunktprogramm 1505 "Mediatisierte Welten"

DFG Deutsche Forschungsgemeinschaft

DFG priority program 1505
MEDIATIZED WORLDS

ISSN 16178432
ISBN 978-3-631-67009-5 (Print)
E-ISBN 978-3-653-06168-0 (E-Book)
E-ISBN 978-3-631-69740-5 (EPUB)
E-ISBN 978-3-631-69741-2 (MOBI)
DOI 10.3726/978-3-653-06168-0

PL Academic Research is an Imprint of Peter Lang GmbH.
Peter Lang – Frankfurt am Main · Bern · Bruxelles · New York · Oxford · Warszawa · Wien

This publication has been peer reviewed.
www.peterlang.com

Contents

Part 3: Integration of Twitter in political strategies in different national contexts

Alex Frame, Arnaud Mercier, Gilles Brachotte & Caja Thimm

General Introduction

In the course of the past six to eight years, Twitter has rapidly imposed itself as one of the major digital PR tools used by politicians in many countries around the world, and in several cases, politicians and journalists have been early adopters (Grant, Moon, & Busby Grant, 2010). Much research carried out into the kinds of information tweeted by politicians, in various countries, suggests that the tool is often used by politicians principally for self-promotion, especially during electoral periods, in the traditional top-down style of political communication (Grant et al., 2010; Larsson & Kalsnes, 2014). As such, Twitter provides new impetus to the *personalization of politics* especially as its design, affordances and network structure allow politicians to "expand the political arena for increased personalized campaigning" (Enli & Skogerbø, 2013: 758). One reason for politicians' self-presentation practices on Twitter is that of 'easy marketing': Especially during election times, candidates who have a Twitter presence are more likely to post their own messages rather than relying on a "well-resourced media staff" (Bruns & Highfield, 2013: 669). In the context of local campaigns, social media can also be used to promote the action of militants and to recruit new ones. The candidate congratulates them publicly, often by retweeting their messages and pictures (Mercier, 2015). In addition, Twitter's functionality as a dynamic information distribution tool offers politicians the possibility to cross-promote and shape their online-identities, for example by linking to their personal blogs, Facebook pages or an online-newspaper article about them (Enli & Skogerbø, 2013).

Twitter's information and networking function, which make political (self-) marketing opportune, is also seen as a key factor for politicians when interacting with others – especially on the institutional level. Strategic exchange with journalists, bloggers or fellow politicians is a central practice of politicians' Twitter activity during election times (Nuernbergk & Conrad, 2016; Thimm, Anastasiadis, Bürger & Einspänner, 2014). In this context, several studies raise the concern that Twitter develops into an exclusive medium, which is–against the hopes of "e-democracy-enthusiasts"–mainly used among a well informed and well educated online-elite (Grant et al., 2010; Block, 2013; Ekman & Widholm, 2015) and thus reflects power inequalities known from the pre-internet era (Gerhards & Schäfer, 2010; Carpentier, 2012). However, while networks between "informed elites" like politicians and journalists on Twitter can be described as close, they are "not closed" (Verweij, 2012: 690): On the one hand, the Twitter public sphere seems to be dominated by the politically interested and engaged but on the other hand, "its influence extends far beyond" (Grant et al., 2010: 599). This means that one has to take into account the role of the passive participants on Twitter, so-called lurkers, who may not actively tweet or retweet but who read along and gather information relevant for their own deliberative processes. Yet Twitter research in this area still is an intention (e.g., Bechmann & Lomborg, 2013; Himmelboim, McCreery & Smith, 2013), as mapping and profiling "passive" audiences on social media is a difficult task. Moreover, between political elites and the passive audience, there is a category of Twitter users for whom the network is a tool for unconventional political participation. Derision towards the rulers and political forces, media criticism and the development of more participatory forms of engagement, are all ways of using Twitter as a counter public sphere (Mercier, 2016), and which often appear problematic to politicians and their staff.

Therefore, the focus of current political Twitter research is on the detectable, like structures and practices of politicians' and users' interaction. A central question in fact is that of Twitter as a more direct platform for dialogical communication between politicians and their voters; thus it is a question of Twitter's potential as a tool for digital democracy. While politicians themselves often claim (or report an idealistic motivation) to use social media like Twitter for connecting with voters and discuss politics with them, studies show that they actually seldom manage to interact with them in practice (Enli & Skogerbø, 2013, Frame & Brachotte (eds), 2015, Thimm et al., 2016). Twitter has, up until now, only rarely been used by politicians to exchange information, debate or give insights into political processes (Golbeck, Grimes, & Rogers, 2010; Lawless, 2012; Vergeer & Hermans, 2013). However, some authors have found evidence of differing styles of Twitter use among politicians, depending on their personal profile (Dang-Anh, Einspänner, & Thimm, 2012; Thimm et al. 2016; Jackson & Lilleker, 2011; Sæbø, 2011) and others have proposed evidence of maturing patterns of usage (Frame & Brachotte, 2013; Grant et al., 2010), cross-media usage (Mercier, 2013) and of the influence of a small political elite within a national Twittersphere (Ausserhofer & Maireder, 2013; Grant et al., 2010).

All in all, the *mediatization of politics* (Block, 2013; Esser & Strömbäck, 2014; Thimm, Dang-Anh & Einspänner, 2014) and the underlying developments like politicians' ubiquitous media presence, the high availability of political information and the various possibilities for "micro-participation" online might suggest an overall better accessibility of and interest in politics. However, when looked at the facts that testify "real political participation", i.e., voter turnout, the low numbers in some western societies prove otherwise (Franklin, 2004; Blais, 2006). Reasons for increasing or decreasing voter turnout over time in various countries are mainly due to different variables like the respective voting system, voting age and rules (Franklin, 2004). While those institutional variables are set, much focus nowadays is on the practical question of how to mobilize voters and increase voter turnout – in short: on candidates' campaigning efforts. The importance of a sophisticated campaigning strategy especially becomes visible in the US presidential elections, where candidates (and their campaign teams) virtuously employ all sorts of online and offline media in order to mobilize their voters (Burton, Miller & Shea, 2015; Benoit, 2016).

The European parliamentary elections can be considered a particular challenge for political candidates (Maarek, 2012), as EU elections in general attract less attention among media and citizens than national elections (De Vreese, Banducci, Semetko, & Boomgaarden, 2006). In 2009, overall voter turnout averaged a mere 43 % of over 375 million eligible European citizens. The 2014 EU elections even had the lowest voter turnout on record with 42.5 % (euroactiv.com) although it has been the largest election for the European Parliament that has ever been held with over 12,000 candidates from almost 450 parties from 28 member states (Treib, 2014). In the absence of a clearly distinguishable European public sphere (Dacheux 2003; De Wilde, Michailidou & Trenz, 2014), getting citizens to discuss European issues, rather than domestic ones, often appears a particularly delicate task. Tendencies of fragmentation became especially vivid in the run-up to the 2014 elections, where many anti-European voices made themselves heard. While Eurosceptic parties won seats in the Parliament in 23 out of the 28 member states, however, it has to be distinguished between "hard and soft Euroscepticism" (Treib, 2014: 1543): The former rejects the whole idea of the European Union in principle, the latter accept the idea of the EU project but oppose specific policies of the EU. Eurosceptic parties are found within the whole political spectrum–from the radical left and centrist to moderate right and radical right (Treib, 2014).

The use of social media and Twitter in particular has been an important asset during the European elections for all candidates, but especially for Eurosceptic parties. A study of over 1.2 million tweets sent in English, French, and German during the EU elections 2014 suggests that national parties "with an explicitly anti-EU or anti-Euro platform generated the most attention" (Pew Research Center, 2014). When looking at the campaigning strategies of selected candidates from Eurosceptic parties a great networking effort can be observed: Marine Le Pen from the French Front National for example tries to restrict her Twitter followers to party members and supportive voices (Thimm et al., 2016). Also, the German

Eurosceptic party Alternative for Germany (AfD) tries a more informative than dialogical way of tweeting (ibid.). Overall, current Twitter research gives the impression of highly diverse patterns of individual tweeting strategies among EU candidates, but for the prospective representatives of an institution often portrayed in European media as being distant from domestic voters, Twitter and other social media can at least be used to give the image (rightly or wrongly) of a tool cutting across barriers and favouring direct communication with voters. However, politicians need to be aware of the dangers of using the participatory features of Twitter in a purely cosmetic way. Already the renewal of democracy through participatory procedures was a promise most often not fulfilled. They must be careful not to create additional democratic disenchantment with social networks.

This volume: Twitter as a political practice

This volume is a collection of papers which examine the way Twitter was used by candidates from different countries, during the 2014 European Parliamentary Election campaign. All of the contributors took part in an international research project to compare Twitter use during these elections in five different countries: Belgium, France, Germany, Italy, Spain and the United Kingdom. All of the tweets sent by or to all of the candidates in these countries were collected during a month around the election date, as well as others which mentioned the candidates themselves, or used hashtags associated with the elections. On the basis of the 50 million tweets collected, processed and divided into national corpora, the different teams worked to establish the specificities of Twitter usage between candidates, parties and countries, looking at a whole range of aspects and of research questions. The current volume brings together the first set of results from the project.

The book has been designed to interest researchers or academics studying the way Twitter is used during European or other elections. Since the project team brings together colleagues working in communication studies, political science and computer science, it has developed integrated solutions and methodologies for collecting and studying Twitter data, using various qualitative and quantitative techniques. The volume builds on the experience of the project team to highlight the difficulties encountered when conducting this kind of research, and how they were overcome. Thus it presents methodological discussions and solutions (Part 1), as well as more theoretical parts dedicated to argumentation styles (Part 2) and political communication strategies in the various countries (Part 3).

In the first chapter of the section outlining methodological challenges and solutions to studying the use of Twitter during political campaigns, Éric Leclercq, Marinette Savonnet, Thierry Grison, Sergey Kirgizov and Ian Basaille outline some of the difficulties encountered in developing SNFreezer, the open source tool which they produced and integrated as a platform to help researchers collect, store and analyse large quantities of tweets. Written from a computer science perspective, the chapter discusses the technical constraints faced by teams seeking to capture numerous posts via Twitter's programming interface, and explains how a multi-paradigm platform can fulfill the requirements of building a corpus of tweets (selecting, harvesting and storing tweets) and can reduce the waiting time for researchers to perform analysis on data. It highlights issues such as the scalability of the architecture that is collecting tweets, as well as its failover mechanism. The originality of this approach is to combine concerns about data harvesting, data storage and data analysis into one platform. The resulting polyglot storage system supports a relational database, graph database or structured files and a set of tools that can provide a suitable solution for mixing different types of algorithms in order to maximize knowledge extraction. The chapter describes the software architecture of the platform and shows how it uses the Twitter APIs and how end-users can select the best data model according to their analysis.

In chapter two, Dario Compagno outlines a mixed methods approach to analysing "families of practices" based on Twitter use by different French candidates during the 2014 European campaign. The approach used here is to apply unsupervised learning techniques to let clusters of candidates emerge from the Twitter data, using operators interpreted by Twitter (hashtags, retweets, hyperlinks, mentions) as variables for clustering. The chapter gives details of the families of uses identified in this way: for example, while some candidates prefer to tweet links to online resources, therefore recognizing the informative potential of the social platform, others tweet many more mentions than links, in a sort of relational "style". It could be inferred that candidates belonging to different families of uses conceive Twitter differently.

In the third chapter, Tatiana Kondrashova and Alex Frame take previous work done on "Twitter Styles" as a starting point to develop a conceptual model seeking to qualify the "dialogical dimension of political tweets". This approach is based on a qualitative analysis applied to the UK corpus, taking into account the notion of "reach" in order to discuss political use of Twitter without simply referring to the traditional and sometimes misleading categories of "informative vs interactive". Chapter 4, written by Nanta Novello Paglianti, looks qualitatively into the use of Twitter by selected Italian candidates during the campaign, in order to characterise the communication strategies adopted, and to seek to define the form of the contemporary political tweet.

The second part of the volume focuses more precisely on forms of argumentation on Twitter. Chapters 5 and 6 both address the question of the rhetorical construction of the Other in campaign discourse on Twitter. In chapter 5, Arnaud Mercier analyses the French corpus from the angle of different figures of "the enemy" in the pro- or anti-European context, and Marina Villa presents similar results for the Italian corpus in the following chapter. They emphasize the polemical usage that candidates make of tweets and underline the strong homology between electoral tweets, and soundbites produced for traditional media.

Elena Albu adopts a linguistic approach to political tweets in chapter 7, examining the various ways in which candidates from the UK Independence Party use calls to action in their tweets, via the #VoteUKIP hashtag. By studying the linguistic strategies and grammatical forms associated with these calls to vote, the chapter identifies the importance of the position of the hashtag and its accompanying elements in influencing its apparent function in individual tweets. The author highlights differences between informative and argumentative calls to action, establishing a typology which allows her to characterise the tweets according to how explicitly and directly the reason for voting UKIP is presented.

The articles in the third part of the book look more generally at the ways in which Twitter has been integrated into the political communication strategies of candidates in four of the countries studied. In chapter 8, Gilles Brachotte and Frédéric Junger provide a quantitative overview of data in order to discuss and characterise the way the microblogging platform was used in the French context by the different parties in competition during the European elections and by individual candidates, in order to differentiate them based on their Twitter metrics and the underlying patterns of usage.

Caja Thimm, Jessica Einspänner Pflock and Mario Anastasiadis discuss the results of their analysis of the German corpus in chapter 9. They discuss the affordances of Twitter for political discourse with a focus on Twitter usage during the EU elections in Germany. The quantitative and qualitative analyses of tweets collected during a specified period of four weeks were carried out on the basis of the functional operator model of Twitter. The model serves as a framework for assessing users' tweeting styles, which can range between personal-interactive and topical-informative. They show the differences between individual politainment strategies but do also question the candidates' alleged efforts to enter into dialogue with their voters. The authors conclude that politicians used Twitter during the EU election mainly as a tool for self-marketing and establishing themselves within a communication infrastructure of their own, outside traditional media.

Vittorio Cobianchi, Maria Francesca Murru and Marina Villa, in chapter 10, look more precisely at the question of Twitter use as "second screen" during televised political debates in Italy. A content analysis of tweets created by political parties before and during the appearance of their candidates on TV shows Twitter's function as a tool to amplify and multiply political messages conveyed through the medium of television. In addition, an analysis of the tweets created by the Twitter audience during the broadcast of the Italian talk show "Porta a Porta" underpins the hypothesis that second screen communication on Twitter conveys patterns of self-representation and opinion stating, especially against or in support of the political candidates on TV.

Finally, in chapter 11, Fernando Bonete Vizcaino, Elena Cebrián Guinovart and Tamara Vázquez Barrio focus on the use of Twitter by the leader of the Spanish political formation *Podemos*, Pablo Iglesias. They ask to what degree the promise of renewal in politics and political discourse which this new formation embodies can be detected in the use of Twitter by its leader. They take into consideration Iglesias's tweets, the main themes addressed and the comments received in order to offer a detailed analysis of this particular leader's political communication strategy on Twitter.

References:

Ausserhofer, J., & Maireder, A. (2013). National Politics on Twitter. *Information, Communication & Society*, *16*(3), 291–314.

Bechmann, A. & Lomborg, S. (2013). Mapping actor roles in social media: Different perspectives on value creation in theories of user participation. *New Media & Society 15*(5), 765–781.

Benoit, W.L. (Ed). (2016). *Praeger Handbook of Political Campaigning in the United States.* Santa Barbara: Praeger.

Blais, A. (2006). What Affects Voter Turnout? *Annual Review of Political Science (9)*, 111–125.

Block, E. (2013). A Culturalist Approach to the Concept of Mediatization of Politics: The Age of "Media Hegemony". *Communication Theory 23*, 259–278.

Bruns, A. & Highfield, T. (2013). Political Networks on Twitter. Tweeting the Queensland State Election. *Information, Communication & Society 16(5)*, 667–691.

Burton, M.J., Miller, W.J. & Shea, D.M. (2015). *Campaign Craft. The Strategies, Tactics, and Art of Political Campaign Management.* Fifth edition. Santa Barbara: Praeger.

Carpentier, N. (2012). The concept of participation. If they have access and interact, do they really participate? *Revista Fronteiras – estudos midiáticos 14*(2), 164–177.

Dang-Anh, M., Einspänner, J., & Thimm, C. (2012). Mediatisierung und Medialität in Social Media: Das Diskurssystem „Twitter ". *Sprache ind Kommunikation im Technischen Zeitalter: Wie viel Internet (v) erträgt unsere Gesellschaft?*, *2*, 68.

Ekman, M. & Widholm, A. (2015). Politicians as Media Producers. *Journalism Practice 9*(1), 78–91.

Enli, G.S. & Skogerbø, E. (2013).Personalized Campaigns in Party-Centred Politics. Twitter and Facebook as Arenas for Political Communication. *Information, Communication & Society, 16*(5), 757–774.

Esser, F. & Strömbäck, J. (2014). *Mediatization of Politics: Understanding the Transformation of Western Democracies.* Palgrave Macmillan.

Dacheux, E. (Ed.). (2003). *L'Europe qui se construit : réflexions sur l'espace public européen.* St Etienne: Publications de l'Université de St Etienne.

Frame, A., & Brachotte, G. (2013). Les campagnes des compagnes: Mise en scène de la vie publique et privée. In S. Zlitni & F. Liénard (Eds.), *La communication électronique en questions* (pp. 387–402). Brussels : Peter Lang.

Frame, A., & Brachotte, G. (Eds.). (2015). *Citizen Participation and Political Communication in a Digital World.* New York: Routledge.

Franklin, M.N. (2004). *Voter Turnout and the Dynamics of Electoral Competition in Established Democracies Since 1945.* Cambridge University Press.

Gerhards, J. & Schäfer, M.S. (2010). Is the Internet a Better Public Sphere? Comparing Old and New Media in the USA and Germany. *New Media & Society 12*(1), 143–160.

Golbeck, J., Grimes, J. M., & Rogers, A. (2010). Twitter use by the U.S. Congress. *Journal of the American Society for Information Science and Technology, 61*(8), 1612–1621.

Grant, W. J., Moon, B., & Busby Grant, J. (2010). Digital Dialogue? Australian Politicians' use of the Social Network Tool Twitter. *Australian Journal of Political Science, 45*(4), 579–604.

Himmelboim, I., McCreery, S. & Smith, M. (2013). Birds of Feather Tweet Together: Integrating Network and Content Analyses to Examine Cross-Ideology Exposure on Twitter. *Journal of Computer-Mediated Communication 18*, 154–174.

Jackson, N. A., & Lilleker, D. G. (2009). MPs and E-representation: Me, MySpace and I. *British Politics, 4*(2), 236–264.

Jackson, N., & Lilleker, D. (2011). Microblogging, Constituency Service and Impression Management: UK MPs and the Use of Twitter. *The Journal of Legislative Studies, 17*(1), 86–105.

Larsson, A. O., & Kalsnes, B. (2014). 'Of course we are on Facebook': Use and non-use of social media among Swedish and Norwegian politicians. *European Journal of Communication.*

Lawless, J. L. (2012). Twitter and Facebook: New Ways for Members of Congress to Send the Same Old Messages? In R. L. Fox & J. Ramos (Eds.), *iPolitics: citizens, elections, and governing in the new media era* (pp. 206–232). New York: Cambridge University Press.

Mercier, A. (2016). Twitter as a Counter Public Sphere. Polemics in the Twittersphere during French Electoral Campaigns. In A. Frame, G. Brachotte (Eds.), *Citizen Participation and Political Communication in a Digital World* (pp. 139–152). London: Routledge.

Mercier, A. (2015). L'intégration de Twitter au répertoire d'action électorale des campagnes municipales françaises de 2014. In F. Liénard, S. Zlitni (Eds.), *La communication électronique: enjeux, stratégies et opportunités* (pp. 149–168). Limoges: éditions Lambert-Lucas.

Mercier, A. (2013). Avènement du Twiléspectateur et hashtags contestataires. In P. J. Maarek (Ed.), *Présidentielle 2012 : une communication politique bien singulière* (pp. 165–200). Paris: L'Harmattan.

Sæbø, Ø. (2011). Understanding Twitter Use among Parliament Representatives: A Genre Analysis. In E. Tambouris, A. Macintosh, & H. de Bruijn (Eds.), *Electronic Participation* (pp. 1–12). Springer Berlin Heidelberg.

Stanyer, J. (2013). *Intimate Politics: Publicity, Privacy and the Personal Lives of Politicians in Media Saturated Democracies.* London: John Wiley.

Thimm, C., Dang-Anh, M. & Einspänner, J. (2014). Mediatized Politics - Structures and Strategies of Discursive Participation and Online Deliberation on Twitter. In F. Krotz & A. Hepp (Eds.), *Mediatized Worlds: Culture and Society in a Media Age* (pp. 253–269). London: Palgrave Macmillian.

Thimm, C., Anastasiadis, M., Bürger, T. & Einspänner, J. (2014). *#Gehwählen: Der Bundestagswahlkampf 2013 auf Twitter.* Bonn: Bonner Akademie für Forschung und Lehre angewandter Politik (BAPP): http://uni-bonn-medienwissenschaft.de/wp-content/uploads/2015/03/BAPP_Bundestagswahl2013_ Screenklein.pdf.

Thimm, C., Frame, A., Einspänner-Pflock, J., Leclercq, E. & Anastasiadis, M. (2016). The EU-Election on Twitter: Comparison of German and French Candidates' Tweeting styles. In C. Holtz-Bacha (ed.): *Europawahlkampf 2014: Internationale Studien zur Rolle der Medien (pp. 175–203).* Wiesbaden: VS Verlag.

Treib, O. (2014). The voter says no, but nobody listens: causes and consequences of the Eurosceptic vote in the 2014 European elections. *Journal of European Public Policy 21*(10), 1541–1554.

Vergeer, M., & Hermans, L. (2013). Campaigning on Twitter: Microblogging and Online Social Networking as Campaign Tools in the 2010 General Elections in the Netherlands. *Journal of Computer-Mediated Communication, 18*(4), 399–419.

De Vreese, C. H., Banducci, S. A., Semetko, H. A., Boomgaarden, H. G., 2006. The News Coverage of the 2004 European Parliamentary Election Campaign in 25 Countries. *European Union Politics, 7*(4), 477–504.

De Wilde, P., Michailidou, A. & Trenz, H.-J. (2014). Converging on euroscepticism: Online polity contestation during European Parliament elections. *European Journal of Political Research* 53, 766–783.

Online Sources:

Euroactiv.com: *It's official: Last EU election had lowest-ever turnout.* http://www.euractiv.com/section/eu-elections-2014/news/it-s-official-last-eu-election-had-lowest-ever-turnout/.

Pew Research Center (2014). *The EU Elections on Twitter. Mixed Views about the EU & Little Passion for the Candidates.* http://www.journalism.org/2014/05/22/the-eu-elections-on-twitter/.

Part 1: Studying Tweet campaigns: methodological issues

Éric Leclercq, Marinette Savonnet, Thierry Grison,
Sergey Kirgizov & Ian Basaille, Laboratoire LE2I – UMR6306 –
CNRS – ENSAM, Univ. Bourgogne Franche-Comté

1. SNFreezer: a Platform for Harvesting and Storing Tweets in a Big Data Context

Abstract
In this chapter we show how a multi-paradigm platform can fulfill the requirements of building a corpus of tweets and can reduce the waiting time for researchers to perform analysis on data. We highlight major issues such as the scalability of the architecture that is collecting tweets, as well as its failover mechanism.

1.1 Introduction and Objectives

In general, analysing complex interaction networks including Twitter data requires different types of algorithms with different theoretical foundations such as graph theory, linear algebra, or statistical models. Regarding tweet analysis, intrinsic links built by operators (i.e. hashtags denoted by #, user mentions denoted by @, reply, and retweets) have a strong impact on the data model and on the performances of the algorithms being used.

Addressing a scientific question often requires mixing different classes of algorithms using different data models that retrieve data from different storage structures. For instance, graph-based algorithms using a matrix adjacency representation are useful for discovering community structure; a Laplacian matrix is useful to evaluate centrality. In general, graph-based algorithms are near-sighted, they do not take into account contextual information. Linear algebra algorithms can be used to identify large scaled structures, for instance clusters can be found using Singular Value Decomposition (SVD) or Principal Component Analysis (PCA). Machine learning algorithms and statistical models are used to predict links or behaviors, to detect anomalies or events. In a context of massive datasets, the most efficient storage structure should be used according to the selected algorithms, knowing that different kinds of algorithms are usually mandatory.

Analysis of tweets can be performed at different levels of granularity: at an individual level like influence assessment, sentiment analysis, by extraction of features that are not explicit; and at a corpus level, through emergence of groups of users exhibiting similar behavior. Thus, possible outcomes of the analysis are the discovery of social structures, social positions, i.e. the role of individuals.

Our contribution is an open source platform named SNFreezer (https://github.com/SNFreezer) that supports the management and the analysis of social data with different paradigms. We have developed a polyglot storage system to store and retrieve tweets in different structures that are able to scale up to the data flow requirements.

1.2 New Paradigms for Data Management Systems

Most enterprise business applications rely on relational database management systems (RDBMS). This technology is mature, widely understood and adapted. However, some issues have recently emerged:

- RDBMS may not have adequate performance for massive datasets;
- RDBMS cannot provide the scalability required by online social network applications;
- The structure of the relational model can be too rigid or not relevant to deal with the variability of complex data networks;
- SQL was not designed to perform explanatory data analysis queries which does not provide exact results.

Explicit and implicit links between social data can also be a hindrance to the use of RDBMS if they are combined with massive data. Explicit links are usually used by path queries that require joining tables, but when the length of the path is not known, SQL often needs to be embedded in a programming language. Implicit links can be discovered by data analysis but the schema of the relational database cannot be quickly and easily updated according to newly discovered relationships.

Considering these drawbacks, a number of systems, not following the relational model paradigms, have recently emerged. They are often denoted under the umbrella term of NoSQL databases (Moniruzzaman 2013).

In general, NoSQL databases rely on schema-less data models and scale horizontally. Their common features are scalability and flexibility in the structure of data. NoSQL database management systems provide different solutions for specific problems: the volume of datasets is addressed in the column-oriented NoSQL or key-value (HBase[1], Cassandra[2]); documents and links management is supported

1 http://hbase.apache.org/
2 http://cassandra.apache.org/

by document databases (CouchDB[3], MongoDB[4]); high density of links, nodes and properties are taken into account in graph database management systems (GDBMS) which are also ideal for performing queries that walk down hierarchical relationships (Neo4j[5], HypergraphDB[6]). XML oriented databases provide a highly extensible data model but lack scalability in the context of social networks.

NoSQL databases can be accessed by different APIs and different query languages, so Atzeni and al. (2014) propose a common programming interface to NoSQL systems hiding the specification details of the various systems for developing applications. The TinkerPop project[7] adopts a similar approach for graph databases. It introduces a graph query language, Gremlin, which is a domain-specific language based on Groovy[8], supported by most GDBMS. Unlike most query languages that are declarative, Gremlin is an imperative language focusing on graph traversals.

The multi-paradigm principle tends to generalize these different approaches. In modelling, multi-paradigm approaches address the necessity of using multiple modelling paradigms to design complex systems (Hodge et al. 2011). Indeed, complex systems require the use of multiple modelling languages to: 1) cope with the inherent heterogeneity of such systems; 2) offer different points of view on all their relevant aspects; 3) cover different activities of the design cycle; 4) allow reasoning at different levels of detail during the design process (Hardebolle and Boulanger 2009). As a result, multi-paradigm modelling addresses three orthogonal directions of research: 1) multi-formalism modelling, concerned with the coupling and transformation between models described in different formalisms; 2) model abstraction concerned with the relationship between models at different levels of abstraction; 3) meta-modelling concerned with the description of classes of models dedicated to particular domains or applications called Domain Specific Languages (DSL). Multi-paradigm data storage or polyglot persistence uses multiple data storage technologies, chosen according to the way data is used by applications and/or algorithms (Sharp et al. 2013). As Ghosh states in (Ghosh 2010), storing data the way it is used in an application simplifies programming and makes it easier to decentralize data processing. ExSchema (Castrejon et al. 2013) is a tool that enables automatic discovery of data schema from a system that relies on multiple documents, graph, relational, column-family data stores.

3 http://couchdb.apache.org/
4 https://www.mongodb.org/
5 http://neo4j.com/
6 http://hypergraphdb.org/
7 http://www.tinkerpop.com
8 http://groovy.codehaus.org/

1.3 SNFreezer Architecture

In order to collect tweets during the political campaign, we have started by analysing existing solutions and we retained the project YourTwapperKeeper[9] (YTK), an open source project that claims to provide users with a tool that archives data from Twitter directly on a server. After a period of tests and code review, we identified some major drawbacks. YTK was not able to collect tweets in various languages; the choice of the database engine limits the volume of datasets; and it does not retrieve information on accounts such as the list of following/followers nor the timeline of the users. Thus, we chose to enhance YTK with a real storage layer and to add database connectors in order to allow analysis tools such as R to retrieve data directly from SNFreezer repositories.

1.3.1 The Storage System

To address the problem of tweet storage, both in terms of performance and interoperability (i.e. easy connection of third party tools) we have specified and developed a storage layer. The proposed polyglot persistence storage layer includes relational databases (RDBMS), a graph data store (GDBMS), and a scalable document database management system (DDBMS) that can be used simultaneously (figure 1).

Figure 1. SNFreezer architecture

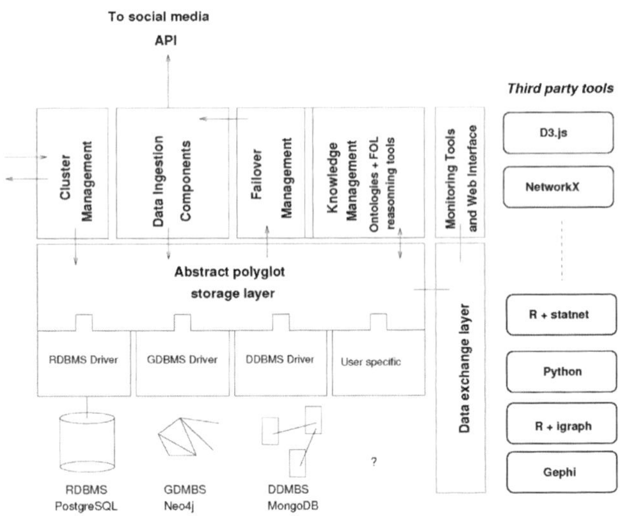

9 https://github.com/540co/yourTwapperKeeper

The configuration of the storage layer allows duplicating information in different storage systems according to the planned analysis so Neo4j or PostgreSQL ready to use databases are available during the collect. Developers can add their specific drivers for other storage systems. The data harvesting is provided by the data ingestion module connected to the Streaming and Search APIs of Twitter using two main processes that run continuously. Two other processes are used to collect the followers/following information at a defined frequency and to retrieve all the possible tweets from the timeline of the users. According to the needs and type of information to be analyzed, one can choose between various storage structures:

- For computing global metrics (e.g. number of tweets/retweets/mentions per user), a relational schema in PostgreSQL can be used.
- In the case of high traffic, it is preferable to store information in a non-normalized database scheme (one table for tweets and a few others for followers) or in JSON files or in MongoDB.
- In the case of the study of linked information (for example social network type data structure), a Neo4j graph database is suitable.

The choice of storage backend can be cumulative (both relational normalized databases and JSON files for example). We also propose a set of tools that implement model transformation to asynchronously transform data from one storage system to another.

1.3.2 Storing Tweets

Tweets coming through the Twitter APIs are JSON strings[10] that contain information on the tweet itself, but also the user who sends or retweets (table 1). JSON strings can be stored in MongoDB or directly in the filesystem.

Table 1: Example of a tweet in JSON

[created_at] => Mon May 05 16:58:20 +0000 2014
[id] => 463362068553674752
[id_str] => 463362068553674752
[text] => RT @JeunesavecBLM : .@Bruno_LeMaire est ce soir à Thionville pour un meeting avec @Nadine__Morano @AnneGrommerch @ArnaudDanjean # EP2014 http…
[source] => <a href =" http:// twitter .com/ download / iphone " rel =" nofollow "> Twitter for iPhone </a>
[truncated] =>

10 JSON (JavaScript Object Notation) is a lightweight data-interchange format.

[in_reply_to_status_id] =>
[in_reply_to_status_id_str] =>
[in_reply_to_user_id] =>
[in_reply_to_user_id_str] =>
[in_reply_to_screen_name] =>
[user] => stdClass Object
(
[id] => 439463212
[id_str] => 439463212
[name] => Arnaud Danjean
[screen_name] => ArnaudDanjean
[location] =>
[description] => Député Européen – Membre de la commission Affaires Etrangères & sous-commission Défense du Parlement Européen – Conseiller Régional de Bourgogne
[url] => http://t.co/ tOt2Mb2YUb
[entities] => stdClass Object …….

JSON strings are not stored directly in RDBMS (in a single attribute). First of all the string is changed into a tuple with different attributes (one tuple = one tweet). Attributes that are extracted from this JSON string are stored in a table named *gtweets*. The *gtweets* table contains more than 40 attributes, for example the most significant are:

- the id of the tweet (*id*), the content (*text*) and the mailing date (*time*), the creating time (*created_at*);
- the id of the twitter account who sents the tweet (from_user_id) and screen name (*from_user*);
- the language of the tweet (*ISO_language_code*), which can give an idea of the language of tweet;
- the source of the tweet (what criteria match the tweet i.e. hashtag, keyword or account)
- optional information on geolocation tweet: point, latitude, longitude (*geo_type*, *geo_coordinates_0, geo_coordinates_1*)
- the link to the user's profile image (*profile_image_url*)
- the id of the user the tweet replies to (if it exists) (*to_user_id*)
- the id of the tweet to which it answers (*in_reply_to_status_id*);
- the id the initial tweet if retweet (*initial_tweet_id*) ;
- the text of the original tweet if retweet (*initial_tweet_text*) ;
- the user's initial tweet (*initial_tweet_user*) ;
- the list of mentioned accounts (*user_mentions*) ;
- the list of hashtags (*hashtags*);
- the list of URLS (*urls*).

Table 2: An entry in gtweets *according to JSON based on the example given in Table 1*

flag	stream
text	RT @JeunesavecBLM : .@Bruno_LeMaire est ce soir à
	Thionville pour un meeting avec @Nadine__Morano @
to_user_id	AnneGrommerch @ArnaudDanjean # EP2014 http ..
from_user	Arnaud Danjean
id	463362068553674752
from_user_id	439463212
iso_language_code	fr
source	<a href =" http:// twitter .com/ download / iphone "
	rel =" nofollow "> Twitter for iPhone </a>
profile_image_url	http://pbs.twing.com/profile_images/1698849326/Capture_
geo_type	d__cran_2011-12-17__21.37.16_normal.png
geo_coodinates_0	0
geo_coordinates_1	0
created_at	Mon May 05 16:58:20 +0000 2014
time	1399309100
……	……….

Tweet Relational Database Schema

The *gtweets* table is complex (many attributes) and voluminous, so queries can become difficult to write. For obvious reasons of querying performance, interesting objects for data analysis are transformed and stored in separate tables (figure 2):

- The *Tweet* table contains tweets and retweeted tweets. The *Tweet* table is connected (by foreign keys) with hashtags (*Tweet_Hashtag* table), URLs (*Tweets_URL* table), symbols (*Tweet_Symbol* table) and query sources, i.e. presence of a keyword, a hashtag or an account in the tweet (*Tweet_Source* table).
- *Retweet* and *Mention* are tables that represent relationships between users and tweets. The *Retweet* table contains the user that retweeted, the id of the retweeted tweet and the date. The *Mention* table connects a tweet with the mentioned users.
- The *User* and *Identity* tables represent information about users. The *User* table represents information that cannot change in a Twitter account (*id*, *created_at*), other information can be updated by the user and are represented as an *Identity*.

Figure 2. Storing tweets in multiple relational tables

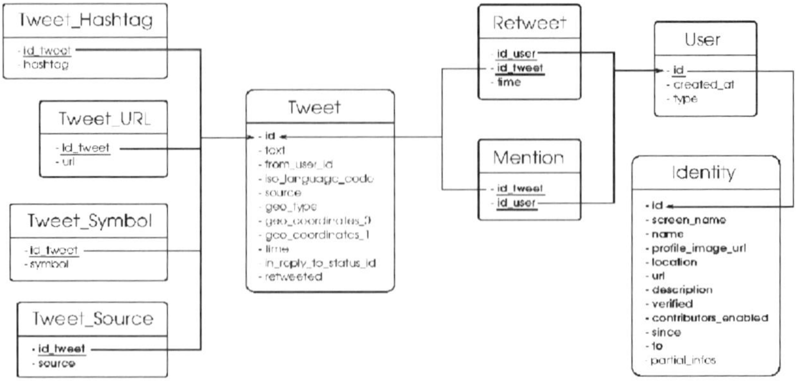

1.3.3 Tweet Graph Database

In a graph database, objects (tweets, users, hashtags, etc.) are nodes with properties, and relationships are described by edges with properties (figure 3). The relationship *use* is not materialized, it may be deducted by composition. The schema has been implemented with Neo4j.

Figure 3. Storage of tweets in GDBMS

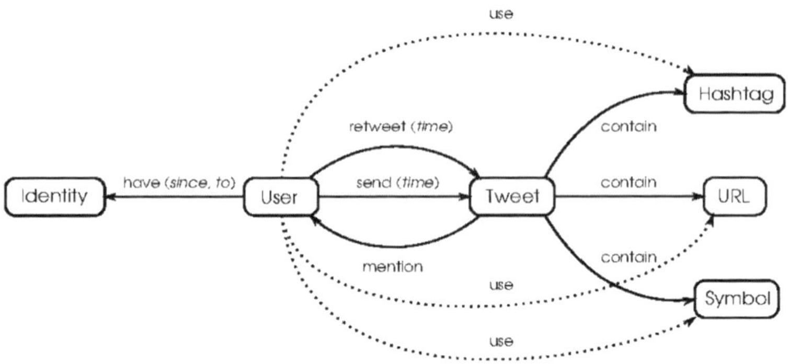

Cypher is a query language for Neo4j, which works by using patterns on the graph database. Operators are optimized for queries requiring graphs traversal, and notably allow finding relationships between nodes despite their separation by several links (which would have required costly joins by SQL). The query in table 3 shows a simple example of what can be expressed using Cypher, here we wish to find the identifiers of the users who retweeted '@Europarl_FR' and the number of retweets.

Table 3. A query example using Cypher

```
match (u: user) -[: USER_HAVE_IDENTITY ]->(i: identity)
where i. screen_name = '@Europarl_FR '
with distinct u as europarl_fr
match europarl_fr -[: USER_SEND_TWEET ]->(t: tweet) <-[:
USER_RETWEET_TWEET ]-(urt: user)
return urt.id , count (t);
```

The first three lines of the query request that, a user node corresponding to the identity with the screen name 'Europarl_FR' should be stored as a variable u. Line 5 retrieves Users (urt) having retweeted a tweet sent by 'Europarl_FR'. Finally, line 6 returns results grouped by user and counts, for each user, the number of his retweets.

1.3.4 Cluster Mode and Fail Over

Cluster and failover modes have been developed to overcome some limitations of the Streaming and Search APIs of Twitter. For instance, one application can only retrieve tweets matching one of the conditions called source query (attribute querysource in database), in a set of 400. Each account on Twitter can define applications, but for each IP address hosting the application the previous limitations apply. However, some projects require more than 400 query sources. To fulfill this requirement we have developed a cluster management module.

In the cluster mode, several virtual machines, in which instances of the data harvesting processes are deployed, can be used in a project to collect tweets using matching criteria in a set of several thousand source queries. Source queries can be defined on each virtual machine using a web interface or can be imported automatically using scripts and import files submitted to one of the virtual machines that acts as a master. In the cluster mode, it is assumed that there will be a high volume of tweets, thus the storage layer can use a non-normalized schema on PostgreSQL (*gtweets* table described in section 3.2), or can store data in MongoDB or in JSON files. Figure 4 gives an example of the cluster deployed to collect tweets during European Election campaign of 2014.

Figure 4. Cluster mode

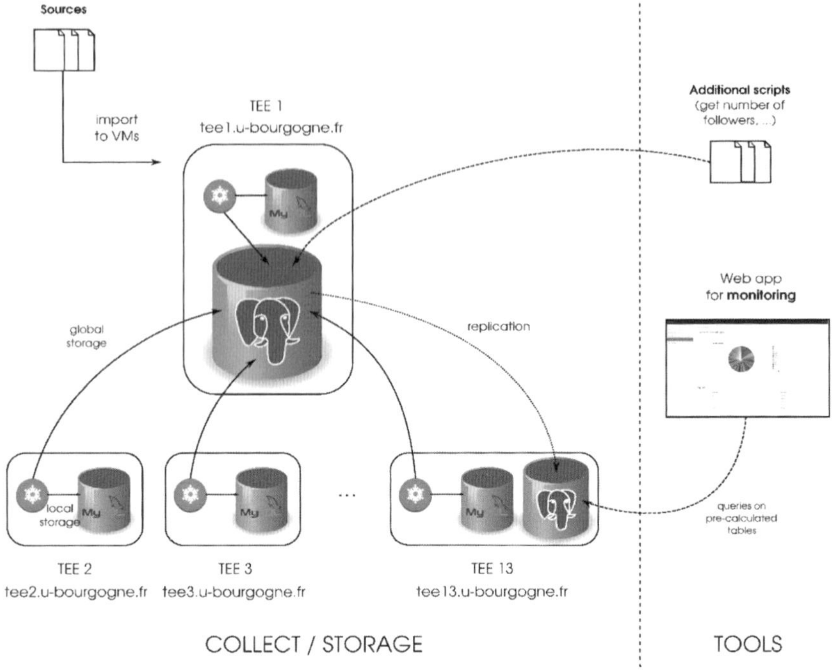

In case tweet harvesting was interrupted for any reason, the process in charge of the Search API can retrieve tweets for a period of seven days. Automatic emails are sent to the administrator with a notification of the failure (storage, networks, etc.) and when the harvesting process is restarted, the latest tweet ID is checked and the process in charge of the Search API starts collecting any lost tweets. Moreover, it is possible to include a local database on each virtual machine using MySQL as a temporary backup, and a global database using PostgreSQL.

Tools were also developed in order to monitor tweet harvesting and the instances of the different local storage in each virtual machine of the cluster. They indicate, amongst other things, the number of tweets for a given period of time, the most used hashtags or the most active users and can send alerts by email to researchers or administrators. In the case of a high volume of tweets, a replica database is used to calculate general statistics for the monitoring tools.

During the TEE2014 project this architecture allowed to harvest more than 50M tweets and the resulting database with non-normalized schema is about 50GB without indexes. For the French corpus, experiments have been performed using Neo4j. Starting from a normalized schema of 5M tweets and a database size of 7GB we obtain a graph database of 20GB.

1.4 Connection with Analysis Tools and Web Applications

A specific data exchange layer is dedicated to application services, and third party tools are plugged in according to the expected analysis. Connectors have been developed to analyse data with third party software such as *R* and *igraph*[11] and to display results with *D3.js*[12]. If a connector is not available, the layer provides export files for the different classes of algorithms such as files containing adjacency matrix, graph triple, multidimensional array or CSV (Comma-Separated Values) for spreadsheet. In the following subsection, we give some key elements for starting analysis.

In order to perform explanatory analysis on the corpus we have developed some web tools. For example, figure 5 is a component that displays the timeline of a user and shows the frequency of tweets or retweets in a period. By clicking on a point, users can display the tweet or retweet. Figure 6 depicts the interface of an algorithm to detect and characterize events. We have proposed to use a simple method that finds local minima and maxima of temporal density of tweets. This method finds the moments after which the number of published tweets begins to increase (or decrease). The method has only one parameter (bandwidth) allowing us to smoothly change the mode of the event detection: when the bandwidth is small, micro-events can be detected, and when it is large only macro-events appear. This method, by itself, does not give any description of the event, except its start and end times. Thus, in order to describe an event, we split the data using hashtag decomposition: for each hashtag of interest, we draw a temporal density plot, and we combine all these plots in the same image, which allows us to compare them. The difference in hashtag frequencies can be regarded as a first approximation of the semantic event description. A part of the program source code (detection of local minima and maxima of temporal density) is available on github[13].

11 http://igraph.org/
12 http://d3js.org/
13 https://github.com/kerzol/changepoint-pelt-vs-timedensity

Figure 5. A web component to display user's timeline

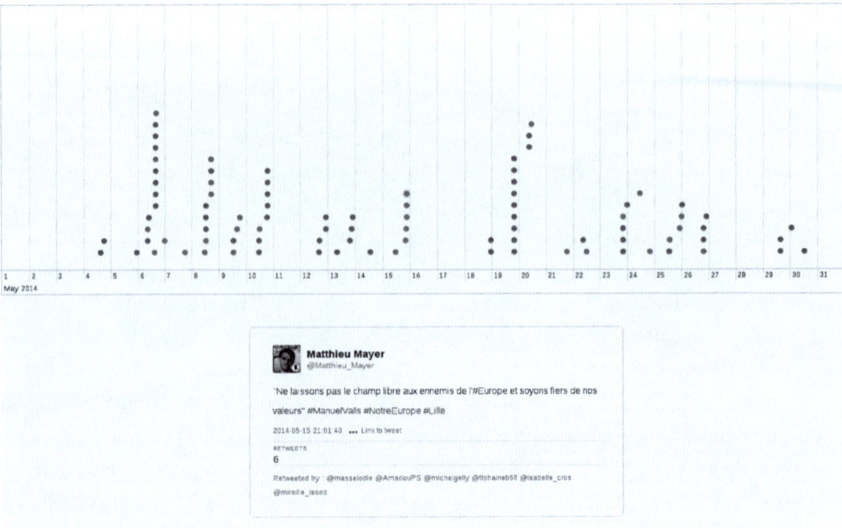

Figure 6. A web component to detect and analyse events

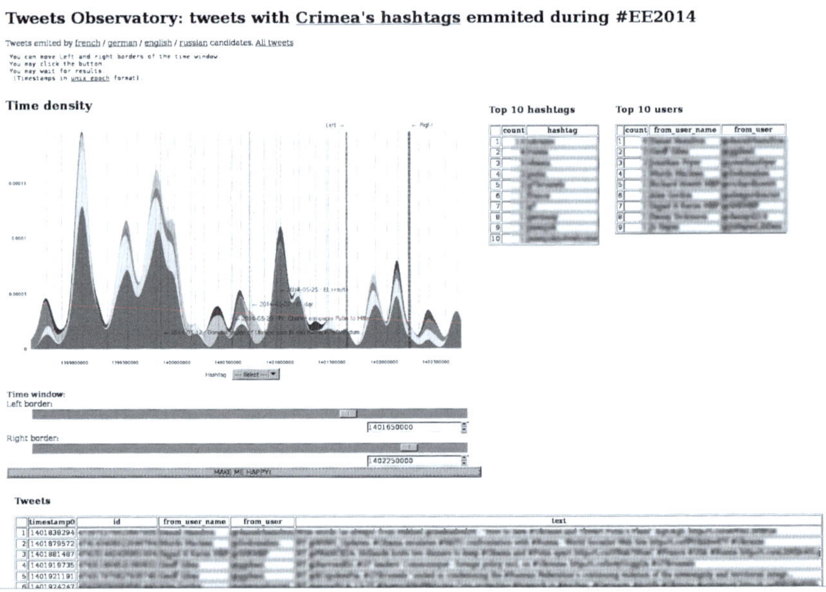

1.5 Conclusion

In this chapter, we have presented an open framework integrating a polyglot scalable storage system that support different analysis algorithms. Different analysis tools have been implemented on the top the platform to perform iterative and incremental analysis through a dedicated web application. We plan to add new web components such as community analysis or heat map clustering representations, that can connect to the different data repositories in to build an observatory that can be used to perform explanatory analysis in real time.

References

Atzeni, Paolo / Bugiotti, Francesca / Rossi, Luca: "Uniform access to NoSQL systems". Information Systems, 43, 2014, pp. 117–133.

Castrejon, J. / Vargas-Solar, G. / Collet, C. / Lozano, R.: "ExSchema: Discovering and Maintaining Schemas from Polyglot Persistence Applications", 29th IEEE International Conference on Software Maintenance (ICSM), 2013, pp. 496–499.

Ghosh Debasish: "Multiparadigm Data Storage for Enterprise Applications", IEEE Software, 27(5), 2010, pp. 57–60.

Hardebolle, Cécile / Boulanger, Frédéric: "Exploring Multi-Paradigm Modeling Techniques", Simulation, 85(11–12), 2009, pp. 688–708.

Hodge, Bri-Mathias S. / Huang, Shisheng / Siirola, John D. / Pekny, Joseph F. / Reklaitis, Gintaras V.: "A multi-paradigm modeling framework for energy systems simulation and analysis", Computers &Chemical Engineering, 35(9), 2011, pp. 1725–1737.

Moniruzzaman, ABM / Hossain, Syed Akhter: "NoSQL database: New era of databases for big data analytics-classification, characteristics and comparison", International Journal of Database Theory and Application, 6(4), 2013.

Sharp, John / McMurtry, Douglas / Oakley, Andrew / Subramanian, Mani / Zhang, Hanzhong: "Data Access for Highly-Scalable Solutions: Using SQL, NoSQL, and Polyglot Persistence", In: Microsoft patterns & practices, 2013.

Acknowledgements

The authors gratefully acknowledge Arnaud Da Costa, engineer in charge of the server infrastructure which was used during the TEE2014 project and Jonathan Norblin who developed the major parts of SNFreezer during the final internship of his masters degree in computer science.

Dario Compagno, Univ. Lorraine

2. Families of practices. A bottom-up approach to differentiate how French candidates made use of Twitter during the 2014 European Campaign

Abstract
The aim of this chapter is to differentiate how French candidates made use of Twitter during the 2014 European campaign. We apply unsupervised learning techniques to let clusters of candidates emerge from the data. In particular, the variables used for clustering are operators interpreted by Twitter (hashtags, retweets, hyperlinks, mentions).

2.1 Introduction and rationale

The aim of this study is to understand how French candidates made use of Twitter during the 2014 European elections. In particular, we are interested in identifying a few families of practices, or "Twitter styles", based on the operators found in the tweets. To this end we adopted a bottom-up approach, based on unsupervised learning (clustering). As a result we found three main "poles" defining the field of Twitter practices: some candidates tweet as a means for getting in direct contact with citizens, others diffuse hyperlinks to websites, while others still make an extensive use of the participative operators allowed by Twitter, such as hashtags, retweets and mentions. The results of this study permit to understand which practices are more common and to characterize them in accord to other variables such as the preferred tweeting interface of a candidate, his or her political party and the content of the words used in his or her tweets.

2.2 Corpus and methodology

The corpus used in this study was extracted from the TEE2014 database[14]. The database collects all the tweets produced by Belgian, English, French, German,

14 TEE2014 Project: http://msh-dijon.u-bourgogne.fr/recherche-msh/les-programmes/547-twitter-aux-elections-europeennes-une-etude-contrastive-internationale-des-utilisations-de-twitter-par-les-candidats-aux-elections-au-parlement-europeen-en-mai-2014-tee2014.html

Italian and Spanish candidates to the European Elections 2014 during the campaign. Our corpus includes all messages tweeted by French candidates. In total, around 72.000 tweets by 467 users have been collected. We decided not to consider for our analysis 106 candidates who tweeted less than 15 tweets during the campaign, and 4 candidates who tweeted more than 1000 tweets, leaving a more homogeneous corpus of 357 candidates.

Data treatment, analysis and plots in this study have been realized with the open source statistical software *R* (R Core Team 2015), including the *dplyr* (Wickham / Francois 2015), *ggplot2* (Wickham 2009) and *cluster* (Maechler et al. 2015) packages[15].

Our study focuses on candidates instead of on individual tweets. Therefore we began by summarizing for each candidate the proportion of tweets including an operator interpreted by Twitter (Thimm 2012, Einspänner / Dang-Anh / Thimm 2013). To calculate these proportions we have preferentially considered the meta-data present in the TEE2014 database, which in turn are based on the Twitter REST API (Twitter Inc. 2015) and on dedicated extraction algorithms. However we have recalculated these meta-data whenever needed by the ends of our research. The operators used in this analysis are the following:

1. The *retweet operator* "RT": identifies retweets;
2. The *hashtag operator* "#": identifies tweets containing hashtags;
3. The *hyperlink operator* "http": identifies tweets containing links to webpages;
4. The direct message or reply operator "reply", referred to as *DM/reply operator* from now on: identifies tweets starting with an "@" character;
5. The *source operator* "via": identifies tweets ending with "via @" followed by a twitter account;
6. The *mention operator* "@": identifies tweets including mentions in their text that are no retweet, DM/reply or source operator.

Other meta-data considered in the study are the candidate's *party name* and the *tweeting interface* most often used by him or her. The choice to focus just on operators to perform a clusterisation of the candidates in our corpus has been determined by past works on the TEE2014 database (Mercier / Villa 2015, Thimm / Einspänner / Gautier 2015) and by a previous exploratory research confirming the importance of operators as features to differentiate among the candidates' tweeting practices (Compagno 2015).

15 The script and the aggregated data are available for reproducibility by contacting the author.

The aim of figure 1 is to show how many times each media logic operator has been used by French candidates. The ratio of tweets by a candidate that made use of a media logic operator is plotted on the x-axis of the facets: therefore a value of 0 means that a candidate never used a certain operator, a value of 1 that he or she used it in every tweet, and a value of 0.5 that we find that operator in every second tweet produced by the candidate. On the y-axis we find the number of candidates distributed according to the ratio of their tweets employing each of the six operators.

Figure 1. Use of media logics operator by candidates

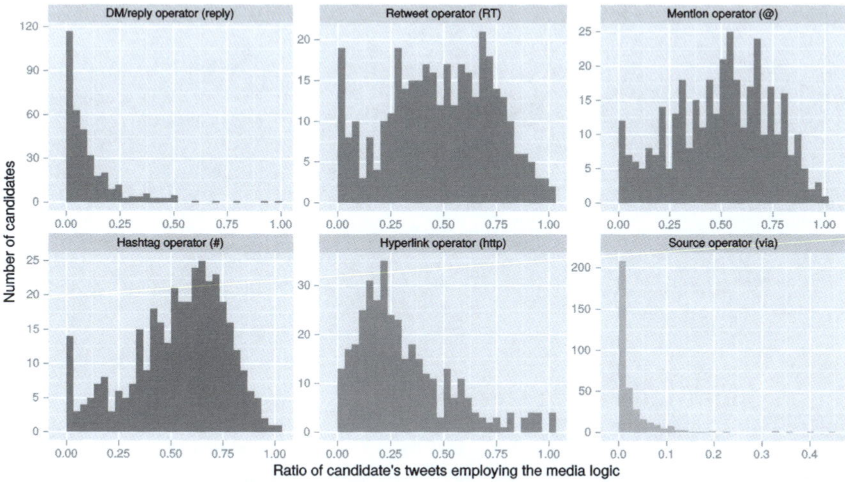

We can observe that the ratios of retweet and mention operators are centred and approximately normally distributed. The hashtag operator is slightly skewed to the left, suggesting that hashtags are often used in tweets. The hyperlink operator is instead more heavily skewed to the right, suggesting that there is a large number of tweets in our corpus not pointing to external webpages. This applies even more to the DM/reply and to the source operators: the vast majority of tweets are neither replies nor direct messages, and just a very small number of tweets in our corpus points to a source at the end of their text. However, we decided to isolate source operators, instead of considering them just as a kind of mention, because they correlate with the presence of hyperlinks in tweets, and would have acted as confounders in clusterisation.

Figure 2 permits to compare these different distributions more easily by plotting the median fraction of tweets per candidate that employ the operators. It is evident that retweet, mention and hashtag operators are found approximately in every second tweet. Instead hyperlinks and especially DM/reply and source operators are much rarer and found respectively in one tweet of four, of fifteen and of one hundred.

Figure 2. Global use of media logics operators

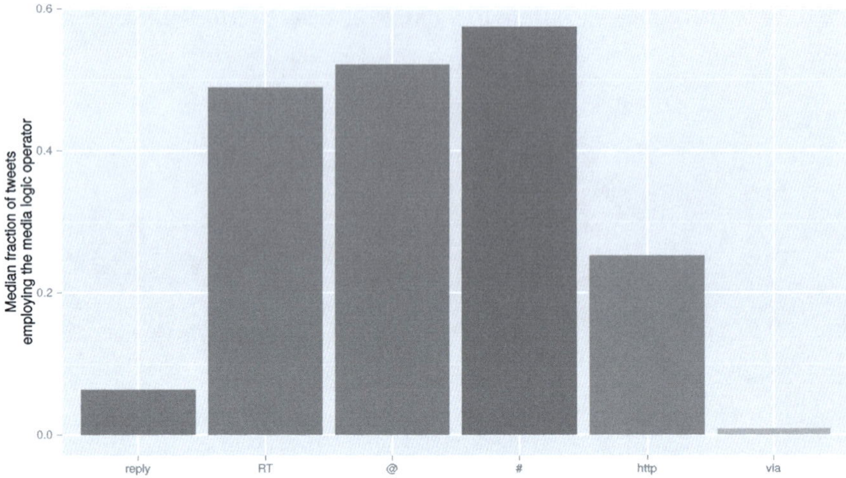

2.3 Exploration and clustering

In order to explore the relationships among the different operators, we performed a principal components analysis (PCA) using chi2 distances[16], of which the results are shown on the left half of figure 3. PCA creates a space of representation in which observations (in this case candidates) can be positioned. The position of each point is determined by its preference to one or another operator. PCA therefore helps to understand if operators characterize mutually exclusive uses of Twitter. The first two factors of PCA, used as coordinates for our plot, explain respectively 40 % and 20 % of the point variability.

16 The function used to convert euclidean distances into chi2 ones has been developed at the *Laboratoire d'informatique théorique et appliquée* (LITA) de l'Université de Lorraine, that we would like to thank.

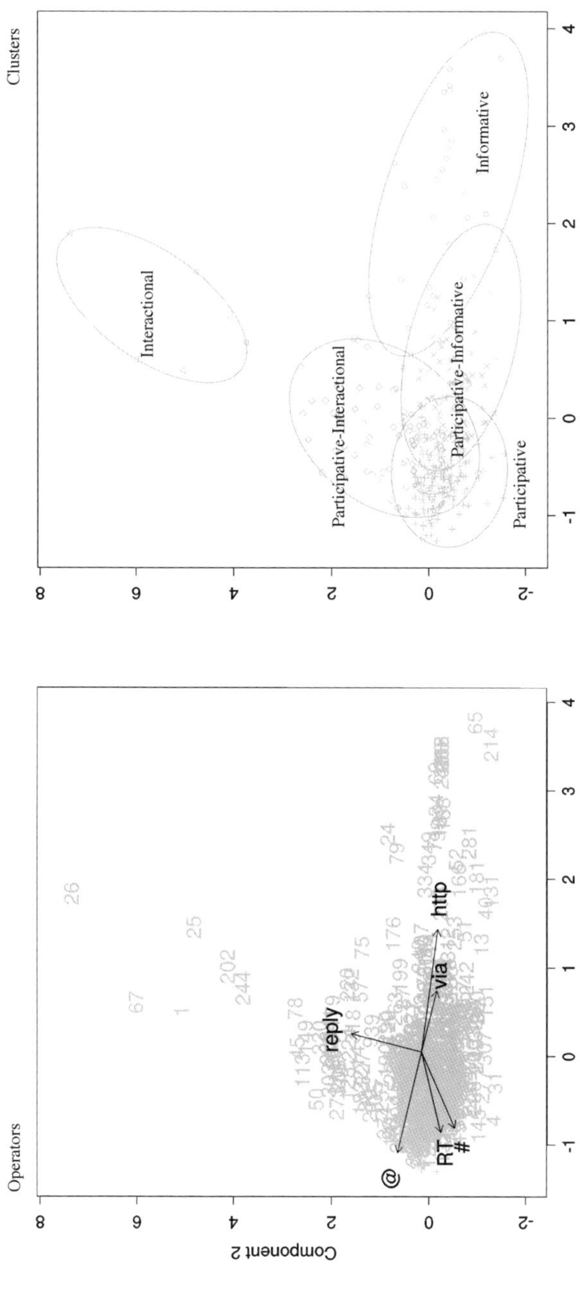

Figure 3. Principal components analysis

PCA shows that hyperlink and mention operators tend to be mutually exclusive: if a candidate makes a large use of the first, he or she will not often use the second, and vice versa. Source operators are positively correlated to hyperlinks: in fact, they are often automatically added to the end of the tweets produced by tweet buttons in news and other websites.

Hashtag and retweet operators tend to be used by the same family of candidates. We can see that this third family does not make use of direct messages and replies, nor publishes many links to webpages. Conversely, those who make heavy use of DM/reply operators or of hyperlink operators do not insert many hashtag or retweet operators in their tweets.

We begin to form an idea of the main trends in the use of Twitter by French candidates in the 2014 campaign: the majority of them, represented at the lower-left corner of figure 3, used hashtags and retweets but did neither tweet many hyperlinks nor engage in direct conversations. We notice two other tendencies: some candidates, at the lower-right side of the diagram, used Twitter mainly to diffuse hyperlinks, while some other candidates, at the top, got more involved in direct exchanges.

To get a better understanding of this insight we performed an agglomerative hierarchical clustering on our data. This technique produces a segmentation of the observations into a predetermined number of classes, according to the preferences that the candidates show about the use of operators. After exploring several different partitions, we ended up with a five-classes clustering. The clusters are plotted on the right half of figure 3, on PCA coordinates. We notice three "extreme" groups of users and two intermediary ones.

The clusters are variable in size, as shown in figure 4. The largest, in the middle, that we called "Participative", includes 164 candidates out of 357. The two small clusters at the extremes of the diagram, named "Interactional" and "Informative", include respectively 6 and 33 candidates. The remaining two intermediary, medium-sized clusters named "Participative-Interactional" and "Participative-Informative" share what remains in two groups of 78 and 76 candidates each.

2.4 Interpretation of the clusters

Let us now enter into the details of the interpretation of these clusters. Figure 5 plots for each cluster the median fraction of tweets employing the media logic operators. This profiling helps us to understand what the candidates in each group have in common, and therefore to interpret these results. We chose not to plot the source operator at this stage because it is not useful to differentiate the five clusters.

Figure 4. Size of the clusters

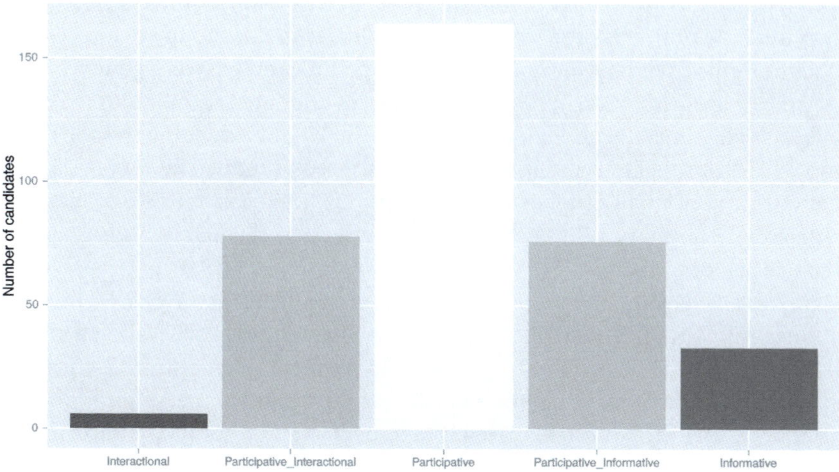

Figure 5. Profiling of the Twitter Styles

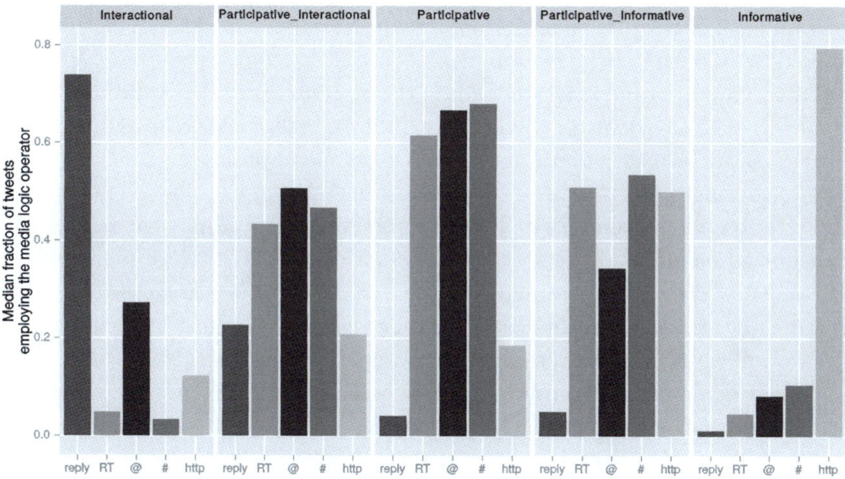

We named the first cluster on the left "Interactional" because the candidates in it used Twitter mainly to engage into direct conversations with other users. More than the 70 % of tweets produced by the candidates in this group are direct messages or replies. On the contrary, hashtag, hyperlink and retweet operators were very rarely used. Mention operators are found in one tweet of four. This tweeting style is highly unconventional, exploiting to the largest extent one minor function of Twitter (that of sending messages addressed to individual users). And in fact only a very small number of candidates, six, used Twitter in this manner. With some irony, we could say that tweets are seen by the users of this group as a substitute for SMS.

Moving to the other extreme of the diagram, to the farthest right, we find the "Informative" group. These candidates used Twitter almost exclusively as a means to diffuse information produced elsewhere, in the form of hyperlinks. They made a very modest if any use of all other operators. With another metaphor, we could say that Twitter is seen by this group's members as a kind of RSS publisher and reader: they post links to websites but do not make use of other operators specific to Twitter. This cluster is the second smallest, including 33 candidates, and represents a second "deviant" use of Twitter – opposite to the first interactional one. Both these tweeting styles constitute radical exceptions to the most common use of Twitter, and they play an important role in shaping the spectrum of alternative uses allowed by this social medium.

At the centre of the diagram we find the largest cluster. The candidates in it made heavy use of hashtag, retweet and mention operators. We named this cluster "Participative" because these operators are meant to promote participation in larger exchanges and discourses: hashtags are anchors to certain events or topics, retweets are instruments of Twitter's polyphony, repeating what was said by others, and mentions invite specific users (and their followers) as interlocutors. Participative candidates rarely engage in direct conversations and do not publish many links to external resources. They play with the operators most specific to Twitter: retweets, hashtags and mentions were born on this social medium and appear to define its most common use. We could say that these candidates practice "pure tweeting", with no immediate interactional nor informative ends.

The "Participative_Interactional" cluster is an intermediary between pure interaction and pure participation. A fifth of the tweets produced by the users in this group were direct messages or replies, which is thrice as much as the global median. In addition to this, hashtag, retweet and mention operators are found each in 40 to 50 percent of their tweets. These candidates participate to the "meaning game" proper to Twitter, but also interact individually with other users.

The last remaining group, "Participative_Informative", is also an intermediary one. One of two tweets produced by the members of this cluster contains a hyperlink. Hashtag and retweet operators are found with the same frequency. Mentions are used slightly less, around a third of the times. Candidates in this cluster use hyperlinks twice as often as the global median, and also participate with hashtags, retweets and mentions.

2.5 Structuring the Tweeting practices of French candidates

These considerations could be thought as a way to give a structural description of the norms regulating the use of Twitter by French candidates during the 2014 campaign. The statistical tools make some of the semiotic norms visible, allowing the researcher to access new aspects of this practice. Rastier (2011) refers to the discourse norms made visible by corpus analysis as "new observables". In our case, the clusters built on the use of the operators help to define the norms active in this field of tweeting practices.

The five families of tweeting practices are organized around *three poles*: the *participative*, the *informative* and the *interactional*. The three "pure" clusters are each close to one pole and far from the other two, while the two intermediary clusters are each close to two poles and far from the remaining third. It should be noticed that no candidates adopted a style close to the informative and to the interactional poles while being far from the participative one. It means that, in our corpus, informative and interactional uses of Twitter are mutually exclusive (there is no "Interactional-Informative" style).

This configuration allows us to talk about *two opposite tendencies*: an interactional and an informative one. When referring to a tendency, we will talk about both pure and intermediary clusters (for example, both the informative and the participative-informative clusters constitute the informative tendency). Schema 1 resumes the configuration of poles and tendencies.

It should be noticed that even if Twitter could have been used by candidates at the same time as a means to send personalized messages (to interact) and messages with a broader reach (to inform), no candidate used it in this way. Also, the diffusion of hyperlinks is very rarely accompanied by personalized mentions, excluding from the observed field of practices the possibility of a "hybrid" between interaction and information. Twitter was not an instrument to send personalized links to websites.

Schema 1. Poles and tendencies

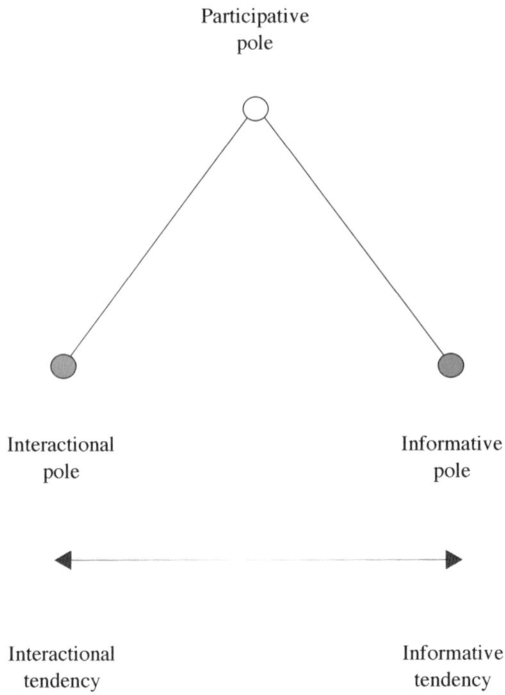

Candidates preferred either a more personalized approach or a more impersonal one, therefore showing that they conceptualized the medium in two very different ways, exploiting different aspects of its potential. It would be interesting, in future research, to further explore the structure of different fields of practices, and compare them. This could result in a better understanding of how technical potentials are reduced to a smaller set whenever their use is filtered by social and semiotic norms. The patterns of this reduction would point to some of the logics of culture and communication, regulating human exchanges.

Twitter *per se*, as a technology, allows a number of different uses: with Eco (1979) we could say that the Twitter *model user* is broadly defined, permitting many potential uses to co-exist. However what matters the most in this case is the transition between the model user and the *empirical uses*: the individual uses of the social medium. What characterize this transition are the norms, made visible in our diagrams, that cause just a limited number of families of uses to actually exist. If it is true that every candidate behaves differently, and if it is also true that

Twitter gives the same potential to all candidates, we still manage to identify a few main patterns. Therefore it is exactly *in the constitution of these patterns* that we may see the effect of the social and semiotic norms responsible for reducing the large virtual potential of Twitter to a small number of actual families of uses.

French political communication showed difficulties merging two tendencies: the informative and the interactional. Maybe French candidates consciously perceive these two tendencies as mutually exclusive, and believe that a hybridization would be seen as contradictory by citizens. Another hypothesis could be that merging information and interaction, for example by sending to individual users many personalized references to websites, would simply be a costly activity.

2.6 Associations between clusters and tweeting interfaces

The five clusters have been calculated exclusively on the recurrence of operators in the candidates' tweets. Therefore, we may now look for further associations between those families of practices and the other variables at our disposal. This may help us to better understand the tweeting styles and also to characterize the other variables' levels on the base of what we have discovered.

We are going to start by observing how the clusters are associated with the preferred tweeting device of each candidate. This is important because different interfaces may produce different experiences of the medium, exposing users to subsets of the Twitter flux or making the use of some operators easier. Figure 6 plots the number of candidates using each tweeting interface most often. The colours of the bars indicate to which tweeting style the candidates belong.

We notice immediately that one interface (Twitter for iPhone) is more frequently used than all other ones (by 154 candidates in 357). The second most popular one (the Twitter website accessed with a web browser) is used by 71 candidates. Twitter for Android is used preferentially by 50 candidates, making it the third most popular. We find three other interfaces preferred each by 8 to 17 candidates (Facebook, Twitter for iPad, tweet buttons embedded in websites) and a higher number of interfaces used each by less than 8 candidates (summing up to 41 candidates and represented as the column "Other" in the diagram).

Figure 6. Interfaces preferentially used for twitting

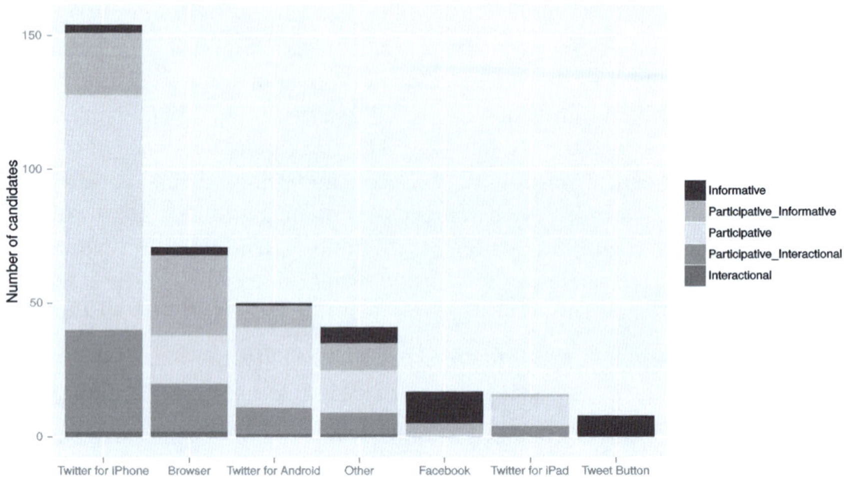

The three major interfaces are used by candidates in all clusters. However, we see that the proportions vary. The candidates using Twitter with an app for smartphones or tablets (either on iOs or on Android) tend to be more participative, and use Twitter to inform as much as to interact with other users. Candidates using iPads in particular use Twitter only rarely to distribute hyperlinks. Instead, the candidates tweeting from a web browser tend to be more informative than participative: as many of them are found in the informative cluster as the sum of those found in the participative and interactional ones.

This tendency becomes predominant for users tweeting from a Facebook application or from tweet buttons found directly on websites: almost the totality of these candidates use Twitter prevalently to distribute hyperlinks. In particular, a small subset of 7 candidates in the informative cluster makes a noticeable use of the source operator (in one tweet of three). This subset mostly uses tweet buttons to tweet, rather than Facebook or other interfaces. Finally, candidates using prevalently other interfaces seem to make the most balanced use of Twitter, as the distribution of clusters in this group closely resembles the global one.

Do the interfaces facilitate a certain approach to the medium, or is there another explanation for the association between the candidates' tweeting styles and their preferences for a certain interface? Candidates using tweet buttons and Facebook application to tweet may actually not fully master the operators specific to Twitter (hashtags, mentions) and therefore adopt an informative tweeting style just because they tweet as a "residual", secondary activity, in which they are not that confident or competent. On the other hand, iPhones and other mobile devices do allow a continuous scan of the Twitter flux, and so they may invite the user to retweet more often, or help to internalize the use of hashtags. Our study points to some potential paths that should be verified, either with experimental procedures, or with the analysis of dedicated datasets, accompanied by a semiotic comparison of the tweeting interfaces (Zinna 2004).

2.7 Associations between clusters and political parties

The families of Twitter practices that we have identified are not homogeneously distributed among the political parties of the candidates. Figure 7 shows the number of candidates for each of the major parties (with at least 15 tweeting candidates in our corpus), and the colour of the bars identifies the family to which the candidates belong.

Figure 7. Distribution of clusters among parties

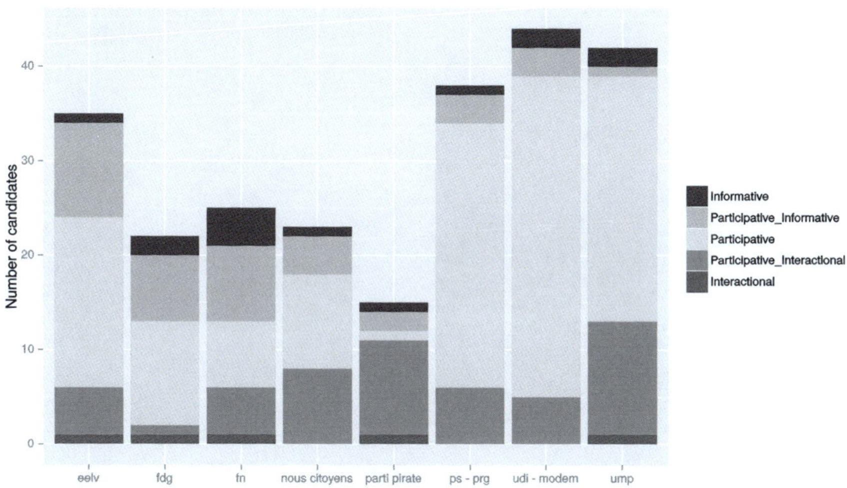

Two of the largest parties, PS-PRG ("Parti socialiste – Parti radical de gauche") and UDI-MODEM ("Union des démocrates et indépendants – Mouvement démocrate"), show a similar distribution. Around 75 % of their candidates belong to the participative cluster, and the remaining ones are equally divided between the informative and the interactional tendencies. The candidates of the UMP ("Union pour un mouvement populaire") party are more attracted by the interactional pole: around 62 % of them adopted a participative style, while 31 % were more interactional and 7 % more informative. The fourth largest party, EELV ("Europe écologie les verts"), was instead more attracted by the informative pole (51 % participative, 31 % informative tendency, 17 % interactional tendency).

Among the four smaller parties, the Parti Pirate shows the most pronounce bias towards the interactional pole, with around the 75 % of its candidates tending towards it; just one in fifteen candidates has been classified as purely participative and the other three show an informative tendency. The FDG ("Front de gauche") shows the opposite configuration, with 50 % of participative candidates and 41 % of informative ones. The candidates of the FN ("Front national") were more informative (48 %) and almost equally participative and interactional (28 % and 24 % respectively). Last, Nous Citoyens was mainly participative (43 %), and more interactional (35 %) than informative (22 %). Figure 8 resumes this information with a PCA plot.

Figure 8. Principal components analysis (parties and tendencies)

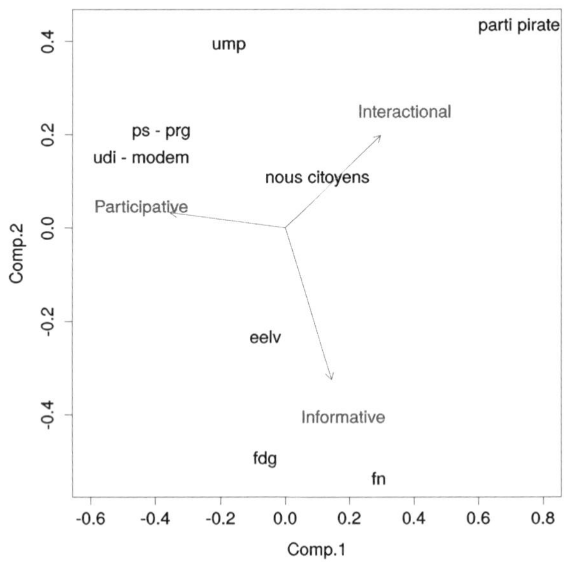

We can observe that the Parti Pirate is the most interactional, while the FN and the FDG are the most informative, and the PS-PRG and UDI-MODEM the most participative. The UMP is equally interactional and participative. It is not possible to associate a certain tweeting tendency to the leftist or rightist orientation of a candidate. We remark that the most extremist parties (FN, FDG) adopt more informative styles, while the moderate ones (PS-PRG, UDI-MODEM, UMP) tend to be more participative. However it should be noticed that the moderate parties are also the largest ones.

2.8 Classification of tweets based on textual analysis

In the last step, we wanted to know if our clusters could be further characterized on the basis of the discourses realized by the candidates in their tweets. Thanks to the software Iramuteq (Ratinaud 2009), we performed to this end a classification of the tweets' texts, based on the co-occurrence of words (Reinert 1983). As a result of this classification, the tweets in our corpus have been preferentially related to one of two ample classes of co-occurring words. Similitude diagrams for the two classes, realized with Iramuteq, are shown in figure 9.

The left half of the figure describes the first of the two classes, that we have called "Political Issues". The words in this class are mainly related to political topics, such as the relationship between France and the European Union, the conduct of the French prime minister François Hollande, the relationships between the three main French parties PS, UMP and FN. Economic issues were also mentioned during the campaign and are included in this class, such as the TAFTA, unemployment and growth. The right half of figure 9 instead describes the lexical class we called "Electoral discourse". It includes hashtags and words used during the campaign to communicate about events, meetings, debates and the elections dates. The two lexical classes are intentionally broad, but give some hints about the contents most addressed by the different parties on Twitter.

Based on the classification of the tweets realized with Iramuteq, we calculated the preference of each candidate's tweets for political issues or for the campaign itself. Figure 10 plots the preferences of the candidates in each cluster.

Figure 9. Lexical classes of the Tweets' texts

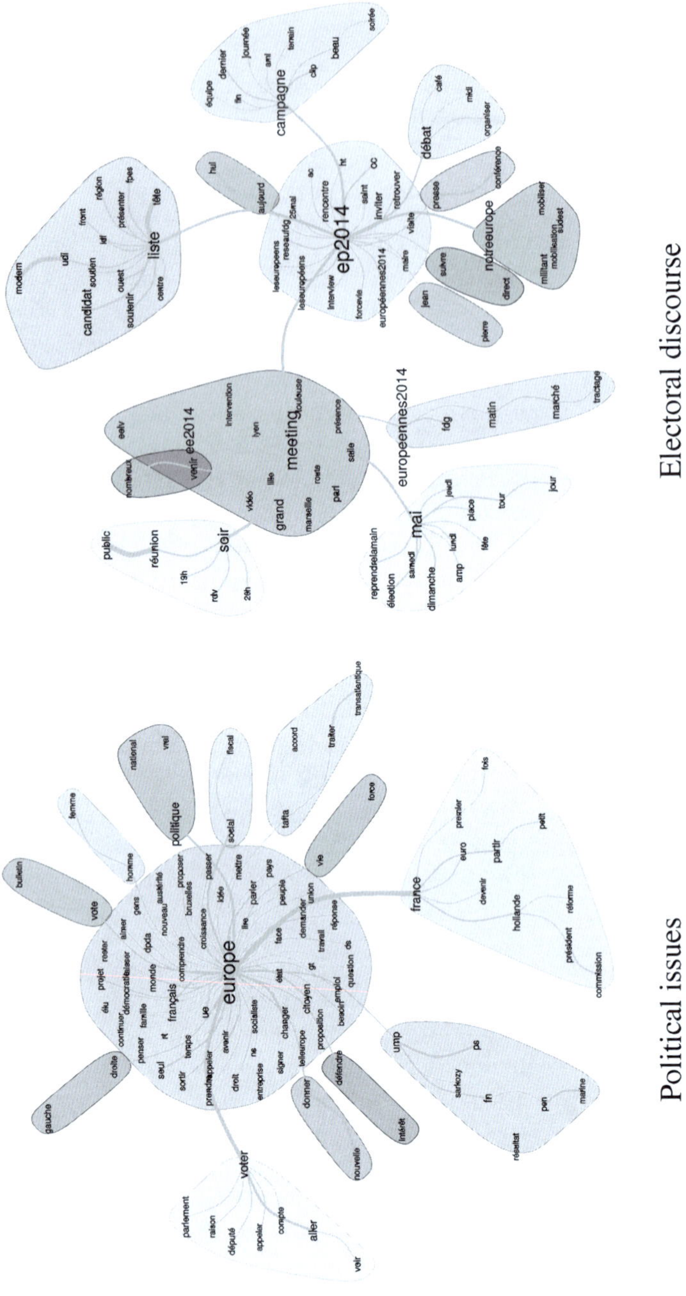

Figure 10. Preference to lexical classes among clusters

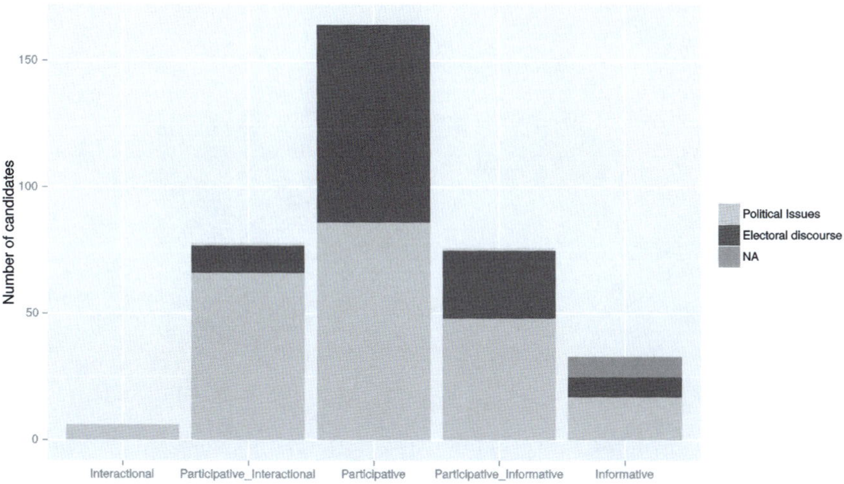

We notice that in the participative cluster political issues and the electoral discourse appear to have the same importance. All the other clusters instead show a preference for the political issues, and this preference is more pronounced on the interactional side than on the informative side. Some of the tweets have not been categorized (they are coloured in green in figure 10), because in most cases they only included a hyperlink without any commentary. The majority of the candidates most often using uncategorised tweets belongs to the purely informative cluster. Figure 11 plots the preferences of each of the major political parties for political issues or for the electoral discourse.

The Parti Pirate is the one most focusing on political issues, followed closely by the EELV. On the opposite, 65 % of the UMP candidates mostly focused on the electoral discourse, followed by the UDI-MODEM (55 % of the candidates). This information should be complemented by the associations between clusters and political parties seen above: the Parti Pirate and the UMP were the most interactional parties; however, it seems that the kind of interaction they perform differs between the two. Our research appears to show that the members of the Parti Pirate use Twitter prevalently to engage in one-to-one conversations about political issues (a *personalized political debate*), while those of the UMP use Twitter to realize a *personalized electoral discourse*, inviting individual users to meetings and other occasions. In these two cases, we can talk of sub-syles of tweeting, defined within the interactional tendency. Textual analysis could be exploited even further to identify more tweeting sub-styles.

Figure 11. Preference to lexical classes among parties

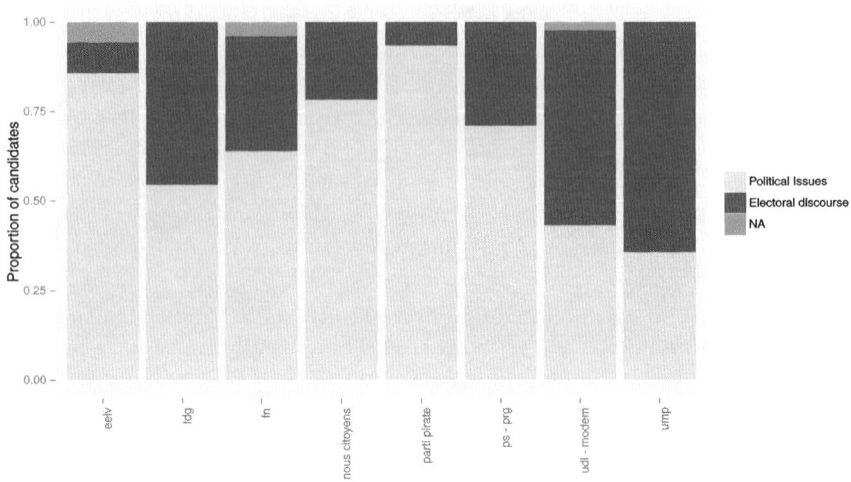

2.9 Conclusion

We have found tendencies in our corpus that show how semiotic and social norms reduce and channel the technical potentials of a social medium. Twitter gives space to many different individual uses, but just a few families of uses, or "tweeting styles", are actually realized. These styles are not homogeneously distributed among the political parties of the candidates. We have also found further associations between the tweeting styles and some other variables, such as the kind of discourse realized in the tweets' texts or the favoured tweeting interface.

The next step of our research will be to perform a similar analysis to other corpora extracted from the TEE2014 database. We want to know if Belgian, English, German, Italian and Spanish candidates use Twitter in a comparable way to the French. Some of the tweeting styles we found in France may not exist elsewhere, or their importance may vary from one country to another. After having extended our research to a larger corpus we may be able to produce a better structural description of the norms guiding the use of Twitter for electoral communication in Europe today.

References

Compagno, Dario: "Families of practices. Employing data mining techniques to differentiate how French candidates make use of Twitter". In: *Twitter at the European Elections 2014*, Metz, February 2015.

Eco, Umberto: *The role of the reader*. Indiana UP: Bloomington 1979.

Einspänner, Jessica / Dang-Anh, Mark / Thimm, Caja: "Computer-assisted content analysis of Twitter data". In: Bruns, Axel / Weller, Katrin / Burgess, Jean / Mahrt, Merja / Puschmann, Cornelius (eds.): *Twitter and Society*. Peter Lang: New York 2013, pp. 97–108.

Maechler, Martin / Rousseeuw, Peter / Struyf, Anja / Hubert, Mia / Hornik, Kurt: *cluster: Cluster Analysis Basics and Extensions*. R package, version 2.0.1. 2015, retrieved 1.6.2015, from https://cran.r-project.org/web/packages/cluster/.

Mercier, Arnaud / Villa, Marina: "The figure of the enemy during the 2014 European tweet-campaign in France and Italy". In: *Twitter at the European Elections 2014*, Metz, February 2015.

Rastier, François: *La mesure et le grain. Sémantique de corpus*. Champion: Paris 2011.

Ratinaud, Pierre: IRaMuTeQ: Interface de R pour les Analyses Multidimensionnelles de Textes et de Questionnaires. 2009, retrieved 1.6.2015, from http://www.iramuteq.org/.

Reinert, Max:. « Une méthode de classification descendante hiérarchique : application à l'analyse lexicale par contexte ». *Les cahiers de l'analyse des données*, VIII (2), 1983, pp. 187–198.

R Core Team: *R: A language and environment for statistical computing*. R Foundation for Statistical Computing: Vienna 2015, retrieved 1.6.2015, from http://www.R-project.org/.

Thimm, Caja: "Political deliberation and the internet: Forms and Functions of civic Participation on Twitter". In: *Communiquer dans un monde de normes. L'information et la communication dans les enjeux contemporains de la mondialisation*, Lille, March 2012.

Thimm, Caja / Einspänner, Jessica / Gautier, Laurent (2015). "German political communication on Twitter during the 2014 European Elections". In: *Twitter at the European Elections 2014*, Metz, February 2015.

Twitter Inc.: *Twitter documentation*. 2015, retrieved 1.6.2015, from https://dev.twitter.com/overview/documentation.

Wickham, Hadley: *ggplot2: elegant graphics for data analysis*. Springer: New York 2009.

Wickham, Hadley. / Francois, Romain: *dplyr: A Grammar of Data Manipulation*. R package, version 0.4.1 2015, retrieved 1.6.2015, from https://cran.r-project.org/web/packages/dplyr/.

Zinna, Alessandro: "L'objet et ses interfaces", *EC*, 2004.

Tatiana Kondrashova & Alex Frame,
Univ. Bourgogne Franche-Comté

3. Exploring the dialogical dimension of political tweets: A qualitative analysis of 'Twitter styles' of UK candidates during the 2014 EU Parliamentary Elections

Abstract

This chapter looks more closely at « informational » and « interactive » communication styles on Twitter, qualitatively examining the multiple and contrasting ways in which different functional operators can be used, and proposing a model based on the "dialogical potential" of the tweet, which aims to avoid some of the more reductive generalisations commonly found.

3.1 Introduction

Since Twitter has become widely used by politicians in many countries, much has been written about the different ways in which this tool is, can and should be exploited (Frame and Brachotte 2015; Jackson and Lilleker 2011; Larsson and Moe 2013; Parmelee and Bichard 2013). Many researchers have denounced a general tendency for politicians to try to reproduce one-to-many communication strategies, tweeting *at* their voters rather than seeking to 'interact' with them in what is often presented as a more appropriate 'web 2.0' style (Small 2010; Vergeer and Hermans 2013). Further attempts have been made to classify communication styles on Twitter, generally ranging between the two poles of one-to-one (interactive) and one-to-many (informational) (Dang-Anh, Einspänner, and Thimm 2012; Eyries and Poirier 2013; Sæbø 2011). This chapter will build on existing approaches to study to what degree the use of different operators on Twitter appears to be correlated with different "Twitter Styles" (Dang-Anh, Einspänner, and Thimm 2012). Adopting a qualitative, context-based approach to analyse messages sent by UK candidates at the European Parliamentary Elections in May 2014, we will seek to further characterise the uses and perceived communicative functions of the Twitter-specific communication operators (*@, RT, #, http*) which contribute to making the micro-blogging network a specific discursive space (Dang-Anh, Einspänner, and Thimm 2012). Anne-Marie Paveau argues that Twitter discourse, as a specific 'techno-discursive' production can be seen to constitute a new genre: "Twitter writing" (Paveau 2012), while Michele Zappavigna sees the discursive dimension of the platform as the key to understanding its "networks of affiliation" (Zappavigna 2012).

Interactions between users on Twitter are the bricks and mortar of the web-based community, the Twittersphere, which, from a technical if not a social point of view, has high potential for generating exchanges in political communication (Ausserhofer and Maireder 2013; Thimm, Einspänner, and Dang-Anh 2012a). When studying online interactions or computer-mediated communication (CMC) it is important to take into consideration interpersonal social interactions (Goffman 1967) but also the specifics of the medium, the technical devices used and their functions (Coutant and Stenger 2010). Compared to face-to-face interactions, the absence of non-verbal means of communication like gestures, mimics, intonation etc. should be taken into account, as well as potential erasing of social distance between communicants, time and place indeterminacy (Bucher 2004). At the same time, the construction of a dialogical situation could be compared to offline communication in terms of the background social and cultural knowledge required to produce and interpret symbolic acts. Language skills and knowledge about the structure and functions of the mediating technical devices are necessary to "release the interactive potential" of the interface (*ibid.*).

In our approach, we do not limit interactions to face to face exchanges (Goffman 1967), but extend this notion to all human activities in which two or more actors are involved (Vion 1992), at least potentially. Publishing tweets in the Twittersphere involves one[17] or more actors, and may create a constellation of "interactants" (Charadeau and Mainqueneau 2002), if we take into account the potential audience of the message posted, or indeed the 'conversations' it generates. The 'presence' of face-to-face interactions is recreated in CMC by various means by which the device allows users to organise their discourse (Bays 1998). Non-verbal interactions are compensated for by other elements inherent to the device's technical structure: in the case of Twitter, these are the communication operators. As Caja Thimm and colleagues have pointed out, each sign becomes a communication operator by taking on different functions within the context of the Twittersphere, as characterized here:

17 The use of the term "interaction" to describe a tweet sent by one person may seem inappropriate. However, we consider it justified by the idea that the person composing the tweet has in mind a potential audience: it is a social act in Goffman's sense, obeying Bakhtinian principles of dialogism (*infra*).

Figure 3.1 Classification of communication operators (Thimm, Einspänner, and Dang-Anh 2013)

Operators	Text	Function
@ (addressing, mentioning)	Name of account, locational reference, emoticons, part of e-mail address	Personal reference, creating attention, dialogicity/interaction, contacting, responsivity, intertextuality, coherence
# (indexing)	Lexeme, key word, occasionalism, abbreviation, acronym, cumulated phrases	Contextualization (cue), discourse organization, topical referencing, tagging, creating ad hoc publics, rhetorical branding
http:// (hyperlinking)	Other websites: internal and external links, pictures/photos (e.g. Twitpics), videos (e.g. YouTube)	Information diffusion, argumentation, illustration, quasi evidencing
RT (Retweet) (redistributing)	Citation, comment	Diffusion, reference, citation, creating attention

Based on their analysis, Thimm and colleagues distinguish two major "Twitter styles": the interactive-personal style, characterised by tweets which invite interactions and interpersonal exchanges, and the thematic-informative style, more concerned with distributing information (Thimm, Einspänner, and Dang-Anh 2012b). The former is characterized by an abundant use of @ and RT operators, while the latter favours external links. In order to simultaneously question and further characterise these styles, this chapter focuses not only on the communication operators, but on their functions as deployed in a specific tweet which can be interpreted in its technical and communication environment and in relation to a wider social and political context. We can ask, for example, whether a journalist who systematically adds to her professional tweets the Twitter handle of the newspaper for which she works, *@Telegraph*, should accurately be described "interactive": she is most probably not seeking a reaction from the newspaper but looking to give her tweets more visibility while underlining her professional affiliation. Similarly, if someone tweets a link in order to provoke reactions from friends, are they employing a solely "informational" strategy? This chapter will endeavour to propose a heuristic framework allowing us to better take into account such specificities.

3.2 Twitter styles revisited

In order to further characterize the Twitter styles, by building on various approaches and trying to limit the overall number, we can list a certain number of partially overlapping major communication functions: addressing, mentions or referencing, contextualisation, argumentation, and passing on information. These can then be related to the communication operators, as presented in Figure 2: each communication operator posesses a main function but could partially fulfill the adjacent functions as well.

Figure 3.2 Five major communication functions correlated with operators

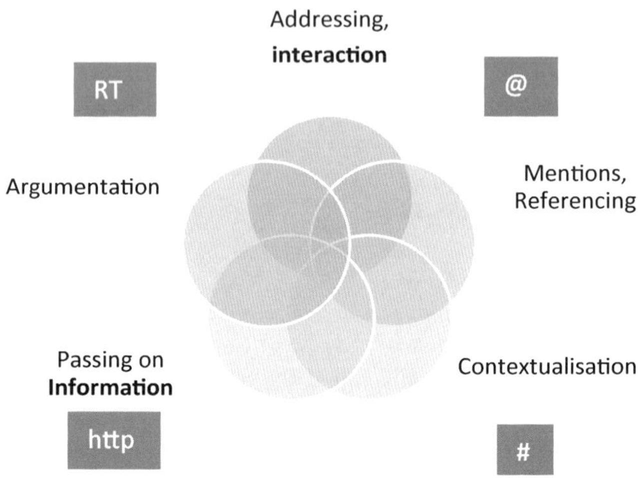

A slightly different way of thinking about the interaction/information continuum is to consider the potential reach of a tweet. A tweet's reach is defined as the number of accounts to which it is potentially visible. A tweet sent by an account (x) becomes potentially visible to another (y) when any of the following conditions are fulfilled:

(a) the account owner of y follows account x;
(b) the tweet sent by x contains the name of account y (an "@ mention");
(c) an account followed by y retweets the tweet sent by x;
(d) the tweet sent by x contains a # which y searches for (or follows using a specific tool);

Some tweets, for example addressed by one account with relatively few followers to another, may have very low reach, potentially being seen by only a few other users. On the other hand, a tweet including very popular twitter handles, plus common or trending hashtags can potentially be seen by millions. Although a lot depends on the actual contents and context of the tweet itself, the functions previously listed can be roughly correlated with their potential reach or the visibility they may give to a particular tweet, as resumed in Figure 3:

Figure 3.3 Relative potential reach of major communication functions

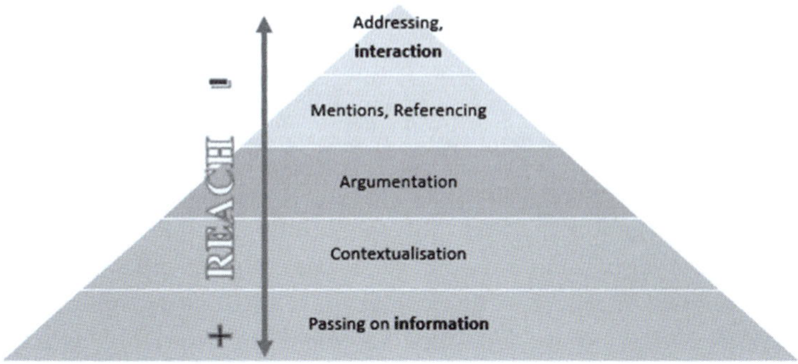

In other words, depending on a communication operator and its contextual function, as well as the element with which the operator is directly combined, its neighbouring elements and their occurrences and significations in a wider context, we can consider that a tweet will have greater or lesser potential reach. It is the technical nature of the operators and the way they function in this particular medium, in relation with the communication environment, that allows us to talk of a 'techno-discursive platform', where the technical elements mobilised in a given interaction contribute to produce pre-programmed dialogical configurations. Their previously-accumulated knowledge about how these technical elements function will allow Twitter users to employ them to seek to achieve certain functions and effects within the Twittersphere. This is close to the dialogical situations encountered in offline communication where participants seek to anticipate potential acts and utterances from their partners, and indeed this conscious or unconscious intersubjective anticipation takes place alongside more technical calculations within the Twittersphere too. Whether the partner is fictive or virtual, the way discourse is constructed is guided by principles of dialogue. From a Bakhtinian perspective (Бахтин 1996), dialogism is a characteristic phenomenon of all speech, even in the case of a monologue.

Indeed, political tweets correspond completely to Bakhtin's logic: the meaning attributed to any tweet is linked to the accumulated tweets of the Twittersphere, and politicians try to take into consideration their potential audience(s). By looking at the way tweets are constructed, we can reason in terms of Bakhtin's logic of the double dialogical extension of discourse (Бахтин 1996). This concept has been used to analyse political discourse online (Bonhomme and Stalder 2006), and allows us to bring together all of the elements that favour a (supposed) dialogue online: producer, potential receiver, different codes of communication (e.g. @, # in case of Twitter), other discourses. Figure 3 (*supra*) can be used to illustrate the different degrees of dialogism which can potentially be associated with different communication functions, and to underline the applicability of this concept to the Twittersphere. In our analysis we will use it in order to evoke the degree of involvement of a Twitter user in a potential dialogue through a tweet. Following on from this discussion, we can formulate two hypotheses:

1. "Twitter styles" are not determined only by the prevailing number of communication operators in a tweet but especially by the correlations of operators' functions as actualized in discourse (the tweet and its wider context).
2. Based on the concept of the dialogism applied to Twitter (Figure 3), we hypothesise that the more determined a potential receiver is (low reach), the higher the degree of implication in a dialogue (dominantly interactive tweet) and, conversely, that the larger the potential audience (high reach), the less the dialogical function is actualized in a tweet (dominantly informational tweet).

These hypotheses were tested by applying them to the corpus of tweets sent by UK candidates during the European Parliamentary Elections, collected within the framework of the TEE2014 project.

3.3 Methodology & results

The corpus consists of all of the tweets of the 309 Twitter accounts which were identified as belonging to UK candidates for the European Parliamentary elections on 22nd May 2014, sent in the three-week run-up to the Elections and in the week following the vote (1st May to 27th May). 72 860 tweets were collected overall. From this corpus, we selected all candidates who had produced more than 50 tweets during the period, this being considered a minimum number for us to be able to usefully characterise the Twitter styles of a particular candidate. This query resulted in a list of 213 candidates. The final step was to reduce this list to a smaller number of candidates enabling us to carry out qualitative analysis to gain insights into the way particular operators and functions were being used. In order to obtain a varied selection of accounts, we chose to take the two candidates whose tweets had the highest percentage of each communication operator, the two candidates with the lowest percentage and two balanced accounts which seem to have close to average numbers of each communication operator (n=18 accounts).[18] The profiles of these accounts are as follows

1. Abundance of communication operators: highest percentage[19] of media[20], RT, http, hashtags and @ (8 accounts).
2. Balanced accounts where the number of each communication operator varies between 25 and 60 percent (2 accounts).
3. Lowest percentage of communication operators (8 accounts).

The first fifty tweets collected for each account were analysed (n=900 tweets). The accounts selected are presented in Table 1, along with the number of communication operators used by each candidate, and the percentage of tweets in which each communication operator was used:

Table 3.1: General information about candidates and statistics about communication operators used

Twitter_handle	local_list_name	place_on_list	Total_tweets	Total_RT	RT %	Total_urls	urls %	Total_#	# %	Total_at	at %
@LindaMcAvanMEP	Labour	1	53	32	60	4	7	28	52	34	64
@SimonDarbyGB	British National Party	5	54	1	1	53	98	0	0	1	1
@EnzaFerreri	Liberty GB	2	58	2	3	56	96	0	0	1	1
@OlwenHamer	Labour	5	61	52	85	1	1	22	36	49	80
@JonathanArnott	UKIP	1	64	0	0	32	50	13	20	16	25
@DianeDoddsMEP	Democratic Unionist	1	67	24	35	3	4	19	28	27	40
@cpasoutheast	Christian Peoples Alliance	1	80	1	1	67	83	1	1	0	0
@yes_edin_south	Scottish National Party	3	116	69	59	33	28	53	45	66	56
@hudghtonmepSNP	Scottish National Party	1	130	120	92	21	16	103	79	86	66
@ansar_ali_khan	Labour	4	140	114	81	4	2	44	31	126	90
@jayne_shotton	Labour	3	145	68	46	56	38	44	30	66	45
@KSillsEngDem	English Democrats	1	163	1	0	155	95	2	1	16	9
@jackbuckby	Liberty GB	3	246	6	2	24	9	1	0	147	59
@kev927riddy	English Democrats	1	322	5	1	297	92	2	0	19	5
@maryhoneyball	Labour	2	342	208	60	29	8	102	29	319	93
@JillEvansMEP	Plaid Cymru	1	388	349	89	86	22	196	50	333	85
@DavidoOrr	British National Party	2	397	200	50	10	2	317	79	80	20
@guydessoy	Animal Welfare	7	447	110	24	152	34	368	82	126	28

The candidates are classified by number of total tweets produced during the period of analysis. The selection criteria resulted in a fairly even spread of parties

18 Where several candidates had the same score for a particular communication operator, the first one in the list of results was selected.

19 The percentage is calculated in relation to the total number of tweets produced by a candidate during the period of analysis.

20 By "media" we understand all photos & videos that were used by a candidate in her/his tweet.

and constituencies being retained, although candidates close to the top of their particular list appear to be overrepresented. It should be highlighted that in some cases (@LindaMcAvanMEP) the abundance of one communication operator is associated with high use of another (high rate of RT and @, > 60 %), while in other cases (@KSillsEngDem) there is a considerable preponderance of one type of communication operator (almost) exclusively. Several accounts fulfilled several criteria at the same time, for example that of @EnzaFerreri had the highest percentage of http, as well as the lowest of # and @.

Discourse analysis of the 900 selected tweets was carried out in the following steps:

1. A communication operator (@, #, httpor RT) was selected.
2. On the basis of the influence of neighbouring elements on the communication operators' function, operators were manually coded using Nvivo, depending on their accompanying element; For example, @Telegraph = @+name_of_media_source.
3. The whole syntagm was analysed, including the neighbouring elements such as prepositions, names of other people, adverbs or other communication operators that could define, change or complete the first function.

Once coded, the tweets, the communication operators and their functions were analysed manually, while Nvivo was used to give insights into word frequency.

3.4 Results and Analysis

3.4.1 The operator @

We began by seeking to establish the degree to which the operator @ can be seen as marker of an "interactive style". A first set of tweets were coded as **@+name of a personal account**. It should be noted that some accounts, such as @Skooshbag, are less transparently personal accounts than others which simply prefix the @ operator to the first name and surname. Most of the time, the account profile description allowed us to clarify this. These tweets often seem to show @ in its primordial function of addressing:

(1) @meljomur @votingyes @Skooshbag @Celebs4indy I wasn't there unfortunately but this post covers general feedback https://t.co/kfuXpYzihz[21]

---

21 Because of the way in which the data was collected, it was unfortunately not possible to reproduce screenshots of all tweets showing them in their original context. For this reason, only the text of the tweets is reproduced here.

(2) @votingyes @Skooshbag @meljomur @DRossborough @Celebs4indy all the more reason to take the positive case to these areas.
(3) @roseleaarran me too!

The first tweet has a neighbouring element http(1) to introduce a supportive argument, the second (2) and third (3) ones obviously have a responsive character. The second tweet illustrates various types of accounts associated with an @ operator, with different degrees of dialogical potential depending on the nature and character of the account: @votingyes = **@+name of community**, @Skooshbag= **@+name of a personal account**. From a political communication perspective, this type of @ also includes politicians' personal accounts: **@+name of a politician**, as in (4) and (5).

(4) RT @CllrAlexander: Great turnout for Dundee… http://t.co/mCDQXhK0I8
(5) @CllrAlexander this for talks as a rally or a big work session?

In the fourth case @ is arguably not a simple marker of interactivity any more (4), since its function has been changed through the presence of another communication operator RT. The goal of this retweet would appear to be referential rather than to enter into a dialogue, though in practice, since the original account is automatically notified of any retweets, this can also be considered as a particular form of dialogical interaction. The counter-example of a tweet using the same operator **@+name of a politician** (5) but accompanied by a question and not a RT radically changes its character and it can much more easily be seen as a part of a dialogue.

It is interesting to note that there are several cases of non-use of the operator **@+name of a personal account**, where opponents refer to the name of the opposite party's member without using the corresponding Twitter handle (6). In contrast to this tendency, political allies are more likely to be introduced directly with @, for instance (7), addressing or referencing a fellow member of Scottish National Party.

(6) So Farage thinks all Romanians are people smugglers & Tory MEP cand Ian Duncan thinks Scots Chinese all eat cat. Fundamentally flawed people
(7) @ToniGiugliano on why we must be independent in Europe: http://t.co/kx20mtbNji #ep2014 *http://t.co/MQoTPwpNTi*.

It is unclear whether the use or non-use of a communication operator here is premeditated or just fortuitous, as counter-examples exist, yet it would appear to make sense as a political strategy designed both to expose one's own message to a sympathetic public which does not necessarily follow one's own account, or indeed to avoid a hostile audience in the case of non-use of an opponent's Twitter handle. It could also be seen as a way to draw attention to an ally's account, but not to that of a political opponent.

The operator @ was very frequently used in its so-called "gratification function" when accompanied by a neighbouring element such as "thanks" (8) (9) or in its localising position accompanied by a preposition of localisation "with" (10).

(8) @AmranHussain @LondonLabour @ClaudeMoraesMEP @Lucy4MEP @SebDance Very many thanks Amran!
(9) @DaveCharnley1 @AnneFairweather @ClaudeMoraesMEP @Lucy4MEP v many thanks Dave
(10) Campaigning with @BarnetLabour & going to Hale ward with @sebdance @giampialhadeff

The construction **@+name of a personal account** + thanks, with, etc. could not be considered as completely non-interactive, because the person in question is addressed (8) (9) or at least mentioned (10), nevertheless its dialogical potential would appear to be relatively lower than in cases of questions or answers (3).

It should be highlighted that constructions of the type **@+name of a tweeting candidate** retweeted by the candidate him/herself are widespread in the political Twittersphere.

(11) RT @redstarneil: Thank u @maryhoneyball et al 4 supporting @QPLabour today. Look forward 2 working with more of you! #labourdoorstep http:/…

The degree of the implication in a dialogue appears here to be low (11). The function of this communication operator, in relation with its neighbouring elements, seems to aim more at gaining visibility rather than interaction. In a similar function we find another type of @: **@+party name**.

(12) Did Labour and the Conservatives do well for the North East 2006–2012? Don't vote for more of the same, vote @UKIP. http://t.co/s6o28eJgk8

In the example (12) the dialogical potential appears seriously limited, and the tweet seems to aim rather at increasing the visibility of the party in question by mentioning it, or indeed at attracting new followers to the author's own account by showing party affiliation. This is an example of a more general strategy which can often be observed.

The last category of @ that we would like to emphasise in this study is **@+name of media source** that seems to reveal the polysemic potential of this communication operator's functions.

(14) Great start for Louise Bours on Question @bbcquestiontime!
(15) @itvnews There's a revolution happening. Many Londoners are planning to #VoteAnimalWelfareParty this Thursday EU elections. Are u following?

(16) "@TheEconomist: Losing America cost King George III his sanity. Mr Cameron thinks losing Scotland would not even cost him his job" losing??

This type of @ usage often appears more informative than interactive. It can be used for argumentation purposes (15) (16) or for passing on information (14).

Through examples 1–16, the @ operator can be seen to potentially fulfil various functions, with different degrees of implication in dialogue. This depends notably on the neighbouring elements that introduce this operator, and the nature of the account with which it is associated: name of a personal account, name of political party or organisation, or name of media.

3.4.2 The operator RT

This communication operator is by nature heteroglossic in Bakhtin's sense, it refers to the words of others, and can be used to pass on information, sometimes accompanied by argumentation. Once again, its exact nature and function are strictly dependant on its context of usage.

In the cases where RT introduces a tweet from a personal account (1), it fulfils its referencing function as a mention that possesses some dialogical potential, and may imply a community of interactants.

(1) RT @tobyperkinsmp: Great to join @WMLabour Euro candidate @ansar_ali_khan & Sir Albert Bore to see Labour investment on Metro extension ht…

Retweeted tweets may also themselves be retweeted (2), possibly with additional comments or reactions, creating a chain of interactions and presenting an interesting case of an enlarged discursive sphere.

(2) RT @ChorltonGreen: RT @ranty_man: Hunt is desperately trying not to alienate former Labour voters #BBCQT; is it working?

Other examples show that when RT introduces the parties' speech (3) (4) (5), it appears to lose much of the dialogical potential of the examples above (1) (2). The goal of such retweets is generally to pass on information, assure parties' visibility or associate oneself with the particular point of view, event, etc. contained in the original tweet. This kind of tweet seems to be less engaging, given that party tweets themselves are generally more neutral that personal ones.

(3) RT @LabourStafford: Euro campaign launch w/ @neenaformep @sionsimon @LW4WM @ansar_ali_khan @katevoteslabour @annieinclover @rowan_draper: h…
(4) RT @AnimalsCount: Results for London 21,092 for #AnimalWelfareParty. Sadly, no seat for us this time. Huge thanks to our amazing supporters…
(5) RT @AnimalsCount: @Djurensparti Best of luck for #EP2014 elections tomorrow. Let's Make History For Animals! #EU2014 http://t.co/Ru79J3rHnT

The last case that we will distinguish in this study is the retweet of a media source (6):

(6) RT @Daily_Record: SNP EU candidate @TasminaSheikh outlines why she and many other Scots-Asians are voting Yes in the #indyref http://t.co/U…

This type of tweet can fulfil both functions of argumentation and contextualisation, but often in the form of quotation.

There are numerous cases of retweets of messages sent to candidates (analysed in the previous section), as shown in example (7), in order to give them more visibility or to show the candidate being addressed in a positive light.

(7) RT @ARUKnews: @maryhoneyball Looking forward to the results of the EU elections. Thanks for your support for medical research #EU4Research

A quote thus deprived of a dialogical dimension can be seen as an instrument of political approbation and argumentation and indeed this dimension is also present in the cases of political parties (3) (4) (5).

3.4.3 The operator

The hashtag is a specific sign that constitutes an important contextualizing element of Twitter discourse, characterized by its terse style. There are several types of hashtags that can be distinguished according to content: **#+phrase** (1) (a syntactically-structured utterance) or **#+word-phenomena** (2) (including acronyms and abbreviations).

(1) Is London ready to **#VoteAnimalWelfareParty** on Thursday at #EP2014 elections? Pls RT if you think yes! http://t.co/YQzlFHEhmj
(2) RT @GlenisWillmott: Labour MEPs fight for LGBT rights in the UK, EU and worldwide **#EP2014** @LGBTLabour @LGBTintergroup http://t.co/U68vnykRXs

However, as in the case of the @ operator, it is not the type of hashtag that determines its function, but the elements it introduces. Both hashtags in the first example (1) present reduced verbal units that aim to contextualize the discourse. The first conveys ideas linked to a particular cause, and the request to retweet aims to encourage people to show their support for this cause. The second might serve to increase visibility of the tweet to all people following the official #EP2014 hashtag. The potential reach of these hashtags is relatively high both because of the wide audience reached by the second hashtag and by the incitation to fellow supporters to retweet the message. The same hashtag used in the second example (2), in a retweet, seems to be more about passing on information, as well as associated references or argumentation through the link.

The dialogical potential of a hashtag also varies depending on its environment. Here are a series of examples using #VoteAnimalWelfareParty. The degree of implication in a dialogue is linked to the construction of the tweet:

(3) @leonalewismusic We want to write a new chapter of history for animals at EU elections this Thurs. Will u join us? #VoteAnimalWelfareParty

(4) @itvnews There's a revolution happening. Many Londoners are planning to #VoteAnimalWelfareParty this Thursday EU elections. Are u following?

(5) This Thursday Londoners have the opportunity to write a new chapter in this history of mankind. Play your part. #VoteAnimalWelfareParty

(6) We need around 140,000 votes from across London to make history for animals on Thursday! #VoteAnimalWelfareParty http://t.co/YQzlFHEhmj

(7) Believe in a better world for all animals? RT this: #VoteAnimalWelfareParty EU Elections May 22 http://t.co/fWshQGIgKF

In these cases, the author tries to appeal to the audience by accompanying the hashtag with linguistic elements such as questions (3) (4) (7) and imperative forms (5). The direct address is a way of trying to increase levels of engagement.

(8) #bbcnews BBC commentators and reporters cannot seem to hide their obvious enthusiasm for UKIP

(9) #bbcnews why is it the bbc are avoiding talking about German results? Maybe it doesn't fit today's agenda as Euro skeptics only got 7 %

The hashtags that name the information source (8) (9) can be compared with previous examples using the operator **@+name of a media source**. The difference would appear to be that using @ is a way of seeking to interact with a media source, whereas the choice of # sets up a conversation *about* the media source, often to criticise it, which can possibly be seen as an invitation to dialogue, either with the representatives of the media source, or among Twitter users who may or may not agree.

The dialogical potential of a hashtag thus depends very much on the hashtag itself: a common hashtag will add visibility to a tweet, but possibly not create much interaction, whereas a more obscure one can be a way of targeting a message to a small group of insiders who don't necessarily follow one's account.

3.4.4 Use of media

When considering use of media in tweets, we can distinguish videos, photos and screenshots.[22] In this chapter we focus solely on the use of photos which are

22 Screenshots of newspapers' sites with relevant information, most often a picture of a candidate, are common. Their use in a tweet may fulfil an argumentative function (reference to an external source) or be a means of self-promotion.

the most common type of media in our global corpus. Photos allow politicians to illustrate their messages and to reinforce their impact on the audience, and can be perceived as having high argumentative and interactive potential, even if this has not been established empirically in the framework of the current study. We can distinguish apparently "spontaneous" photos and others which are more evidently "staged". Examples of photos within the first category concern some sports events, photos of natural scenes or of political debates. The aim of this type of photo seems to be to create a degree of complicity with Twitter users who could potentially be witness to these events. Staged photos often concern events from the campaign trail, possibly aiming to allow absent followers to feel present alongside their candidate.[23]

In individual tweets, the most common way for politicians to introduce photos is: **introductory utterance + spontaneous/staged photo.** The dialogical potential of a photo seems to depend on the nature of this photo and on the content of the introductory utterance.

Photo 1

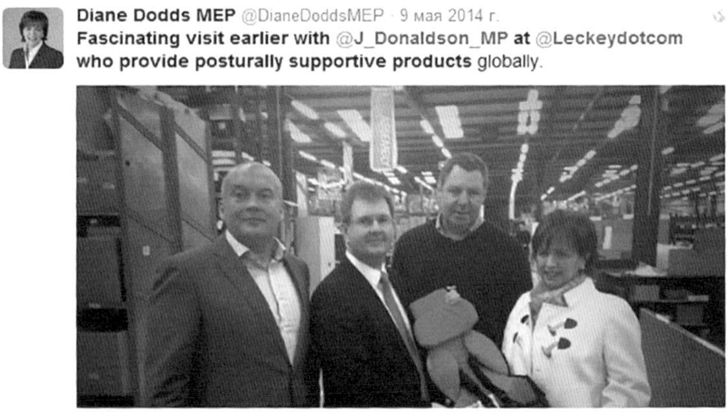

This post (Photo 1) presents a composition of an introductory utterance that contains two @ communication operators: **with + @ + name of politician** and **@ + company name** and a **staged photo**, possibly in the hope of being retweeted, since the dialogical potential seems otherwise to be relatively low.

23 This distinction is of course largely artificial, since even "spontaneous" photos are planned and taken intentionally. The difference here is more precisely as to how explicit the staging appears to be.

Photo 2

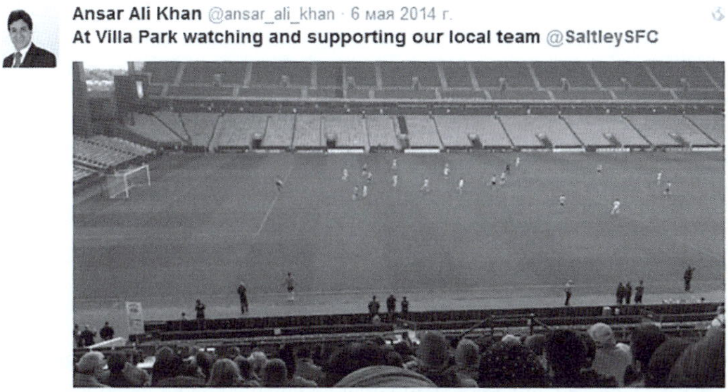

The second tweet also contains an @ communication operator: **@ + football club,** but takes the form of a **spontaneous photo** this time. By choosing this particular @ mention and showing followers of the football team that he was present at the match, it can be assumed that this candidate was seeking to underline their shared allegiances, foregrounding his role of "ordinary" football supporter rather than his role of candidate.

It is interesting to note that the photos posted tend to constitute an integral part of the utterance (nominative sentence completed by Photo 1, elliptic sentence explained by Photo 2). Once again, the complementarity between the introductory utterance and the posted photo underlines the necessity for these two elements to be analysed together. Nominative sentences as illustrated by Photo 1 are recurrent:

(3) Great session with the best team in Birmingham in my own ward WWH + **staged photo**

(4) Lovely afternoon in Stafford with super PPC @kategodfrey @sionsimon @neenaformep @LW4WM and Stafford councillors + **staged photo**

(5) Fantastic 1st day of @balmoralshow – great conversations with people from right across NI & beyond. Roll on tomorrow + **spontaneous photo with a political actor.**

Another common type of introductory utterance: gratification element (thank you) + **spontaneous/staged photo**, # + **spontaneous/staged photo**, as for example

(6) Best wishes to the hundreds of cyclists that just passed my office in Lisburn who are #cyclingagainstsuicide + **spontaneous photo of a sports event**.

The spontaneous photos may seem to be more interactive because they can more easily be shared and understood (2) (5) (6), while the staged photos (1) (3) (4) seem to target Twitter users curious about a precise event. In all cases, both spontaneous and staged photos can be used to convey information or arguments. Their interactivity can be measured only in conjunction with the analysis of an introductory utterance that determines the targeted audience.

3.4.5 The use of links (http)

A hyperlink is a flexible communication operator whose function and associated dialogical potential depend very much on its neighbouring elements, as the content of a shortened link is generally not immediately apparent. The vast majority of links are coded by clickable shortened URLs, which provide few clues to their target or content. This may or may not make people curious to click on them. Sometimes the content of the link is directly integrated in a tweet (for example videos from Youtube (1, below)). Politicians' links often lead to personal or party sites, blogs or Facebook pages, whose objective appears to be to invite people to adhere to their ideas.

There are different ways of introducing (a) **personal links** that lead either to personal sites (3), Facebook pages or profiles, (4) (5) (6), or blogs (2), which can be termed or (b) **external links** leading to external sources (1) (7) (8). The dialogical potential of these links depends in the first place on the neighbouring elements: other communication operators and/or other integrated elements (videos/clickable screenshots of media web pages). Tweets (1) and (2) below illustrate this. Tweet (1) includes an external link to YouTube, yet the whole tweet seems to be more interactive than the second one (2) that leads to a personal link. In spite of the presence of a gratification element, tweet (2) does not seem to address followers in particular, and is incomplete, with followers being implicitly encouraged to click on the link for more information. The first tweet (1) contains a hashtag and a question that seem to increase its dialogical potential, in association with the integrated video.

(1) Believe in a better world for all animals? RT this: #VoteAnimalWelfareParty EU Elections May 22 http://bit.ly/1t3ebBU + **integrated video**
(2) Thanks: A big thank you to everyone who took the time and trouble to vote BNP yesterday. I would also like to… http://bit.ly/1jBUs9M
(3) The second in my week-long series of reasons to vote UKIP on Thursday. Send them a message! jonathanarnott.co.uk/2014/05/reason…

Examples (5) and (6) also contain personal links that lead to Facebook but seem to reveal higher dialogical potential than tweet (1) thanks to the neighbouring elements used, such as @ + **personal account name** (5) or question + integrated article (6). Even an external link to a media source as in examples (7) and (8) could be seen to be interactive depending on the neighbouring elements as @ + **personal account name** + integrated picture (8) or opinion + external link + integrated video (7).

(4) This is the last day before the vote to elect Members of the European Parliaments for Britain, and I cannot… http://fb.me/6qIBKclQD

(5) @meljomur @votingyes @Skooshbag @Celebs4indy I wasn't there unfortunately but this post covers general feedback m.facebook.com/story.php?stor…

(6) *Had enough yet? The system is broken.* http://fb.me/3a9Ba5Lby + **integrated article from Guardian**

(7) Didn't see it on tv news at all but at least @BBCScotlandNews have the pensions confirmed safe article posted on line *m.bbc.co.uk/news/uk-scotla…*+**integrated video**

(8) @ToniGiugliano on why we must be independent in Europe: heraldscotland.com/mobile/comment… #ep2014 + **picture**

In general we can note several strategies used by politicians in order to incite Twitter users to follow their personal sites or external links: imperative phrases (3), broken sentences (4), questions (6) or even direct addressing (8). The dialogical potential of a link does not depend on its nature but on the introductory utterance and the elements integrated afterwards. A link to Facebook or another social media account may also lead sympathetic Twitter followers to follow that account too, thus increasing the candidate's social media visibility and reach in general. The dialogical potential of tweets including social media links thus exceeds Twitter itself, since comments may be left on other platforms, after clicking on a social media link in a tweet.

3.5 Discussion and conclusions

The examples cited of the different communication operators and their functions tend to confirm the hypotheses formulated above. Hypothesis 1, concerning the importance of neighbouring elements in determining a communication operator's function can be validated thanks to the data studied. This suggests that Twitter style classifications should be based not only on the number of each type of communication operator used by a politician, but on the functions of the prevailing operator(s) as actualized in discourse by means of its accompanying elements. This in turn entails close, qualitative analysis of the tweets in question.

The second hypothesis, concerning the degree of implication in dialogue, is also supported by the data considered in this study, although the notion of "dialogue" clearly merits further investigation, which could be carried out by examining the retweets and conversations provoked by a given tweet. Despite this, the notion of implication or reach appears to be a meaningful criterion on which to differentiate tweets qualitatively, ranging from those whose dialogical markers (addressing, questions, exclamations...) and communication operators suggest that they are aimed at one or a few individuals, to those who seem to target a much wider audience. These differences in potential reach often seem to correspond to different strategies, ranging from "authentic" one-to-one dialogue – that Holy Grail of political communication on Twitter when one reads certain analyses – to the use of hashtags or at mentions which seem aimed to ensure a tweet's visibility rather than to provoke direct exchanges with other users. There again, the contents of the tweet (more or less controversial, surprising, inspiring, etc.) and its dialogical markers, as well as the social and / or political context in which it is sent, all need to be taken into account in order to further characterise its dialogical potential.[24] In order to analyse this potential, we propose the following table, applied to different operators, to resume, qualify and exemplify the differing degrees of dialogical implication.

Figure 4: the "I to I" Model

Degree of implication in a dialogue	+++	++	+/-
Dominant communication operator functions	Addressing, Mention, interaction	Referencing, argumentation	Passing on information, contextualisation
Goal/strategy	To involve other persons directly in discussion	To enter into a particular mini-public on Twitter	To share information
Audience concerned by the message	=> limited number of Twitter users	=> some groups of Twitter users	=> large numbers of Twitter users

24 It should be further noted that this "potential" remains a prescriptive idealisation when based on an analysis of the dialogical features of the tweets themselves. Another way to approach the question would be to analyse the actual "impact" of the tweets in the Twittersphere, based on conversations and retweets (*supra*).

Degree of implication in a dialogue	+++	++	+/-
Example[25]	@CllrAlexander this for talks as a rally or a big work session?	RT @ChorltonGreen: RT @ranty_man: Hunt is desperately trying not to alienate former Labour voters #BBCQT; is it working?	#bbcnews BBC commentators and reporters cannot seem to hide their obvious enthusiasm for UKIP
Example of communication using operators	@+name of a person / question @+name of a person / gratification elements	#+question RT+personal commentary[26] @+party name	Popular # RT / @+name of a media source http[without other elements]

The acronym in "I to I Model" stands for "Information to Interaction": often presented as the two extremes of a tweet's potential functions. The model characterises the relationship between four key elements. (i) The **communication operator's function** as mobilized in the tweet which defines (ii) the **audience potentially concerned** by that tweet. According to the audience potentially addressed or actually involved in a conversation, we can talk about (iii) the **reach** of a tweet. Based on the reach, (iv) the **relative dialogical potential** of the message can be estimated. This estimate is not numerical, but simply relative to other contextualised configurations of operators. The figure suggests that the degree of implication in a dialogue is inversely proportional to the number of Twitter users concerned by a tweet. Once actualized in a tweet, communication operators should give a key to understanding a politician's strategy to reach his or her targeted audience.

Although the "I to I model" attempts to associate particular occurrences of operators and their neighbouring elements with different degrees of implication

25 It is not possible to show separate examples for each type of operator, because the functions are actualized by the way of correlations between different operators, thus to extract them from their context does not make sense.

26 One particular limit to characterising the dialogical value of retweets is the difficulty of knowing whether a message is being quoted partially or not, and consequently distinguishing its different authors. While this is possible when working on a corpus, it is much more difficult for users in real time.

in dialogue, we have already noted that this may vary considerably depending on other elements in the tweet and on the wider context. The model thus needs to be further developed and adapted to take into account these factors. Other limits to this preliminary study include sample size and representativeness, and the particular domain (political communication) from which the tweets were chosen. While we would argue that the general principle of taking into account the context of operator use remains equally valid for tweets from other domains of social activity (corporate communications, celebrity fandom…), it is clear that each of these domains is likely to reveal its own specificities.

Future developments of this model will go further into taking into account the use of embedded or linked media (photos, videos) in tweets, as this is a widely-used feature of the platform. The approach also needs clarify how images relate to questions of dialogue and reach.

For all of its limits and the exploratory nature of this approach, we suggest that the "I to I" model opens up new possibilities to let us systematically investigate and characterise the dialogical qualities not only of single tweets, but also, by extension, of individual accounts, political parties, etc., in a more sophisticated way than many of the approaches currently presented in the academic literature. In this respect, we hope that it may help shed light on the ongoing debate in political communication into the relative "(im)maturity" of politicians' use of the medium and the frequent denunciations of their "web 1.0 mentality", whereby they prefer to broadcast information rather than interact. Looking at the relative reach or dialogical potential of their messages may enable us to distinguish more subtly between different strategies, taking into account the different communication functions which specific tweets might seem to fulfil, and the individuals or groups which they ostensibly target, be they political colleagues, journalists or media, activists, citizens, etc. If direct two-way politician-voter interactions may indeed be scarce, with whom do politicians more readily interact and what seems to motivate the different types of tweets they use? The answers to such questions will hopefully give us a more accurate vision of various logics of usage by politicians, which may then be fed back into the wider discussion about the possible construction of a deliberative digital public sphere and the degree to which the adoption of Twitter and other social networking sites by politicians may or may not renew democratic processes.

References

Ausserhofer, Julian / Maireder, Axel: 'National Politics on Twitter: Structures and Topics of a Networked Public Sphere', *Information, Communication & Society*, 3 (16), 2013, pp. 291–314.

Bays, Hillary. 'Framing and Face in Internet Exchanges: A Socio-Cognitive Approach'. 1998, http://www.linguistik-online.com/bays.htm, accessed on 09.09.2015.

Bonhomme, Marc / Stalder, Pia: 'Analyse Sémiotique Des Pages D'accueil Des Sites Politiques Suisse', *La politique mise au net*, no. 80, 2006, pp. 11–23.

Bucher, Hans-Jürgen 2004: 'Online-Interaktivität –ein hybrider Begriff für eine hybride Kommunikationsform. Begriffliche Klärungen und empirischen Rezeptionsbefunde'. In: Bieber, Christoph / Leggewie, Claus: *Interaktivität. Ein transdisziplinärer Schlüsselbegriff*, Frankfurt : Campus. 2004, pp. 132–167.

Charadeau, Patrick / Mainqueneau Dominique: *Dictionnaire D'analyse Du Discours*. Paris: Edition du Seuil. 2002.

Coutant, Alexandre / Stenger, Thomas: 'Processus Identitaire et Ordre de L'interaction Sur Les Réseaux Socionumériques', *Les enjeux de l'information et de la communication*, 1, 2010, pp. 45–64.

Dang-Anh, Mark / Einspänner, Jessica / Thimm, Caja: 'Mediatisierung Und Medialität in Social Media: Das Diskurssystem „Twitter"'. *Sprache Und Kommunikation Im Technischen Zeitalter: Wieviel Internet (v) Erträgt Unsere Gesellschaft?* 2, 2012, pp. 68–91.

Eyries, Alexandre / Poirier, Cassandra: Alexandre Eyries et Cassandra Poirier, « Une communication politique 2.0 », Communication [Online], Vol. 32/2 | 2013, accessed on 14.09.2015. http://communication.revues.org/5001.

Frame, Alex / Brachotte Gilles: 'Le Tweet Stratégique: Use of Twitter as a PR Tool by French Politicians'. *Public Relations Review* 41 (Special Issue: New Digital Publics), 2015, pp. 278–87.

Goffman, Erving: Interaction Ritual: Essays in Face-to-Face Behavior. Chicago: Aldine Pub. Co., 1967.

Jackson, Nigel / Lilleker, Darren: 'Microblogging, Constituency Service and Impression Management: UK MPs and the Use of Twitter'. *The Journal of Legislative Studies* 17 (1), 2011, pp. 86–105.

Larsson, Anders O. / Moe, Hallvard: 'Twitter in Politics and Elections. Insights from Scandinavia'. In *Twitter and Society*, edited by Katrin Weller, Axel Bruns, Jean Burgess, and Merja Mahrt, 219–30. New York: Peter Lang Publishing Inc, 2013, pp. 319–330.

Parmelee, John H. / Bichard, Shannon L.: Politics and the Twitter Revolution: How Tweets Influence the Relationship between Political Leaders and the Public. Lanham, Md.: Lexington Books, 2013.

Marie-Anne Paveau. 'Genre de discours et technologie discursive. Tweet, twittecriture et twitterature'. 2012, https://hal.archives-ouvertes.fr/hal-00824817/document, accessed on 06.09.2015.

Sæbø, Øystein: 'Understanding Twitter Use among Parliament Representatives: A Genre Analysis'. In *Electronic Participation*, edited by Efthimios Tambouris, Ann Macintosh, and Hans de Bruijn, 1–12. Lecture Notes in Computer Science 6847. Springer: Berlin Heidelberg, 2011, http://link.springer.com/chapter/10.1007/978-3-642-23333-3_1, accessed on 17.09.2015.

Small, Tamara A. : 'La politique canadienne en 140 caracteres : la vie des partis dans l'univers Twitter'. *Revue parlementaire canadienne* 33 (3), 2010, pp. 41–48.

Thimm, Caja / Einspänner, Jessica / Dang-Anh, Mark: 'Politische Deliberation Online – Twitter Als Element Des Politischen Diskurses'. In *Mediatisierte Welten*. Wiesbaden: VS Verlag fur Sozialwissenschaften, 2012a, pp 283–305.

Thimm, Caja / Einspänner, Jessica / Dang-Anh, Mark: 'Twitter Als Wahlkampfmedium: Modellierung Und Analyse Politischer Social-Media-Nutzung', *Publizistik*, 3 (57), 2012b, pp. 293–313.

Thimm, Caja / Einspänner, Jessica / Dang-Anh, Mark: 'Mediatisierung Und Medialität in Social Media: Das Diskurssystem "Twitter"'. In *Sprache Und Kommunikation Im Technischen Zeitalter. Wieviel Technik (v)erträgt Unsere Gesellschaft?* Berlin: de Gruyter, 2013, pp. 68–91.

Vergeer, Maurice / Hermans, Liesbeth: 'Campaigning on Twitter: Microblogging and Online Social Networking as Campaign Tools in the 2010 General Elections in the Netherlands'. *Journal of Computer-Mediated Communication* 18 (4), 2013, pp. 399–419.

Vion, Robert: La Communication Verbale. Analyse Des Interactions. Paris: Hachette, 1992.

Zappavigna, Michele: Discourse of Twitter and Social Media: How We Use Language to Create Affiliation on the Web. 1st ed. Bloomsbury Academic, 2012.

Бахтин, Михаил: *Собрание сочинений*. Vol. 5. Москва: Русские словари, 1996.

Nanta Novello Paglianti, Univ. Bourgogne Franche-Comté

4. Twitter et la politique : stratégies de communication de candidats et espace public

Abstract
The chapter focuses on the tweets exchanged by two Italian candidates during the European election campaign, analysing how they are using Twitter as a political communication tool, and trying to define the "political tweet" in the light of the current political system.

4.1 Introduction

Traditionnellement Twitter est présenté comme « un service Web de microblogging permettant à ses utilisateurs de diffuser des messages limités à 140 caractères, de rediffuser et de répondre à ceux d'autres utilisateurs[27] ». Inventé par Jack Dorsey en 2006 à San Francisco, ce service a pris de l'ampleur grâce à sa structure multifonctionnelle. Il a réussi à regrouper différentes fonctions avant séparées dans d'autres médias sur une seule interface.

Nous commencerons par nous centrer sur ce medium en tant que support en explorant ses fonctions communicationnelles et ensuite nous étudierons les pratiques de Twitter, les manières dont deux candidates italiennes aux élections européennes ont utilisé ce microblogging. Cette approche s'explique d'une part par la nécessité de comprendre comment ce medium dicte ses contraintes d'interaction avec les utilisateurs et oriente la communication de ses participants, de l'autre par la volonté d'analyser comment les candidates s'approprient ce support et s'expriment à travers leurs tweets. Peut-on vraiment parler de stratégies de communication à l'intérieur de l'agora de Twitter?

Nous nous intéresserons aux pratiques sociales dictées par ce support : peut-on examiner des « manières de faire » d'usagers ? Plutôt qu'approcher Twitter comme un texte en cherchant des limites presque impossibles à cerner, nous allons le considérer comme une pratique[28] dans le sens qu'on s'intéressera au cours d'action

27 Emilie Ogez & Jean-Noel Chaintreuil, *Twitter, 101 questions*, Strasbourg, Ed. Diateino, 2012, p. 21.

28 « On fera donc l'hypothèse que les pratiques se caractérisent et se distinguent principalement par le rôle du cours d'action dans la production de formes signifiantes, et spécifiquement des *valeurs pratiques*, suscitées et exprimées par la forme des cours d'action, dans le « grain » le plus fin de leur déploiement spatial, temporel, aspectuel,

que Twitter va produire, à la dynamique activée par ce medium. Ce sont les étapes de l'action qui produisent du sens, les objectifs que les utilisateurs vont atteindre et qui sont remaniés continument dans la pratique des usagers. Twitter est à ce propos un exemple pertinent pour l'observation des usages collectifs des réseaux sociaux et pour la construction du sens des « expériences en acte [29]».

Si Twitter dicte, sur le plan de l'expression certaines configurations figées (obligation d'écriture brève, emploi de symboles spécifiques, de hashtags, etc.), les candidats construisent-ils un *modus operandi* cohérent, spécifique à l'usage de ce microblogging ?

4.2 Le cadre de la recherche

Nous avons constitué et étudié un corpus de tweets échangés par les candidats italiens de la liste Tsipras et de celle du Movimento Cinque Stelle (M5S) pendant la campagne électorale européenne 2014[30]. Notre corpus a été recueilli grâce à une méthode quantitative qui a pu rassembler les tweets et les hashtags envoyés par les candidats italiens des listes officielles de la campagne électorale européenne de 2014. Malgré l'utilisation d'un logiciel qui a rassemblé tous les tweets et les hashtags émis par les candidats de chaque liste de différents pays d'Europe (Allemagne, Angleterre, Belgique, Italie, Espagne), nous avons choisi, dans ce papier, de nous focaliser sur un seul pays : l'Italie.

La multiplicité des données a permis une analyse comparative des corpus dans la volonté de comprendre les styles des campagnes électorales, le croisement des stratégies des candidats et l'étude des contenus des tweets échangés[31]. Twitter est-il un outil d'autopromotion des candidats ? S'agit-il d'une nouvelle façon de rester au plus près des électeurs ?

Pour le moment, nous allons nous concentrer sur une analyse qualitative en rassemblant les tweets envoyés par quelques représentants italiens de la liste Tsipras et celle du Movimento Cinque Stelle (M5s).

---

modal et passionnel », J. Fontanille, « L'analyse du cours d'action. Des pratiques et des corps », NAS, 114, 2011, consulté le 28/06/2015.

29 Pour un approfondissement sur la pratique en sémiotique, je renvoie à J. Fontanille, Pratiques Sémiotiques, Paris, Puf, 2008, p. 26.

30 Il s'agit du projet ANR (2012–2015) « Twitter at the European Elections 2014 » (TEE 2014), piloté par le laboratoire CIMEOS de l'Université de Bourgogne (A. Frame). Cette étude réunit différents laboratoires internationaux autour de la question « Formes et fonctions de participation politique dans un monde numérique ».

31 La récolte des données s'est achevée une semaine après le vote européen le 1er juin 2014.

Enfin, le but ultime de cette recherche sera celui de comprendre la nature d'un tweet politique, si l'on peut en parler à juste titre pour comprendre ses conditions d'existence et d'échange. Pourquoi certains tweets sont-ils plus suivis ou retweetés que d'autres ? Quelles sont les conditions de succès d'un tweet ?

4.3 Twitter: structure, matérialité et fonctionnalités

Chaque forme de média se caractérise et se distingue de ses pairs à la fois par son support et par les fonctionnalités qui lui sont spécifiques. Pour comprendre les contraintes d'un medium, dans sa composante paradigmatique et surtout dans ses déploiements syntagmatiques, nous souhaitons, comme précédemment annoncé, nous occuper du microblogging Twitter en l'appréhendant à différents niveaux.

Tout d'abord, nous allons partir de certaines contraintes matérielles et fonctionnelles de Twitter pour comprendre l'influence et l'incidence du support sur son emploi par les usagers (ergonomie de l'interface, accessibilité, points d'intervention, etc.). Il s'agit notamment de s'intéresser aux outils techniques mis à disposition par le système informatique même permettant de « faire-faire », au sens sémiotique du terme[32], à l'usager différents parcours actantiels.

Ensuite, en recentrant l'attention sur son aspect communicationnel, nous tenterons de caractériser Twitter par rapport à d'autres médias. À partir de ce medium multimodal déterminé comme d'autres par la présence de l'image, de l'écrit, du son et de liens interactifs, nous allons comprendre les interactions qui seront induites par Twitter et qui vont le différencier du SMS, du chat ou de l'email. Il s'agit de comprendre les usages générés par ce support qui le déterminent par rapport à d'autres, dans sa circulation médiatique. Twitter peut par exemple partager la même structure rhizomique typique des réseaux sociaux mais seulement certaines de ses fonctionnalités peuvent être activées par rapport à d'autres supports médiatiques.

Après l'inscription obligatoire sur le site (twitter.com), l'utilisateur a la possibilité de personnaliser son profil avec une phrase (un slogan), un avatar et comme dans d'autres interfaces, customiser sa « mise en scène de soi [33]». Le contrôle du profil reste semblable à d'autres interfaces comme Facebook dont on peut, dans l'onglet accueil, connaitre le nombre de tweets envoyés, les abonnements, les abonnés et retweeter un message. Déjà parmi ces premières possibilités, il

---

32 A. J. Greimas/J. Courtés, *Dictionnaire raisonné des sciences du langage*, Paris, Hachette, 1979.

33 E. Goffman, La mise en scène de la vie quotidienne. La Présentation du soi, Paris, Ed de Minuit, 1973.

s'instaure un pouvoir faire commun soit au courriel soit à la messagerie instantanée ou chat : l'écriture et l'échange. Il s'agit d'un vrai binôme : l'un n'a plus de sens aujourd'hui sans l'autre. Plus que pour l'échange épistolaire traditionnel, on assiste à un « dialogue écrit » en temps réel, marqué, comme pour Facebook, par la réciprocité et l'instantanéité.

Pour ce qui concerne le retweet, nous pouvons parler d'une vraie et propre pratique d'usage[34] dans le sens que l'internaute fait une expérience des textes dans sa sélection, dans sa manipulation[35] et dans la ré-énonciation. Le retweet est la republication d'un tweet d'une autre personne, jugé particulièrement intéressant par son contenu. Il s'agit d'un partage ciblé aux abonnés (aux followers) ou à une liste (à un groupe de personnes plus ou moins restreintes réunies par une ou plusieurs thématiques communes) ou à l'ensemble du réseau. Le symbole « RT » signifie bien que la personne n'est pas auteur du message mais un simple véhicule de transmission de l'information. Cette opération, qui à l'intérieur d'un courriel est une procédure relativement banale, sur Twitter prend une autre signification. L'usager qui décide de retweeter n'abuse pas de cette procédure. Le principe n'est pas celui d'une rediffusion massive mais au contraire ciblée et marquée par une valeur ajoutée. Le message retweeté apporte de l'appréciation, du crédit soit à son auteur soit à la personne qui « trie » l'information en la diffusant. Cette valeur est simplement la marque énonciative RT souvent suivi d'un ajout, d'un commentaire ou de quelques mots emphatiques qui ont le but de renforcer le texte source. L'utilisateur peut ajouter au texte du retweet un commentaire et signer le texte en le personnalisant. Cette procédure peut se réaliser maintes fois. Une question se pose : à qui appartient le contenu textuel d'un tweet ?

Toujours dans l'onglet d'accueil, l'usager peut écrire un message privé à un autre usager ou un tweet visible, sauf restrictions particulières à tout le monde. La restriction de 140 caractères est toujours valable, détail qui le différencie du mail ou de Facebook où l'espace d'écriture est majeur. Nous pouvons considérer le tweet comme une forme brève de communication dans le sens décrit par I. Pezzini : « Il s'agit de formes délibérément mineures, où le mineur n'est pas un repli mais un genre comme un autre[36] ». Les tweets sont des textes autonomes contenant des supports multimodaux tenus ensemble par une même source énonciative : l'énonciation du tweet.

---

34 J. Fontanille, *Pratiques sémiotiques*, PUF, 2008.

35 A. J. Greimas/ J. Courtés, *idem*, 1979.

36 I. Pezzini, *Trailer, spot, siti, banner*, 2002, p. 17. (traduction personnelle).

Twitter ne permet pas la constitution de groupes privés gérés par un seul leader mais cela ne signifie pas que certains followings (personnes que l'utilisateur a décidé de suivre en s'abonnant à leur compte) n'assument pas ce rôle. L'effet « avalanche » reste présent dans Twitter du moment que plus un usager est suivi plus il sera connu, diffusé, lu et en tout cas présent dans le réseau. La gestion du profil public/ privé relève de ce que D. Cardon appelle le modèle de visibilité « post-it ». Selon l'auteur, « les participants rendent visibles leur disponibilité et leur présence en multipliant les indices contextuels, mais ils se réservent leurs accès à un cercle relationnel restreint [37]». C'est le cas de Twitter, caractérisé par une panoplie d'indices laissés par les utilisateurs comme la localisation géographique permanente et leur présence soulignée par la mise à jour de leurs tweets postés en temps réel. Pour continuer à favoriser l'échange écrit Twitter impose dès l'inscription, l'emploi d'un pseudonyme suivi du symbole de l'arobase (@). La valorisation de l'écrit, comme pourrait être pour d'autres sites celle de l'image (par exemple Flickr), passe aussi par la reconnaissance de mêmes symboles qui facilitent l'interaction en étant déjà employés ailleurs.

Enfin, une des dernières fonctionnalités de ce blogging qui se présente à l'utilisateur, est l'onglet nommé « découvrir ». Il se remarque par cinq possibilités. L'usager se trouve dans la position de choisir des propositions déjà filtrées par ses connaissances, il peut s'abonner aux contacts favoris de ses amis ou laisser à Twitter la suggestion de thématiques les plus retweetées du moment. Nous observons différentes sections : une première nommée « tweets » qui regroupe « Ce qui se passe en ce moment, personnalisé pour vous [38]». Il s'agit d'un choix de tweets, les plus diffusés, sélectionnés selon la localisation géographique de l'utilisateur. L'information est proposée par des followers que l'usager suit régulièrement, elle est « triée » par d'autres usagers et annoncée presque en temps réel sans « effets d'annonce » particuliers. Deuxièmement, nous trouvons la section « activité qui permet de voir ce que les autres usagers ont fait, modifié de leur compte », affichant les nouveaux tweets dans la time -line (TL) de l'utilisateur. L'inactivité est bien évidemment bannie de cette rubrique parce que la mise à jour instantanée, la découverte d'un tweet curieux et insolite est le but ultime. La concurrence s'exprime par un simple commentaire ou par une énonciation de ce qui est déjà connu. Il s'agit de souligner ce qui est arrivé dans le monde entier. La fonction phatique de Jakobson[39], la volonté de maintenir le contact avec l'usager par le

37 D. Cardon, « Le design de la visibilité : un essai de typologie du Web 2.0 », *Internet Actu.net*, 01/02/2008, consulté le 05/06/2014.

38 https://twitter.com/i/discover, consulté le 05/06/2014.

39 R. Jakobson, *Essais de linguistique générale*, Paris, Ed. de Minuit, 1963.

simple fait d'être présent sur le réseau, est un des objectifs de Twitter. Ce qui fait dire à Ogez & Chaintreuil : « assez rapidement le slogan de Twitter est passé de 'What are you doing ?' à 'What's happening ?'[40] ».

La troisième possibilité comprend les « suggestions », le suivi en temps réel des comptes abonnés et d'autres nouveaux susceptibles d'intéresser l'usager pour leur affinité thématique. Cet onglet se présente comme une liste de propositions sous forme d'un menu déroulant marqué par la postille « suivre ». Cette dernière est prête à être activée par l'utilisateur. Un simple clic permet d'initier l'abonnement et suivre le flux continu des tweets. Le libre accès à cette fonction invite l'utilisateur à entrer dans d'autres comptes en sachant que plus il sera abonné, plus il aura la possibilité de participer à l'univers de Twitter en tant que membre actif.

Le quatrième onglet rassemble les « comptes populaires » les plus suivis par l'actualité contemporaine. Cette liste d'adresses non exhaustive change au fur et mesure de l'actualité. Elle est divisée par genre comme par exemple : la musique, le sport, l'humour, la télévision, le divertissement, la politique, les voyages, etc. Elle présente une différente organisation de l'information par rapport à l'onglet « suggestions ». Il s'agit toujours d'évoquer, jamais de contraindre, des comptes à suivre mais d'une façon indirecte en présentant des sujets assez larges, traités par différents comptes. Par exemple pour la thématique « semaine des musées » nous trouvons la possibilité de s'abonner aux accounts des musées majeurs européens. Ces suggestions se présentent, au contraire des comptes, sous forme d'un menu horizontal visible que par les photographies des accounts. Il s'agit de la carte de visite du compte officiel, la marque de fabrique de l'institution ou d'un privé. Ce regroupement est encore plus large et exhaustif que le simple compte en permettant de découvrir et implicitement de s'abonner à un ensemble de followings. Différentes logiques opposent ces deux possibilités de découverte des nouveaux comptes : la première recherche un compte spécifique qui ensuite peut renvoyer à d'autres similaires, la deuxième s'ouvre à une thématique générale pour trouver des comptes spécifiques privés ou publics. Le but est par une voie ou par une autre d'intéresser les usagers en proposant deux parcours narratifs différents. Le premier concerne l'usager qui sait quoi chercher, un compte précis d'un following et qui arrive directement à sa source d'information. Le seconde s'adresse à l'utilisateur intéressé par un thème mais curieux de découvrir des propositions similaires, ouvert à différentes possibilités en restant focalisé sur un sujet précis.

Nous pourrons ajouter dans la barre horizontale du menu de Twitter l'onglet « rechercher » qui reste toujours présent dans la structure du site pour pouvoir

---

40 *Idem*, 2012, p. 22.

explorer l'univers des informations. Le recherche se fait par simple écriture d'un mot-clé précédé ou pas par le hashtag « # ». Ce symbole, redevenu à la mode (2007), permet d'annoncer un mot-clé qui regroupera la thématique indiquée et tous les tweets envoyés par les twitteurs contentant ce sujet. La fonction de l'hashtag est englobée dans une tension permanente entre informer l'usager d'une manière précise sur le sujet et trouver d'autres utilisateurs avec lesquels interagir sur le même centre d'intérêt[41]. Le hashtag semble condenser quelques fonctions typiques du titre : la fonction d'identification et celle intertextuelle[42]. La première permet de comprendre de quel sujet le tweet va traiter ; en revanche le contenu textuel n'apparait pas au lecteur. L'usager doit cliquer sur le hashtag pour pouvoir y accéder et lire son contenu. Cette dématérialisation du texte ouvre des ambigüités sémantiques par rapport à l'emploi plus « traditionnel » du titre dont le texte suit, à l'intérieur la même page, le titre. Le hashtag apparait comme un mot-clé condensant plusieurs arguments qui fait référence à une multitude de plans du contenu. Comme le souligne Hoeck : « Il existe pour tout titre une phrase explicite performative qui doit avoir la forme suivante : «je déclare à toi que ce texte s'appelle X». A la surface nous ne trouvons que X[43] ». Il s'agirait pour l'auteur de l'apparition sur le plan de l'expression du titre qui se présenterait comme un indice et une condensation du texte dont le plan du contenu serait beaucoup plus large qu'un texte traditionnel.

La deuxième fonction, d'ordre intertextuel, est plus exploitée par le hashtag et le microblogging Twitter plus en général. Le hashstag est mis en relation avec les autres textes circulant à l'intérieur du réseau Twitter et potentiellement avec tous les liens hypertextuels présents dans les tweets. Il entre en dialogue avec d'autres textes que seul l'usager va activer en construisant son parcours textuel. Nous pouvons parler d'une pratique exploratoire du texte qui désormais repose sur une structure « rhizomatique » et non plus linéaire.

Brièvement le cinquième onglet offre la possibilité de « trouver des amis » en important les contacts de ses propres adresses électroniques ou en invitant un ami à découvrir Twitter.

---

41 Nous avons différents sites qui aident les usagers à trouver les hashtags plus populaires et à en créer d'autres selon les buts recherchés comme par exemple hastags.org, hastagify.me ou wthashtag.com.

42 Leo.H. Hoeck, « Pour une sémiotique du titre », *Documents de Travail et prépublications* XX–XXI, Centro Internazionale di Semiotica e Linguistica, Université de Urbino 1973, pp. 1–48.

43 *Idem*, p. 25.

L'importation de liens faibles[44] qui sont en réalité les plus présents sur les microblogging, alimentent automatiquement le site de Twitter qui vit grâce à cet afflux constant de réseautage amical.

Nous avons pu expliquer quelles sont les caractéristiques de cette « page-écran »[45] et les points d'intervention[46] du site, qui techniquement permettent de faire intervenir le sujet sur l'interface graphique de Twitter. Ce microblogging qui cherche « à éveiller un vouloir [47]» dans notre cas spécifique de connaissances, de nouveautés et plus globalement d'information.

Nous allons comprendre à travers quelles stratégies de communication ce vouloir se met en place pour favoriser le fameux « clic » ou abonnement aux followings.

4.4 Twitter en action : focus sur les fonctions communicationnelles

Si concrètement la gestualité requise par l'interface de Twitter reste relativement simple (déplacement avec la souris et clic sur les liens, pratique commune aussi à d'autres supports électroniques), la communication avec l'usager se met en place de diverses façons.

Tout d'abord, dès la création d'un compte Twitter, l'usager voit apparaitre dans son profil le texte suivant :

Prenez 2 minutes afin que Twitter soit plus proche de vous. Notre suggestion : suivre plus de personnes. Oui, plus. C'est grâce à vos abonnements que vous construirez votre fil d'actualité. Construire un bon fil est au cœur du fonctionnement de Twitter. En construisant un fil qui vous reflète ainsi que vos intérêts, vous verrez avec quelle rapidité Twitter devient une partie inestimable de votre vie[48].

L'utilisateur est placé au centre du processus de communication en devenant actant[49] de la construction de son réseau. Ce qui est demandé est d'accomplir

44 Pour la distinction entre liens forts et liens faibles je renvoie à A. Casilli, *Liaisons numériques, Vers une nouvelle sociabilité?*, Paris, Seuil, 2010.

45 Nicole Pignier, « De la vie des textes aux formes et forces de vie. Texte, sens et communication, entre esthésie et éthique », Revue *Actes Sémiotiques*, Ouvrage de HDR, Presses Universitaire de Limoges, http://epublications.unilim.fr/revues/as/4786, 2012, p. 126. Consulté le 06/06/2014.

46 Nous empruntons cette expression à A. Zinna, « Les objets d'écriture et leurs interfaces. Textes interactifs et hypertextes. Décrire et comparer les nouveaux phénomènes de sens », ouvrage de HDR, Limoges, 2001.

47 Nicole Pignier, *idem*, p. 113.

48 https://twitter.com/, consulté le 06/06/2014.

49 A.J. Greimas/J. Courtés, *idem*, 1979.

une performance grâce au vouloir faire de l'usager. Twitter favorise un accès facile au contenu informatif. Le sujet possède tous les outils techniques comme le moteur de recherche, la découverte des hashtags, le classement par genre pour se construire son propre savoir personnalisé selon ses goûts et ses envies. Le but officiel de ce microblogging est apparemment celui de s'informer et de se tenir au courant de l'actualité mais en réalité le savoir se construit en tant que partage de contacts, de circulation et ensuite de connaissances. L'idée de partage est valorisée beaucoup plus que le contenu de ce qui est véhiculé. La métaphore omniprésente de l'icône Twitter, un oiseau qui gazouille, qui survole et qui émet de courts messages semble bien représenter l'esprit du réseau. La centralité de l'échange ne signifie pas forcément partage de l'information. L'individu est un transmetteur de l'information et un interprète de cette dernière. La charge émotionnelle, le ressenti véhiculé, les prises de position permettent de faire émerger des « leaders d'opinion[50] » très actifs, à court et long terme, à l'intérieur du microblogging. Par exemple, les tweets peuvent contenir de brefs textes de 140 caractères suivis de liens électroniques abrégés ou pas qui permettent de retrouver l'intégralité du propos sur d'autres pages web, ou simplement incitent à visionner des fichiers multimédias (photos, vidéos, fichiers sonores) hébergés sur d'autres sites. Ces pages renvoient souvent à des pages personnelles qui explicitent les idées et invitent à « approfondir » le profil de la personne.

La rapidité et l'instantanéité sont les mots d'ordre de Twitter. Les informations se présentent sous forme d'agence de presse, presque en continu du moment que le nombre d'abonnements s'élargit et que la personne ajoute ses contacts. Ce format est désormais présent sur les chaines d'information télévisuelles et à la une des journaux en ligne sous forme de « flash ». Nous avons différents exemples de circulation rapide de l'information à travers Twitter pendant des situations de révolution politique ou de catastrophes naturelles[51].

L'association de fonctions communes au courriel comme celle de répondre, de fowarder, de bloquer ou d'inscrire le tweet dans les « favoris », implique la reprise de la communication écrite associée à un moteur de recherche interne à Twitter et à ses utilisateurs.

---

50 Nous faisons référence aux théories de E., Katz & P. Lazarsfeld, (2008), *Influence personnelle*. Paris: Armand Colin (1955: Personal Influence, New York: The Free Press).

51 Nous faisons référence à l'article de Z. Dahmen-Jarrin, « Tic et mouvement social en Tunisie. Le rôle du téléphone portable et de Twitter dans la mobilisation », *La communication électronique dans la société de l'information*. Quels usages, quelles pratiques ?, sous la dir. de S. Zlini & F. Liénard, Ed. Klog, Mont-Saint-Aignan, 2012, p. 165–174.

Les messages plurisémiotiques se succèdent les uns simultanément aux autres. Le microblogging les relie ensemble dans un réseau intertextuel en créant un macro-texte en évolution perpétuelle.

4.5 Le tweet politique

L'emploi du twitter en politique concerne au moins trois sphères différentes[52] :

1) Les politiques en sens strict, les candidats mêmes (seule partie ici de notre analyse)
2) Les bloggeurs, les personnalités médiatiques, les stratèges de campagne autour des candidats
3) Les organisations qui couvrent la sphère politique

Déjà avec ces données, nous voyons que le champ d'investigation s'élargit de plus en plus.

Un premier point à souligner est malgré le fait que nous analysions un tweet d'une façon spécifique et en « autonomie », nous ne pouvons pas penser qu'il ne soit pas lié à un contexte précis et à un éventuel échange communicationnel qui se caractérisent par une interaction et une thématique spécifique. Ce type d'échange (au moins une émission d'un tweet et une réponse au dit tweet) n'est pas très fréquent dans les tweets de nos candidates qui n'instaurent pas beaucoup d'échanges communicationnels avec leur public. Par contre, ce sont les interactions entre twitteurs qui construisent le champ sémantique et qui définissent l'interaction même et la textualité qui reste par définition ici « ouverte ». En effet, l'écriture des tweets et l'émission des tweets autour du même argument créent une circulation de l'information éphémère qui permet de reconstruire au moins une isotopie. En tant qu'utilisateurs nous comprenons la thématique discutée et les expressions d'un certain nombre de candidats autour d'un thème spécifique.

Toutefois, il faudrait poser une question « Qu'est-ce que un tweet politique » ? Il n'est pas si évident de le définir mais si l'on reste sur l'idée que le dispositif même limite le contenu du tweet, nous pouvons soutenir qu'un tweet politique est un tweet attribuable aux accounts officiels des figures politiques dans un moment historique donné appartenant officiellement à un parti politique précis. Cette définition se veut encore vague mais le contenu lui-même ne peut pas être utile à la définition même. Encore, le tweet politique émis ou retweeté par le candidat est une sélection de l'information publique que le /la candidat(e) diffuse ou relance autour

52 Inside the Political Twittersphere A look inside Twiter's use for politics, October 2009 By Sysomos Inc. Alex Cheng, Mark Evans and Nick Koudas, consulté le 27/06/2015.

d'un évènement concernant la sphère publique à un moment précis. Souvent il s'agit d'un événement qui marque l'actualité et que le candidat va reprendre pour commenter ou l'employer comme cible polémique et pour proposer une contre réponse. Il aurait au moins deux emplois majeurs du Twitter imputables la sphère politique mais expansibles au fonctionnement même du médium. D'une part, on assiste à la diffusion ou rediffusion d'une information, souvent pas commentée et qui provient d'autres sources médiatiques. Il s'agit de remettre dans l'arène publique une nouvelle qui a été divulguée sur d'autres médias ou même sur Twitter mais qui est republiée sans commentaire de la part de l'expéditeur. Ce dernier rend visible sa source primaire, grâce aussi aux hashtags, et devient un simple diffuseur de la nouvelle. Les marques subjectives sont présentes à travers l'adresse Twitter de l'utilisateur et la personnalisation du profil. La communication se construit, ici, plus comme une caisse de résonance, de diffusion d'une thématique qui pourra s'élargir très vite et alimenter l'écriture des tweets. Ce n'est pas le contenu qui souvent fait rebondir l'information mais la rediffusion qui réactive le mécanisme de circulation même. Le retweet n'implique pas forcément un commentaire, ni une prise de position mais une réactivation à un moment précis d'une actualité souvent provenant d'ailleurs (presse en ligne et/ou papier, d'autres sites internet). Ce phénomène qui est consubstantiel au médium a instauré une vraie pratique, un vrai faire–faire à l'utilisateur. Elle prend le nom de retweeter.

D'autre part pour ce qui concerne le deuxième emploi, une intervention directe d'un twitteur est une prise de parole immédiate sur un évènement ou en tout cas l'expression d'une opinion. Le medium, vu les contraintes de 140 caractères, ne permet pas de formes d'expression longues mais plutôt succinctes grâce aussi à la présence de hashtags qui réduisent l'espace d'expression. Les prises de position directes et à la première personne n'encouragent pas forcément le dialogue ou la construction d'une interaction dialogique. Le tweet peut recevoir des réponses ou pas, peut être transféré ou pas ce qui dit de son intérêt peut-être ou de son succès médiatique.

En tout cas, le contenu du tweet n'implique pas forcément de réponses de formes d'interaction. Si l'on peut se permettre une métaphore un peu triviale, on pourrait comparer le tweet à une bouteille à la mer : son contenu circulera certainement mais il pourra être ou pas relevé. A ce propos, Cervulle et Pailler, en citant G. Deleuze, parlent de « production de rapports d'affection[53] ». Les auteurs sou-

53 M. Cervulle & F. Pailler, « #mariagepourtous : Twitter et la politique affective des hashtags », *Revue Française des Sciences de l'Information et de la communication*, [En ligne], 4 | 2014, mis en ligne le 15 janvier 2014, consulté le 20 mai 2015. URL : http://rfsic.revues.org/717.

lignent que « Affecter c'est exercer une force au sein d'un champ de relations. Appréhender les réseaux sociaux numériques comme le lieu de rapports d'affection permet de considérer que les échanges en leur sein dessinent des lignes de tension et de partage aussi bien au niveau des sociabilités que des discours ». Il s'agirait de travailler plus sur les rapports qui se tissent entre les différents échanges autour d'une thématique que sur l'argument principal. On pourrait conclure qu'un tweet réussi est celui qui a été retweeté et qui a « touché » un large public.

Pour Twitter, tweeter (écrire), retweeter (rediffuser, partager un contenu), être un follower d'un account (suivre une personne ou une liste de diffusion) font partie de la participation en ligne. Les degrés de cette « participation[54] » plus ou moins actifs ou passifs, permettent globalement de suivre des traces de visibilité et de présence de l'internaute à l'intérieur du microblogging. En tout cas le suivi des débats politiques sur Twitter ne se résume ni à l'activisme politique ni à la circulation de l'information hors ligne. Même si l'on peut trouver des rapprochements et des compénétrations continues entre les deux sphères, pour comprendre en quoi les réseaux sociaux influencent les comportements politiques, nous sommes obligés d'étudier des pratiques d'usager en ligne mises en relation avec des supports médiatiques qui révèlent de la même substance de l'expression : le médium internet et en particulier le web 2.0, c'est-à-dire les réseaux sociaux.

4.6 Un rappel des bonnes pratiques

Ce que nous intéresse ici est de rappeler d'une façon très succincte les quelques règles de bon usage qui sont instaurées par Twitter même, pour « avoir succès » et réussir ses propres tweets[55]. Il existe une pléthore de manuels de conseils et d'astuces de la création d'un compte jusqu'à son bon fonctionnement. Brièvement, nous pourrions dire que :

1) Indispensable est le choix de sa propre ligne éditoriale : partager des informations appétissantes et centrées sur un domaine pointu
2) S'exprimer à travers des mots-clés représentatifs de la personne et d'un contexte. La personne sera plus facilement « re-diffusée »
3) Promouvoir une animation quotidienne et un engagement du 70 % (informations), 20 % (réponses aux followers, interaction), 10 % (messages personnels)

54 La notion de participation a fait couler beaucoup d'encre. A ce propos on renvoie pour une synthèse du débat à Ch. Barats, *Manuel d'analyse du web*, Paris, A. Colin, 2013, p. 171.

55 Un exemple parmi d'autres : Jean-François Belmonte, *La vie en 140 caractères*, 2013.

4) Respecter les créneaux horaires pour l'mission de tweets : 6h-7h le matin, la pause déjeuner, 17h-18h le tard après-midi et, au maximum 21h le soir (le retweet est recommandé en fin de soirée)
5) Adopter la bonne place pour le lien hypertextuel qui devrait se placer au 25 % de longueur du tweet et pas à la fin
6) Employer les applications liées à Twitter comme : tweetreach.com qui permet de connaitre le nombre de fois où un tweet ou un hashtag a été mentionné et également le nombre de personnes potentiellement touchées ; crowdbooster.com qui aide à suivre le nombre de followers dans le temps, de mentions et de retweets; tweetWhen.com pour savoir quand nous sommes plus retweetés, tweriod.com pour connaître si les followers ont retweetés les messages, clocktwetts pour programmer l'envoi de tweets, etc.

Ces quelques lignes de bonne conduite ne sont pas forcément suivies par les candidates de notre corpus qui semblent plutôt poster des tweets dans l'immédiateté et particulièrement pendant les événements dont ils ont le rôle de participants actifs (meetings, débats politiques, présences à l'ecran). La construction d'une image médiatique des candidats se réalise aussi à travers ce microblogging qui grâce à son instantanéité permet un semblant de participation « live » des followers à la sphère politique et renvoie une image de forte activité de ses participants.

4.7 Analyses des pratiques des candidats : le cas E. Forenza

Comme annoncé précédemment, nous allons repérer des pratiques d'usage de Twitter des candidats aux élections européennes du 22–25 mai 2014. Pour question de praticité et de méthode qualitative nous ne pouvons pas faire un parallèle entre tous les candidats des partis participants à cet événement politique. Nos analyses se veulent sur le plan de l'immanence, ponctuelles, circonscrites autour d'un évènement précis.

Nous nous consacrons à deux candidates femmes : Eleonora Forenza inscrite au Parti communiste italien, candidate de la liste Tsipras pour le Sud d'Italie et Isabella Adinolfi pour le Mouvement Cinq Etoiles (M5S) pour le Sud d'Italie aussi. Nous avons comparé les deux candidates parce qu'elles étaient suivies presque par un nombre paritaire des followers (3.546/4.393) aujourd'hui[56], pour leur âge similaire (1976/1978), parce qu'elles sont inscrites à Twitter depuis la même période (février 2012) et parce qu'elles appartiennent à deux partis différents de la sphère politique de gauche.

56 Septembre 2015.

Nous nous sommes limités à une petite incursion dans le domaine politique, même si bien d'autres seraient possibles, pour comprendre les tweets qui s'insèrent dans ce champ et pour comprendre les relations autour de ces derniers.

Les tweets recueillis débutent le jour du dépôt par le gouvernement italien des listes officielles, le 25 avril 2014, jusqu'à une semaine après les élections, le 1er juin 2014.

Nous allons commencer par regarder de plus près les tweets émis et échangés (retweets) sur le profil Twitter de la candidate E. Forenza dans la période citée. A l'époque, la candidate est suivie par 1.600 followers et se présente en tant que « chercheuse précaire féministe, communiste, qui vit dans le sud de l'Italie, qui aime Gramsci et Lonzi et le pop des années 80 »[57]. La volonté de mêler l'appartenance politique de la candidate (Liste Tsipras) avec ses gouts personnels et ses « maîtres à penser », démontre une approche d'« exposition personnelle » avec ses followers. Une stratégie confidentielle, proche des électeurs qui voie l'élue s'adresser aux internautes dans la volonté de les impliquer dans le combat pour Alexis Tsipras : « Oggi partecipiamo come delegazione dell'@altraeuropa ConTsipras alla riunione del GUE. restiamo uniti, e uniamo ciò che il neolib ha diviso![58] » ou « Dopo la riunione dei candidati, una conferma : l'@altraeuropa continua! Abbiamo una grande responsabilità: non disperdere il lavoro fatto![59] ». Les tweets émis par la candidate soulignent, même après élections, la promesse de changement prise par la liste, la volonté d'entreprendre un combat collectif et le sentiment d'appartenance à une collectivité qui partage des valeurs proches.

Pour ce qui concerne les tweets, nous pouvons affirmer que du début du mois de mai à la fin, la candidate a augmenté son nombre de tweet, grâce à une écriture directe et continue qui marque sa présence sur ce microblogging. Le nombre de tweet a progressé d'une manière constante. La candidate émet plus d'un tweet (une moyenne de 5) par jour. Ces derniers sont émis avec une fréquence très rapprochée (quelques minutes) sans avoir forcément une unité thématique commune. Il

57 En réalité le terme italien que l'élue a employé pour indiquer les régions du sud de l'Italie relève plus de l'oralité et de l'expression familiale que d'un langage " politiquement correct ". Nous ne pouvons pas nous étaler sur les variations du langage oral/écrit, partie qui resterait très intéressante à approfondir.

58 Publié le 10 juin 2014 par E. Forenza : « Aujourd'hui nous participons en tant que délégation de l'altraeuropa con Tsipras à la réunion GUE. Restons unis et unions ce que le néolibéralisme (néolib) a divisé », (traduction personnelle).

59 Publié le 31 mai 2014 par E. Forenza : « Après la réunion des candidats, une confirmation : l'@altraeuropa continue ! Nous avons une grande responsabilité : ne pas disperser le travail accompli ! », (traduction personnelle).

s'agit plutôt de diffuser des informations autour des événements que d'instaurer des interactions. Ce qui rythme leur écriture est pour la majorité un évènement médiatique hors du microblogging.

Autour des jours du vote, la présence et la mise en scène de la candidate sur le microblogging a augmenté sensiblement paradoxalement grâce aux retweets plus qu'aux tweets mêmes. Déclarations, vidéos, photographies et slogans envahissent l'account de la candidate qui laisse ses «traces numériques[60] » avec une fréquence moyenne de 4 fois par jour. A noter que l'émission de tweets et retweets est relativement concentrée dans le temps, les tweets se suivent à intervalles variables de quelques minutes à quelques heures. L'échange est très intense pour ensuite se diluer dans le temps.

Forenza fait de l'autopromotion en publiant le bulletin de vote à employer le 24 et le 25 mai avec son nom déjà écrit et souligné. Tout est à empoigner pour la valorisation de soi : l'appui des amis qui parlent de la générosité de Forenza et même d'un membre proche de la famille (un frère ?) qui affiche une photographie d'un autre temps de la candidate, servent à construire le personnage médiatique.

Les internautes « participent» à la vie médiatique de Forenza qui tweete à ces followers depuis le Parlement européen, qui se réjouit pour les batailles qu'elle commence à mener, qui dévoile son « humanité », en se présentant dans la vie active et en affichant ses émotions et ses passions[61]. La stratégie de la subjectivité et de l'empathie font partie désormais d'une nouvelle façon de faire politique aujourd'hui et Forenza part d'elle-même pour témoigner des actualités de la sphère publique. L'expérience, l'être là qui normalement appartenaient à la dimension du privé, sont valorisés comme points de départ pour appréhender le réel[62]. La candidate implique l'internaute dans sa vie publique pendant la campagne électorale en rappelant des informations techniques sur les élections (lieu, débat,

---

60 B. Galinon –Mélénec & S. Zlitni, *Traces numériques*, CNRS, 2013.

61 Pour l'importance de la composante passionnelle, nous renvoyons à A. J. Greimas & J. Fontanille, *Sémiotique de passions. Des états de choses aux états d'âme*, Paris, Ed. du Seuil, 1991 et aussi à J. Fontanille, *Soma & Séma : Figures du corps*, Paris, Maisonneuve & Larose, 2004. L'étude de la composante passionnelle et en particulier celle corporelle dans l'écriture, l'image et plus en général l'échange sur le microblogging Twitter reste encore une dimension à explorer.

62 Il s'agit d'une nouvelle dimension du partage de la sphère publique et personnelle. A ce propos, nous renvoyons à A. Frame & G. Brachotte : « Les campagnes des compagnes : mise en scène de la vie publique et privée. La présence sur Twitter des compagnes des leaders politiques en France, en Grande-Bretagne et aux Etats-Unis », (sous la dir. de) S. Zlitni & F. Lieanard, *La communication électronique en questions*, Berne, Peter Lang, 2013, pp. 387–402.

initiatives locales) et en cherchant de sensibiliser avec des slogans l'opinion publique sur certaines thématiques (oggi giornata mondiale contro l'omofobia, sta per arrivare il 25 maggio[63]) et en créant un actant collectif animé par la même passion (@romano_tano @altraeuropa grazie! Bravi tutti noi che ci crediamo e non ci arrendiamo mai!; sta per partire il corteo beni comuni, noi siamo qui per appoggiarli; qui sono stati toccati i nodi di fondo di questa campagna[64]).

La candidate exploite Twitter comme désormais est coutume : un outil pour réduire la distance entre citoyens et sphère publique. Comme le soutient J. L. Dader « Ainsi, bien que l'analyse politique ne soit pas rigoureuse, ni le débat politique de qualité, les individus se trouvent plus proches des affaires publiques, de telle sorte que la politique cesse d'être élitiste et ennuyeuse, exclusivité des classes dirigeantes au regard du peuple. L'info-entertaining télévisuel et de la presse à sensation avait déjà créé et mûri progressivement cet effet de la politique pop (Mazzoleni & Sfardini, 2009), mais Internet a contribué de façon exponentielle à son accroissement dans une dimension que les médias du passé, essentiellement unidirectionnels, ne pouvaient pas faciliter[65] ». L'idée d'une « libre » circulation de la parole et d'un échange « directe » amène l'illusion d'une fausse proximité avec le candidat qui se représente d'abord comme un citoyen parmi d'autres.

4.7.1 Le- re-tweet de E. Forenza

Sur cette deuxième pratique, nous assistons concrètement à la publication d'un tweet d'une personne par un autre utilisateur. Il s'agit d'une rediffusion d'un contenu, jugé particulièrement pertinent à un moment donné. Le symbole RT suivi du pseudonyme de la personne qui a retweeté, caractérise cette pratique. Le contenu du message peut être renvoyé tel quel en ajoutant de la valeur au rédacteur du tweet ou il peut se compléter par un commentaire personnel du retweetteur, placé avant le symbole RT. Dans notre cas, Forenza n'écrit aucun commentaire dans le retweet pendant toute la campagne. Les autres supporteurs parlent d'elle mais toujours d'une manière directe mais la candidate emploie le retweet pour

63 (Aujourd'hui journée mondiale contre l'homophobie, le 25 mai va bientôt arriver), traduction personnelle.

64 (@romano_tano @altraeuropa merci ! Bravo à nous tous qui continuions à croire et qui ne cédons jamais ! le cortège autour de biens publiques est en train de partir, nous sommes ici pour les soutenir ; ici nous avons touché les nœuds sensibles de cette campagne électorale), traduction personnelle.

65 J. L. Dader, « La transformation de la politique sur internet : de la politique spectacle à la cyberdémocratie d'activisme citoyen », *Networks and Communication Studies, NETCOM*, vol. 26 (2012), n° 1–2 p. 18.

informer et non pour s'exprimer. D'où toute la problématique d'usage du retweet qui en même temps accumulerait au moins deux fonctions en un seul medium : celle de diffusion des contenus médiatiques, de citation, de focalisateur d'attention sur une thématique et celle de mise en scène de soi, d'expression personnelle[66]. Le fait d'attirer l'attention sous-entend aussi une volonté de surligner un événement dans le but de l'emphatiser, de le remettre au centre pour pouvoir ensuite d'y rebondir. Nous ne pouvons pas oublier qu'une des fonctions de Twitter est justement la veille informationnelle qui s'opère de différentes façons : hashtags, moteur de recherche, mots-clés, etc.

Cette fonction de retweet est de plus en plus employée jusqu'à la fin de la campagne électorale. La majorité de retweets concernent directement ou indirectement la candidate. Il s'agit de messages de soutien en sa faveur, des compliments pour la victoire obtenue, des encouragements de la part d'autres votants, de collectivités et de partis. Les incitations à la candidate n'explicitent pas les raisons du soutien mais ressemblent à des marques personnelles d'estime et d'incitation. Les personnes qui ont porté Forenza ont laissé des tweets, retweetés ensuite par l'élue, comme « témoignage » de leur engagement. Nous passons d'un électorat potentiel à l'assurance que derrière le tweet nous retrouvons des personnes concrètes qui ont appuyé la candidate. En outre, laisser une trace évidente de sa propre énonciation incite d'autres followers à suivre et à encourager la candidate. L'appui à cette dernière se fait aussi grâce à la présence ferme de ces followers qui restent la meilleure preuve du bienfait de la postulante.

Encore, le retweet est employé d'une façon indirecte en tant que « rebond » autour des thématiques chère à Forenza. Il s'agit de citer d'autres déclarations des politiciens pour pouvoir rejaillir de ses propres propos, les développer, les remettre dans la sphère du blogging. Nous avons constaté des liens thématiques évidents entre les propos de Forenza et les contenus des retweets. Par exemple, le message de l'account "L'Antifascista" : « Sta per partite il corteo beni comuni e

66 A ce propos je renvoie à la présentation de A. Frame & T. Kondrashova, « Exploring the dialogical dimension of political tweets : A qualitative analysis of Twitter style of UK candidates during the 2014 Eu Parliamentary Elections », communication présentée au meeting du 5–6 février 2015, université de Lorraine, Metz. Il est question dans cette communication d'opposer le tweet personnel-interactif marqué par la présence de majeur @ et RT à celui informationnel qui serait caractérisé par un nombre majeur de liens hypertextuels. Sur cette division, C. Thimm, J. Einsapnner, Dang-Ahn M., 2012, Twitter als Wahlkampfmedium, Publizistik, 57 (3), p. 293–313.

noi siamo qui ad appoggiarli #primalepersone pic.twitter.com/PznQZsTxJe[67] », a été repris par Forenza pour raconter sa présence à une manifestation autour de toute autre thématique. La mise en valeur de soi passe aussi par le fait de se montrer en plein engagement, dans les feux de l'action sur multiples terrains. Les évènements publics sont rattachés à la candidate et réinterprétés par son idéologie politique. Le contenu informatif d'un retweet fournit l'occasion pour une prise de parole en public qui marque la présence de la candidate. C'est le cas de ce retweet : « Garantire uno standard salariale e il reddito minimo di cittadinanza », suivi par quelques secondes après, « Verso Taranto, con @giakrussospena e @eleonoraforenza per "Tsipras chi?[68]" (11/05/2014).

4.8 Le cas d'I. Adinolfi

La candidate a émis 442 tweets pendant les 4 semaines de recueil de données. Le double par rapport à la candidate précédente. Est-ce que la présence constante et continue sur Twitter permet d'afficher une stratégie communicationnelle plus représentative pour mener une campagne politique en ligne ? Il parait que oui.

D'abord, la candidate est présente avec un nombre de tweets majeurs par jour (une dizaine). Les échanges se font sur une fréquence très courte (quelques minutes) et avec des rebondissements autour de la même thématique. L'idée est de se concentrer sur un thème central de la journée et ensuite continuer à le nourrir pendant la longueur du jour. De la communication de la nouvelle « complète », on assiste à l'expression du point de vue du M5S qui transforme le contenu en « nouvelle virtuelle », centrée autour des déclarations, commentaires, polémiques, débats etc. Nous assistons aux discours autour d'un contenu qui est ensuite oublié pour passer à un autre argument. Les rebondissements médiatiques servent à alimenter les discussions et la présence de la candidate.

Les stratégies adoptées par Adinolfi sont de deux types : d'une part le retweet des nouvelles dont le M5S n'est peut-être pas le protagoniste mais où il veut exprimer en tant que parti ; de l'autre la rédaction constante de tweets qui manifestent l'implication de la candidate pour les causes du mouvement. A ce propos : « @m_ariano5stelle #campaniatour, dopo il diluvio…il sole e @AngeloTofalo ci

67 Publié par Forenza le 17 mai 2014. « Le défilé pour la protection des biens communs est en train de commencer et nous sommes ici pour l'appuyer #primalepersone pic. twitter.com/PznQZsTxJe », (traduction personnelle).

68 « Garantir le minimum salarial et une redevance minimale pour la citoyenneté », « Vers Taranto avec @giakrussospena et eleonoraforenza pour « Tsipras qui » ? », traduction personnelle.

parla del lavoro dei ragazzi del #m5s! http://t.co/VzjbvgGfd7 », « Domani tutti in Molise con il Campania tour[69] ».

Bien évidemment, le style polémique, qui a caractérisé son principal candidat, Beppe Grillo, est présent à travers des tweets comme : « Pool trattativa smantellato, siamo indignati », « In scena il delitto perfetto, non consentitelo, solo rappresentanza massiccia di forze del cambiamento puo' impedirlo[70] ».

Il ne manque pas de propagande pour le parti même comme « Siamo a Tremoli, seguiteci in diretta streaming qui http.. », « in Europa una scelta a cinque stelle », « Per il PD se non hai soldi non vali niente, il M5S è diverso, siamo una comunità [71] », etc.

Nous constatons que la candidate cherche à exploiter toutes les possibilités et les variétés du médium en utilisant les différents niveaux du discours ; de la persuasion à la polémique, à l'emphase.

La présence de retweets (149) reste aussi pour cette candidate majoritaire ; ils sont suivis principalement par les commentaires de la part de la candidate. Malgré la fonction de retweet employée comme auparavant pour rediffuser l'information, Adinolfi commente les actualités par le biais de la coloration politique du M5S. Quelques retweets : « Riordino per il corpo dei #vvf .Ma i criteri seguiti sembrano sempre gli stessi:TAGLI![72] » (23/05/2014), ou « RT @MicFailla: @Isa_Adinolfi @frattademo avete letto le falsità del soporifero editoriale di Salfari? http…73 » (18/05/2014). Les faits divers de l'actualité servent à la candidate pour s'élever comme porte-parole et commentatrice des positions politiques du parti. Toutes les occasions sont exploitables pour montrer l'opinion contrecourant et dénonciatrice du M5S par rapport à la politique actuelle. Bien sûr la volonté « de crier fort » et d'assumer une position d'opposition dans tous les domaines politiques a fait un des succès de ce parti.

---

69 « Après le déluge, le soleil et @Angelo Tofalo nous parle du travail des jeunes… », « Demain tous au Molise pour le Campania tour », traduction personnelle.

70 « Tractations pour le Pool sont tombées, nous sommes indignés », « Nous ne pouvons pas assister à ce délit parfait, seulement une importante présence des forces du changement peut empêcher tout ça », traduction personnelle.

71 « Nous sommes à Tremoli, suivez- nous en direct streaming ici http.. », « En Europe un choix à cinq étoiles », « pour le PD si tu n'as pas d'argent tu n'as aucune valeur, pour le M5S c'est différent, nous sommes une communauté », traduction personnelle.

72 « Rangement pour le corps des vvf. Mais les critères suivis sont toujours les mêmes : Diminution d'argent », traduction personnelle

73 « Entretemps avez- vous lu les faussetés de l'ennuyeux et soporifique éditorial de Scalfari ? », traduction personnelle.

La succession d'intervention de tweets et de retweets n'est pas la même pendant toute la campagne électorale d'où l'intérêt de travailler sur la temporalité de ce microblogging. Il est difficile de stipuler une proportion constante dans le temps mais comme soutient E. Albu[74] la position des éléments comme les liens hypertextuels mettent en relief le contenu pour mieux informer le lecteur sur le topic du tweet en soulignant le rôle actif de la candidate dans la construction et orientation de l'opinion. Il sert aussi à fournir le contexte et donc la source de l'information.

Enfin, un détail important est la présence de mêmes hashtags tout au long de la période observée. A chaque fois que la candidate poste un tweet, on retrouve : #vinciamonoi, #M5S, #Europa ou des hashtags similaires où la notion d'Europe est présente (#EU, #euDebate2014, #EuropeeM5S, #UE, #EP2014, #EUROPA, #EUROPEE, #europa5stelle). D'autres vont s'ajouter à fur et mesure de l'avancée de la campagne électorale comme : #Campaniatour, #adottaunindeciso, #3preferenze, #sonoroschiaffo, #piùsocial, centrés sur des thèmes très précis qu'une fois que le sujet est passé d'actualité, ils sont vite délaissés. La présence des hashtags[75] permet la plus large diffusion possible sur Twitter en sachant aussi que beaucoup de tweets font directement référence au compte Facebook de la candidate où l'on peut trouver le déploiement des commentaires et des informations. Le lien électronique, qui est présent dans l'hashtag, renvoie de manière complète à la source d'information, souvent placée à la fin de la phrase. Ce positionnement fait faire un cheminement au lecteur qui est vraiment intéressé par l'approfondissement de l'information, un lecteur moins impliqué ne serait pas sollicité à l'approfondissement.

4.9 Vers des pratiques « transmédiatiques » ?

Nous avons constaté un emploi différent de Twitter par les deux candidates : nous pouvons affirmer que Forenza emploie Twitter d'une façon informationnelle, Adinolfi d'une façon participative ce qui expliquerait le majeur succès de l'account de cette dernière candidate[76]. La première candidate utilise Twitter plus pour la fonction de retweet, de circulation de l'information, de mise à jour continue sur sa présence en laissant une trace numérique faible. Très peu de réponses, mais

---

74 E. Albu, " Twitter Use at the 2014 European Elections: The Case of the UKIP Candidates ", communication donnée à Université de Lorraine, Metz, 2015.

75 L'analyse de la fonction des hashtags n'est pas pour le moment une composante qui a été étudiée dans ce papier.

76 Pour cette répartition, je renvoie à D. Compagno, « Families of practices. A bottom-up approach to differentiate how French candidates made use of Twitter during 2014 European Campaign », 201, dans ce volume.

seulement un moyen pour pouvoir suivre les activités de cette élue. En revanche, Adinolfi écrit plus des tweets en expliquant son point de vue, ses goûts en n'effaçant pas sa subjectivité. Elle retransmet l'information du parti en soulignant la prise de parole en public. La candidate se comporte en leader d'opinion[77] qui émerge dans des situations où la concentration d'intérêt pour la sphère publique est majeure.

D'où l'importance, ici, des manipulations de l'outil Twitter plus que de leur contenu textuel. Ce qui le caractérise est qui signale le succès d'un candidat est l'exploitation la plus complète possible des possibilités fournies par ce medium. C'est la forme tweet et sa circulation qui créent une sphère dite « politique », grâce aux pratiques de candidates qui s'inscrivent dans cet ethos commun à ce champ spécifique.

Nous ne retrouvons pas de pratiques affichées parmi les candidates qui les déterminent et les distinguent fortement, plutôt des emplois plus ou moins travaillés de ce support. La vraie question devrait peut-être être déplacée. Twitter ne produit des appropriations si remarquables. Ce qui fait par contre la différence est le taux de popularité médiatique qui rend connu un candidat en étant déjà hors twitter un « personnage médiatique ». C'est plutôt la popularité dans la presse ou la télévision qui fait suivre un compte twitter. C'est le cas de Beppe Grillo en tant que leader du parti M5S (38,3 k de tweets et 1,84 M de followers) déjà médiatiquement très présent dans la presse et la télévision italiennes.

La spécificité de ce medium serait celle d'être une caisse de résonnance de l'information, une veille constante qui s'appuie sur une sphère médiatique globale comme le net.

C'est quand la politique occupe la première place dans l'actualité qu'elle se positionne au centre des discussions ordinaires. Ces échanges doivent être appréhendés moins comme des discussions strictement politiques plutôt comme des débats à propos des événements qui marquent l'actualité médiatique[78].

Nous pouvons conclure en listant les différentes pratiques que ce medium met en acte.

Le premier palier est celui qui implique un faire-faire à l'utilisateur c'est-à-dire une pratique technique qui implique le fonctionnement de l'interface Twitter comme ses points d'intervention, ses fonctions, la gestion des contacts et des followers.

---

77 Katz E., Lazarsfeld P. F., [1955], Influence personnelle : ce que les gens font des médias, A. Colin, Paris, 2008.

78 J. Boyadjian, « Twitter, un nouveau « baromètre de l'opinion publique » ? », Revue Participations, 1/2014, Ed. De Boeck, Bruxelles, p. 70.

Le deuxième niveau implique une pratique langagière qui se résume à la scripturalité du tweet, à l'utilisation du langage, au contenu, au style, tous les éléments qui marquent le langage du candidat et les valeurs incarnées par son affiliation politique.

La dernière pratique consisterait dans les médiations que Twitter instaure avec d'autres medias (télévision, presse, etc.). Ce medium fournit des représentations, des interactions, des renvois à d'autres médias appartenant à un environnement médiatique plus global. Il filtre à travers ses valeurs et son ethos tout ce que les médias mettent en circulation d'eux-mêmes.

Références bibliographiques

Albu Elena, "Twitter Use at the 2014 European Elections: The Case of the UKIP Candidates", communication donnée à Université de Lorraine, Metz, 2015.

Barats Christine, *Manuel d'analyse du web*, Paris, A. Colin, 2013, p. 171.

Belmonte Jean-François, *La vie en 140 caractères*, 2013.

Boyadjian Julien, « Twitter, un nouveau « baromètre de l'opinion publique ? », Revue *Participations*, 1/2014, Ed. De Boeck, Bruxelles, p. 70.

Cardon Dominique, « Le design de la visibilité : un essai de typologie du Web 2.0 », *Internet Actu.net*, 01/02/2008, consulté le 05/06/2014.

Casilli Antonio, Liaisons numériques, Vers une nouvelle sociabilité?, Paris, Seuil, 2010.

Cervulle Maxime & Pailler Fred, « #mariagepourtous : Twitter et la politique affective des hashtags », *Revue Française des Sciences de l'Information et de la communication*, [En ligne], 4 | 2014, mis en ligne le 15 janvier 2014, consulté le 20 mai 2015. URL : http://rfsic.revues.org/717.

Compagno Dario, « Families of practices. A bottom-up approach to differentiate how French candidates made use of Twitter during 2014 European Campaign », 2015 à paraître.

Cheng Alex, Evans Mark & Koudas Nick, *Inside the Political Twittersphere A look inside Twitter's use for politics*, October 2009 By Sysomos Inc., consulté le 27/06/2015.

Dader José Luis, « La transformation de la politique sur internet : de la politique spectacle à la cyberdémocratie d'activisme citoyen », *Networks and Communication Studies, NETCOM*, vol. 26 (2012), n° 1–2 p. 18.

Fontanille Jacques, *Soma & Séma : Figures du corps*, Paris, Maisonneuve & Larose, 2004.

Fontanille Jacques, *Pratiques Sémiotiques*, Paris, Puf, 2008.

Fontanille Jacques, « L'analyse du cours d'action. Des pratiques et des corps », *NAS*, 114, 2011, consulté le 28/06/2015.

Frame Alexander & Brachotte Gilles : « Les campagnes des compagnes : mise en scène de la vie publique et privée. La présence sur Twitter des compagnes des leaders politiques en France, en Grande-Bretagne et aux Etats-Unis » (sous la dir. de) S. Zlitni & F. Liénard, *La communication électronique en questions*, Berne, Peter Lang, 2013, pp. 387–402.

Frame Alexander & Kondrashova Tatiana, « Exploring the dialogical dimension of political tweets: A qualitative analysis of Twitter style of UK candidates during the 2014 Eu Parliamentary Elections ».

Galinon–Mélénec Béatrice & Zlitni Sami, *Traces numériques,* Paris, CNRS, 2013.

Greimas Algirdas Julien & Courtés Joseph, *Dictionnaire raisonné de la théorie du langage*, Paris, Hachette, 1979.

Greimas Algirdas Julien & Fontanille Jacques, *Sémiotique de passions. Des états de choses aux états d'âme*, Paris, Ed. du Seuil, 1991.

Hoeck Léo, Pour une sémiotique du titre », *Documents de Travail et prépublications* XX–XXI, Centro Internazionale di Semiotica e Linguistica, Université de Urbino 1973, pp. 1–48.

Jakobson Roman, *Essais de linguistique générale*, Paris, Ed. de Minuit, 1963.

Katz Elihu & Lazarsfeld Paul Felix., *Influence personnelle : ce que les gens font des médias*, A. Colin, Paris, 2008 [1955].

Ogez Emilie/ Chaintreuil Jean-Noel, *Twitter, 101 questions*, Strasbourg, Ed. Diateino, 2012, p. 21.

Pezzini Isabella, Trailer,, spot, clip, siti, banner. Le forme brevi della comunicazione audiovisiva, Roma, Meltemi, 2006.

Pignier Nicole, « De la vie des textes aux formes et forces de vie. Texte, sens et communication, entre esthésie et éthique », Revue *Actes Sémiotiques*, Ouvrage de HDR, Presses Universitaire de Limoges, 2012, p. 126.

Thimm Caja, Einsapnner Jessica, Dang-Ahn Mark, 2012, *Twitter als Wahlkampfmedium*, Publizistik, 57 (3), p. 293–313.

Zinna A., « Les objets d'écriture et leurs interfaces. Textes interactifs et hypertextes. Décrire et comparer les nouveaux phénomènes de sens », ouvrage de HDR, Limoges, 2001.

Part 2:
Tweet campaign argumentation

Arnaud Mercier, IFP / CARISM, Université Panthéon-Assas, Paris

5. Les figures de l'ennemi dans les tweets-polémiques des forces protestataires françaises durant la campagne de mai 2014

Abstract

This chapter looks at the role of polemic in the way candidates used Twitter during their election campaign. The features of Twitter obviously make it a great electoral tool for controversy, especially for anti-system political parties. During the 2014 European elections, significant convergence could be noticed in France between the left and extreme right in (a) how to identify the enemy, (b) the choice of these European enemies and (c) the use of irony and sarcasm to ridicule and weaken them politically.

5.1 Twitter, un excellent outil de polémique électorale

Élargissant la grille d'analyse initiale de Tamara Small, en quatre grandes catégories, sur les usages faits de Twitter par les partis politiques canadiens (Small, 2010), nous en sommes venus à synthétiser les usages de Twitter par les candidats aux élections en six activités distinctes. La ***publicité*** a trait à la diffusion d'informations dans un sens descendant, du parti politique ou du candidat vers les internautes ; la ***mobilisation*** valorise les pratiques militantes de terrain, les remercie publiquement, ou les incite à agir, en s'adressant prioritairement aux sympathisants ; la ***personnalisation*** qui voit le candidat mettre en avant ses traits de personnalité et le plus souvent sous un jour favorable, inédit ou décalé, pour déclencher des réactions d'ordre affectif ; l'***auto-médiatisation*** consiste à jouer des réseaux socionumériques dans une logique de substitution aux médias traditionnels mais aussi parfois pour attirer leur attention, en cherchant à faire le *buzz* ; les ***interactions sociales*** visant à échanger directement avec les internautes, sans médiation, en les interpelant et acceptant d'être interpelé par eux, en initiant débats ou dialogues ; enfin la ***polémique*** car les réseaux socionumériques sont des espaces où le débat politique peut s'exprimer en envoyant des petites phrases cinglantes contre ses adversaires, voire en les interpelant directement. C'est une tribune ouverte pour lancer sous forme de slogans, de phrases chocs, des accusations directes et des messages simples voire simplistes.

Ce dernier aspect retiendra notre attention dans cet article, en focalisant notre étude sur les figures de l'ennemi qui sont diffusées sur les comptes Twitter des candidats français aux élections européennes, issus de forces protestataires, et la manière dont ils sont présentés, dénoncés, combattus.

Plusieurs auteurs nous aident à cerner la notion de polémique, du point de vue d'une analyse argumentative. La polémique sert « à constituer une propagande pour le point de vue du locuteur » écrit Yanoshevsky (2003 : 5). Elle « prend toujours pour objet un discours autre et porte des jugements de valeur sur celui-ci » poursuit Micheli (2011) et « le pathos, la passion, jouent donc un rôle essentiel dans les discours polémiques » parachève C. Kerbrat-Orecchioni (1980 : 10–11). Du coup, poursuit cette éminente linguiste : « en ressortent inexorablement des procédés discursifs relatifs au champ sémantique guerrier que sont l'agressivité, la véhémence, les insultes, etc. Cela va de pair avec une attaque vers la personne plutôt qu'à l'encontre des arguments. Le discours polémique attaque une cible, souvent personnalisée au travers d'une personne ou d'un groupe. En cela, la polémique définit un camp adverse. Elle est alors considérée comme dialogique ». D'où, pour Ruth Amossy (Amossy & Burger, 2011 : 7), le fait que pareille joute verbale soit « un cas limite de communication conflictuelle en ce que domine un désaccord fondamental, radical, et qui semble durable ». On peut en conclure que dans la polémique, tous les coups sont permis, que la mauvaise foi le dispute à l'invective. Tout est bon pour disqualifier la parole de l'adversaire, quitte à falsifier ou surinterpréter ses propos, à le tourner en dérision plutôt que d'argumenter en raison, en détournant des images, en construisant des jeux de mot, en insultant…

Twitter par son format d'expression (limitation à 140 caractères) se prête particulièrement bien au jeu politique médiatique de la petite phrase, de la phrase slogan, qui permet d'énoncer ses idées de façon concise et de dénoncer de façon assez vive ses adversaires. Que ce soit les internautes qui utilisent ce support pour accéder à une parole publique, ou des candidats à une élection, pour en faire un espace de propagande électorale en plus, on trouve un nombre conséquent d'attaques, de piques contre les concurrents électoraux. Une certaine agressivité s'exprime, même si nos constats nés de l'étude de la tweet-campagne des municipales française de 2014 tendrait à montrer que l'agressivité et l'injure sont plus fréquents sur les comptes des citoyens (assez souvent anonymes) que sur les comptes des candidats. Leur statut de candidats, même outsiders et antisystème, semble les contraindre à respecter un minimum de règles de bienséance et à afficher une image pas trop outrancière. Cependant, les jeux de mot ironiques, les sarcasmes, les caricatures, sont nombreux et servent à dévaloriser des adversaires politiques. Dans le cas de la construction communautaire, les candidats hostiles à l'Union européenne ont été virulents, en articulant un habituel discours de rejet de l'Europe supranationale et une vision alternative (il faut construire l'Europe autrement et/ou sortir de la zone euro, par exemple). Leurs adversaires politiques (que ce soit les autres candidats ou les personnes qui concourent à l'édification de l'Union) sont désignés de telle manière qu'ils sont présentés en ennemis à combattre, pas seulement des rivaux respectables, mais des êtres plus ou moins malfaisants et malintentionnés non dignes de respect, incarnant une figure du mal.

Ajoutons que les qualités d'un bon tweet : être bref et nerveux, fait des comptes officiels des candidats un très bon observatoire des discours qu'ils tiennent en campagne. En effet, les partis s'en servent pour énoncer les points clés de leur programme et de leurs propositions. S'ils font du verbatim des meetings ou des émissions auxquels leurs candidats participent, ils en extraient, par définition, la substance, les phrases clés, les arguments chocs. On voit donc émerger au sein de cette masse de tweets, des éléments de langage qui illustrent parfaitement les thématiques des candidats et la rhétorique qu'ils utilisent, souvent simple voire simpliste, pour essayer de convaincre les électeurs. Dans la gangue des milliers de tweets émis, se trouve, très identifiable, la vision du monde des acteurs en présence, leur *weltanschauung*.

Les élections européennes sont régies par une règle que le politologue français Jean-Luc Parodi a appelé la logique « des élections intermédiaires », ces élections qui se déroulent entre deux scrutins nationaux de grande influence sur l'attribution du pouvoir national. Ces élections sont perçues comme de moindre enjeu, singulièrement les élections européennes, ce qui explique à la fois que les électeurs s'abstiennent plus lors de ce scrutin (phénomène observable un peu partout en Europe) et qu'ils en profitent pour sanctionner le gouvernement en place si son action a généré beaucoup de mécontentements, voire qu'ils s'autorisent à voter pour des forces protestataires ou populistes, considérant le résultat du scrutin sans grande conséquence pratique, tout en ayant pu ainsi envoyer un message fort de mécontentement. Du coup, le scrutin européen est aussi instrumentalisé par les forces les plus contestataires, les plus radicales, les plus populistes (même si un des leaders du FN récuse ce terme : « @brunogollnisch Ce que vous vous appelez le populisme, nous on appelle ça la démocratie, la voix du peuple ! ») pour émerger dans l'espace politique national, avec des thématiques de campagne très nationales.

Pour étudier ces mouvements anti-européens français et leur tweet-rhétorique, nous avons choisi de sélectionner trois forces politiques qui ont des positions extrêmement critiques vis-à-vis du projet européen, de ses institutions et des forces et personnalités politiques qui incarnent ou défendent l'UE. Il s'agit de Debout la République / Debout la France (DLR), du Front national (FN) et du Front de gauche (FDG). Ces partis occupent soit des positions atypiques sur l'échiquier politique (refusant le positionnement gauche/droite) soit des positions situées aux extrémités de l'axe gauche/droite. Ils ne sont pas des partis de gouvernement, donc tenus par un principe de responsabilité, obligés de faire preuve de réalisme et d'accepter des compromis intergouvernementaux lors de la prise de décision européenne. Ce sont des partis protestataires, qui dénoncent l'Europe, en jouant sur les frustrations nationales et souverainistes et qui attisent les colères que la politique de l'Union génère parfois. De plus, ils savent habilement mélanger un discours anti-européen avec une critique vive de leurs adversaires politiques nationaux, afin de nationaliser l'enjeu des élections européennes. Le plus souvent cette rhétorique se veut virulente, en utilisant des images et des comparaisons peu flatteuses, voire dégradantes ; en faisant des amalgames souvent grossiers, tout en dessinant, en creux, une contre-vision de ce que devrait être l'Europe.

Il s'agira donc de mettre au jour les discours de dénonciations concernant l'Europe chez ces trois forces politiques. Les forces d'extrême-droite et d'extrême-gauche convergent-elles dans leur vision dénonciatrice de l'Europe ? Ont-elles recours à des procédés rhétoriques identiques pour mettre en cause les artisans de l'Union européenne ? Perçoit-on des convergences des similitudes entre leurs tweet-rhétoriques ? Nous essaierons de répondre à toutes ces questions, en présentant d'abord un tableau statistique global de l'activité de ces forces politiques sur Twitter durant les trois semaines qui ont précédé le scrutin européen et la semaine d'après. Puis nous présenterons et expliquerons les figures de l'ennemi mobilisées.

5.2 Analyse statistique croisée des tweet-campagnes protestataires françaises

Commençons par une perspective globale de notre corpus. Tous les candidats aux élections européennes n'avaient pas en 2014 un compte Twitter. Les candidats sur Twitter restent même encore minoritaires. L'activisme électoral sur Twitter est très disparate, entre les partis et entre les candidats, y compris au sein d'un même parti. Peu tweetent beaucoup, beaucoup se contentent de rediffuser des messages déjà publiés, de retweeter donc.

Figure 5.1 Tweets des 3 forces populistes durant la dernière phase de l'élection européenne

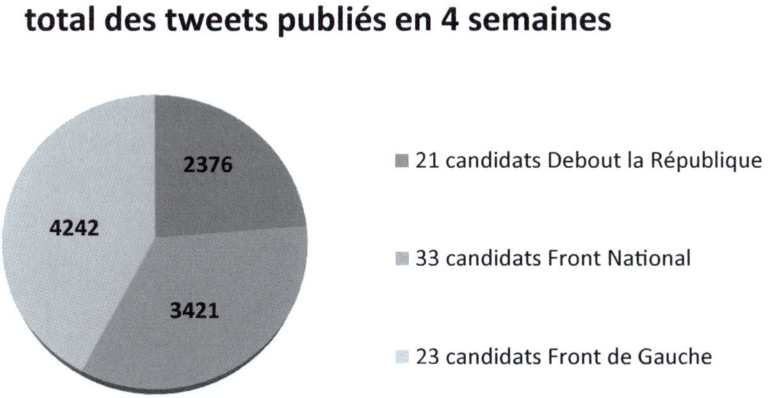

Le niveau de maîtrise tactique des usages du web diffèrent aussi beaucoup et les stratégies de marketing électoral sur Twitter sont encore très disparates, sur un large spectre allant de l'absence de réflexion tactique sur ce qu'un candidat fait (ou ne fait pas) de Twitter à une ébauche de coordination par le parti des titulaires d'un compte, afin de donner une même tonalité (fond d'écran standardisé pour tous, tweets ou retweets dans la même période, valorisation du parti ou du leader…). Pour les trois forces en présence retenues, on voit que la fréquence des messages et le nombre de candidats actifs peut diverger nettement.

Tableau 5–1: Répartition des tweets des 3 forces populistes

Nombre de candidats avec un compte Twitter	Total de tweets	dont total de retweets	Moyenne de tweets par candidat
21 candidats Debout la République	2376	949	113
33 candidats Front National	3421	1394	103
23 candidats Front de Gauche	4242	1922	184

Il en va de même des usages tactiques respectifs, comme on le voit dans le graphique suivant, avec en rouge le Front de Gauche, en noir le Front national, en bleu Debout la France. Les données sont ramenées à un calcul de part relative dans le pourcentage total de tweets de chaque parti, afin de pouvoir établir des comparaisons pertinentes.

Figure 5.2: Présence du parti et du leader dans les tweets de campagne des 3 forces populistes

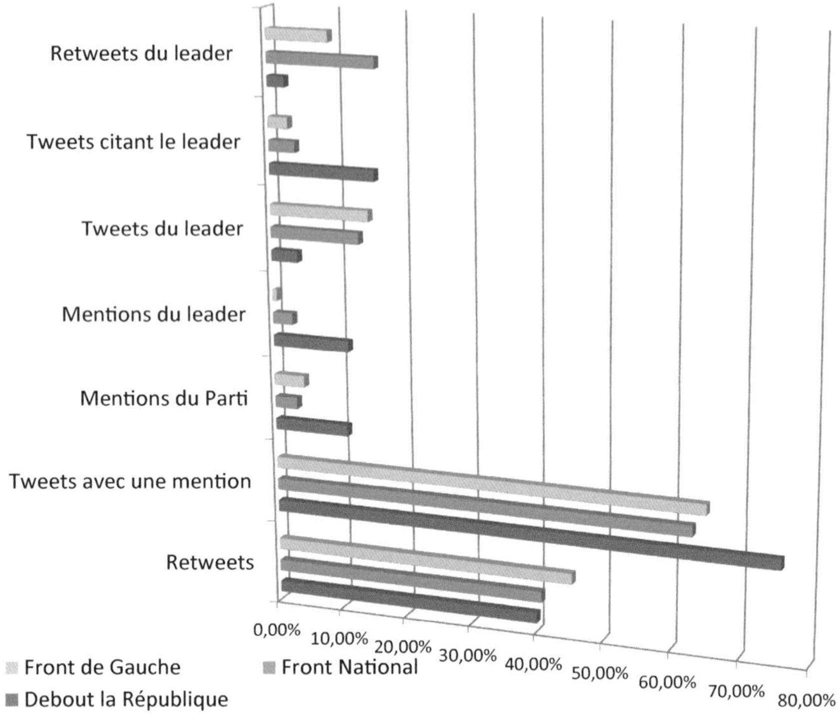

On voit que le poids relatif du leader de la formation et de la liste est sujet à variation. Le Front national et le Front de gauche publient beaucoup plus de messages de leur leader que Debout la France et les autres candidats les retwittent aussi beaucoup plus. Nicolas Dupont-Aignan n'a publié que 93 messages en 4 semaines, contre 462 par Marine Le Pen et 636 par Jean-Luc Mélenchon.

En revanche le nom du leader et du parti sont très massivement cités dans les messages de Debout la France (respectivement 378 et 267 fois), sans doute parce que parti et son leader, Nicolas Dupont-Aignan sont conscients de leur déficit de notoriété, problème que ne connaissent pas les deux autres dirigeants populistes (138 citations de M. Le Pen & 129 de J. L. Mélenchon et 118 mentions du FN & 195 du Front de gauche).

Les différences entre les trois partis s'estompent lorsque l'on additionne le nombre de tweets émis par toutes les têtes de liste dans chaque région (puisque le scrutin était régionalisé) car on voit que les têtes de liste assument pour beaucoup un rôle moteur dans l'émission de message sur Twitter.

Figure 5.3: Part des têtes de liste régionaux dans la tweet-campagne de chaque parti

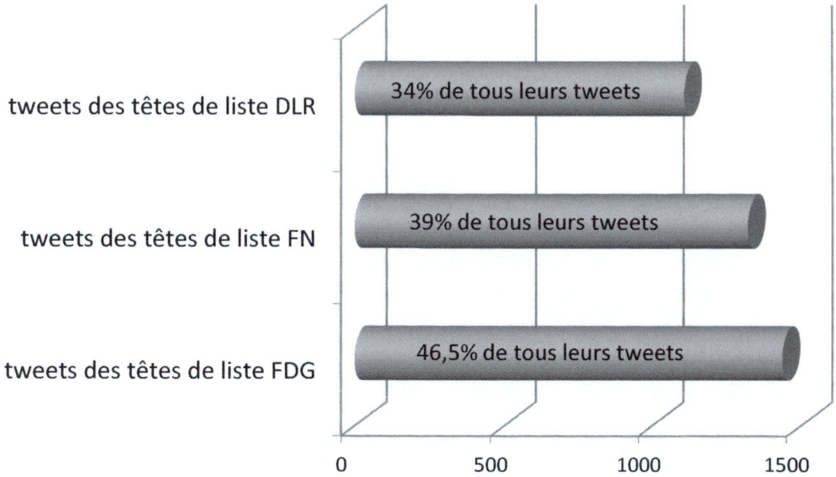

Mais pour ce qui concerne les statistiques générales sur les usages de l'outil Twitter, il n'y a pas de différences majeures sur les équilibres entre les messages originels (tweets) et le repartages (retweets), ou dans le nombre de messages contenant la mention d'au moins un autre compte (personnalités politiques le plus souvent ou publiques). De même, une des constantes de chacun des candidats est d'utiliser de nombreux hashtags (mot accolé à un dièse afin de mettre en exergue un mot clé) pour mettre en valeur des noms de ville (car les réseaux socionumériques sont très utilisés comme support publicitaire pour annoncer les lieux où le candidat se rend ou fait meeting), ou pour mettre en valeur des noms d'émissions ou de médias (car les candidats consacrent beaucoup de messages à autocélébrer leurs passages dans les médias).

Si les usages de Twitter diffèrent donc assez notablement entre ces forces protestataires, en fonction de la notoriété des leaders et des partis, en revanche, de nombreuses similitudes émergent sur l'art rhétorique mobilisé sur Twitter par ces trois forces, quand se ne sont pas de « troublantes » similitudes d'arguments entre des forces qui se déclarent pourtant hostiles les unes aux autres sur l'échiquier idéologique.

5.3 Les figures de l'ennemi dans la rhétorique protestataire anti-européenne

Les accusations contre l'Europe sur Twitter empruntent à plusieurs figures rhétoriques. On retrouve d'abord la dénonciation des travers d'une Union européenne qui ne s'occuperait (très mal) que des normes des biens de consommation, jusqu'à l'absurde : « L'escabeau, chasses d'eau, élevage des poulets, grilles des jardins d'enfants etc… Voilà quelques exemples de règles imposées par l'UE ! » (DLR). Un candidat FN évoque « des normes de technocrates qui ne connaissent rien de la réalité ».

Et de façon plus générale, c'est l'idée que l'Union impose tout, qui est vilipendée. Faisant fi des procédures de codécision entre la Commission, le Parlement et les Etats, l'Union européenne est construite comme un bunker d'où sortent des décisions absurdes ou malveillantes : « La Commission européenne : une oligarchie autocratique » (DLR) et N. Dupont-Aignan (leader de DLR) parle dans ses tweets de « L'Europe de l'esclavage ». Il dramatise alors l'enjeu électoral : « C'est maintenant l'heure du choix de la liberté ou de l'esclavage pour les Français ». Le Front de Gauche va dans le même sens. Un de ses candidats évoque « encore un coup de force : le conseil refuse le choix des urnes » (FDG), accréditant l'idée du « despotisme de l'UE » (FN), de « L'#UE, championne dans l'art de décider contre la volonté des peuples » (FN), de « l'Europe [qui] n'est pas "démocratique » (DLR), de « L'Union Européenne ou le déni de démocratie » (DLR), le FDG appelant à contester « Une soumission au diktat européen ». Même esprit de révolte au FDG, où un candidat se demande s'il faut continuer à « obéir aux injonctions absurdes de Bruxelles ? ». Et un candidat FN se remémore la date anniversaire du référendum contre le Traité constitutionnel européen de 2005, sous les traits d'une libération de l'esclavage : « 29 mai : il y a 9 ans le peuple français par référendum brisait ses chaînes ! #ConstitutionEuropéenne ». Un candidat du FDG y revient aussi, pour souligner que ce vote n'aurait pas été suivi des effets espérés : « la défiance des Français est grande. Ils ont dit non en 2005. Ca n'a pas été respecté ».

Et bien sûr, si les institutions sont néfastes, ceux qui les incarnent sont aussi dignes de mépris ou d'attaques : « @MartinSchulz et @JunckerEU sont les mêmes ! Le choix qui nous est offert est de décider de la couleur de nos barreaux ! » (FN). L'effet dramatique est recherché par le fait de souligner le caractère inéluctable de notre destin avec de tels leaders, qui nous emprisonnent, nous mettent derrière des barreaux. Les dirigeants européens sont présentés comme des nababs (« Les retraites de Nababs des commissaires européens » DLR), des « oligarques européens » (FDG), comme une clique d'exploiteurs (« la clique de dirigeants non élus qui exploitent les peuples », FN). D'où la nécessité d'en « finir avec cette Europe de la soumission et du déclin » (FN). Mais il faut souligner que les candidats de ces trois partis s'en prennent beaucoup moins qu'en Italie ou en Espagne à Juncker, Schultz ou à Angela Merkel. Les attaques nominatives sont plus rares et moins outrancières. On trouve quand même un candidat FDG pour renvoyer les deux candidats à la présidence de la Commission violemment dos-à-dos : « Valls fait campagne pour Schulz contre Junker : la peste contre le choléra » (FDG). Concernant Angela Merkel, c'est plutôt la soumission des autorités françaises face à l'Allemagne qui fait l'objet de tweets incendiaires : « Hollande est nul. Élu par défaut, il est la marionnette parfaite de Merkel » (DLR) ou encore « Ce qui apparente Hollande à Louis XVI c'est sa faiblesse. Il n'osera jamais être ferme face à Merkel » (DLR). Au Front de Gauche, si l'Allemagne est ciblée, c'est parce qu'elle a accédé au rang de symbole d'une politique économique rejetée : « les Allemands spéculent sur les dettes des autres pays » ; « Le modèle allemand, mirage libéral ! ».

Un tel propos introduit à une autre critique forte, la perspective nationaliste et souverainiste qu'on trouve surtout à droite et à la droite de la droite. Un candidat DLR (qui revendique l'héritage du gaullisme) invente la notion de « FFI 2.0 ». Les Forces Françaises de l'Intérieur furent le fruit du regroupement, en 1944, des divers mouvements de la Résistance sur le sol français. Ici, ce front de résistance s'organise sur internet (le tweet renvoyant vers un blog militant très virulent, hébergé en Russie). « FFI 2.0 : La France est occupée, sa destruction programmée ». La patrie est donc en danger. N. Dupont-Aignan (DLR) s'indigne d'ailleurs du fait que « Il ne s'agit plus de "Changer l'Europe" mais de "Changer la France" pour plaire à l'UE ». Au FDG aussi on trouve des références à l'esprit de : « résistance pour pulvériser leur système basé sur des compromis pourris ». Le Front national parle de « destruction des Etats-nations » et un de ses candidats affirme : « Nous sommes aujourd'hui un pays sous tutelle ». L'Union européenne est donc le « broyeur politique de la subsidiarité » (FN), poursuivant une imagerie de la toute-puissance destructrice de l'Europe. « l'#UE qui abolit la diversité culturelle et ruine les communautés nationales » (FN).

Mais ce n'est pas uniquement l'Etat-nation qui serait anéanti par l'Union européenne. Notre civilisation est menacée. Les candidats du FN déclinent cette idée avec diverses formulations : « l'UE méprise les peuples, les nations et la civilisation » ; « menace sur "la civilisation européenne" » ; « L'UE détruit la loi naturelle, la famille et notre socle civilisationnel ! » ; « N'en déplaise au petit cercle mondialiste gouverneur 2 la "province france", les racines chrétiennes sont les fondements 2 notre civilisation ». Les décisions prises au niveau européen menaceraient donc aussi l'idéal de famille traditionnelle et donc notre identité et notre socle commun. D'où la charge très forte : d'un candidat FN qui dénonce « la perversité de cette #UE immorale ». C'est dans ce contexte que le grand prix de l'Eurovision a fait une apparition inattendue dans notre corpus, avec la victoire d'une drag queen autrichienne. Deux candidats FN se moquent de cette personnalité hors norme et en font le symbole de la décadence des valeurs sur notre continent : « #Eurovision. #ConchitaWurst, ou chronique de la mise en œuvre du nouvel ordre mondial » ; « Je trouve que #ConchitaWurst représente parfaitement l'Europe actuelle ». Propos qui converge avec les hashtags mis en circulation par DLR : #stopgender ; #lafamille.

Si on regarde du côté des arguments déployés sur l'économie, on retrouve alors une sorte de front uni des trois mouvements protestataires étudiés. Chacun dénonce avec plus ou moins de violence le libre-échangisme, le néo-capitalisme, les banques… Sachant que le Front de gauche a très tôt décidé d'orienter sa critique sous cet angle. Il a fait de sa campagne une lutte contre « l'Europe austéritaire », jeu de mot contractant le mot austérité et la terminaison de l'adjectif autoritaire. L'Europe des critères de convergence de Maastricht qui impose de ne pas dépasser un certain niveau de déficit budgétaire, est donc dénoncée à la fois comme produisant de l'austérité et en le faisant de façon autoritaire, contre l'avis et l'intérêt immédiat des peuples. Par conséquent : « on vote #fdg contre l'austérité » ! Ou encore, on soutient « la jeunesse qui est sacrifiée par les politiques d'austérité », et on crée « un front du refus de l'austérité et du libre-échange » (FDG). Un candidat Front national fait aussi circuler un hashtag : #euro austérité et un autre s'essaie également au mot-valise, avec le hashtag #eurostérité. Et on découvre à travers tous les tweets étudiés une véritable convergence programmatique de ces trois forces politiques qui se présentent pourtant comme opposées les unes aux autres. Se dégage un même discours de dénonciation de la monnaie unique, des choix néo-libéraux et capitalistes de l'Union, qui détruiraient les pays, leur économie et/ou leurs peuples. On retiendra des tweets convergents comme : « La terrible rançon du fiasco de l'Europe libérale ! » (FDG) ; « Le libéralisme sauvage est l'idéologie poursuivie par l'UE! » (DLR) ; ou pour le Front national, c'est « l'UE machine à délocaliser l'emploi » et « l'UE = désindustrialisation ! » ; « nous vivons les ravages d'une mondialisation de la concurrence libre et non faussée » (FDG).

Pour le Front de Gauche, il faut donc, grâce à ce vote, « Casser les dents aux rapaces de la finance ! », « Il ne faut pas laisser l'Europe aux entreprises et aux banques ». Donc, « Contre l'Europe de la finance et atlantiste, votons #FDG ». Même chose au Front national. Il faut combattre « ceux qui vendent notre pays à la concurrence internationale déloyale », condamner « Cette Europe, instrument du mondialisme » celle qui ne sert que « les intérêts des élites mondialisées » car « L'UE actuelle ne protège pas notre peuple, elle est au service des lobbys et des multinationales » (FN). Même discours à Debout la République : « L'UE est au service des banques et des multinationales, et non au service des peuples #Reveillezvous », « Le président Charles de Gaulle n'aurait jamais accepté une dictature bancaire en Europe ».

« L'Europe a créé une concurrence déloyale entre les peuples », elle est associée au « dumping fiscal et social » (DLR). D'où l'idée émise par une des têtes de liste du FN que « Les patriciens de l'UE prêtent serment de servir docilement le mondialisme ultralibéral ». Un candidat Front de gauche pousse le plus loin l'hyperbole dans la comparaison historique, assimilant les orientations libérales de la commission aux premiers moments du nazisme : « Le nazisme fut le résultat de choix politiques : celui de la domination de l Europe de la finance et des grands cartels industriels » (FDG). D'où l'appel à rejeter « les traités européens qui saignent le peuple » (FDG).

Dans ce contexte, la monnaie unique et la Banque centrale européenne sont des cibles privilégiées. Pour le Front national, le procès fait à l'euro se décline en plusieurs arguments : « Euro rime avec zéro! Zéro emploi, zéro croissance, zéro social ! » ; « Propagande : "L'euro nous protège" – Vérité : C'est dans la zone euro que la crise est la plus sévère et la plus longue ». Et pour étayer la position, on met en circulation des liens URL d'articles pas écrits par des militants du FN : « La BCE refuse que les politiques lui dictent sa stratégie (Le Monde 10/5). Aux peuples de reprendre la main par les urnes ! » ; « Emmanuel Todd : "La zone euro n'est pas du tout une zone de protection mais une zone de guerre économique maximale" (Le Figaro 22/5) ». Mêmes attaques pour DLR : « Depuis 2009, la zone euro a 4 millions de chômeurs de plus, les Etats-Unis 4 millions de moins », « On asphyxie notre économie avec une monnaie trop chère », jusqu'à un angoissant message dramatique : « on a une monnaie qui nous assassine ». Pour toutes ces raisons le FDG appelle à combattre « Le Cauchemar Européen », formule qui permet de synthétiser un amalgame de divers reproches comme formulé ici : « Le fumeur de poulet à la javel et la vache aux hormones au sommet de leur haine des peuples et de leur amour des banques! » (FDG).

Un point de crispation a construit la campagne convergente de ces trois partis anti-européens : le projet de traité commercial transAltlantique. Que ce soit par idéologie nationaliste ou en raison d'une idéologie communiste et anticapitaliste, les États-Unis font l'objet en France depuis longtemps d'un fort rejet (Revel, 2002) y compris après les attentats du 11 septembre, sur le mode du juste retour des choses contre eux (Mercier, 2002). Pour DLR « L'Europe ne doit pas être vendue aux États-Unis ! », pour le FN « TAFTA rendra la France esclave économique des USA ! » et « Les États-Unis nous ont contaminé du virus libéral, tout en continuant à se protéger ! », et pour le FDG « L'Union européenne sans diplomatie véritable est inféodée aux États-Unis et à l'Otan ». Cet accord en cours de négociation possède la vertu de permettre d'amalgamer absolument toutes les critiques : la décision technocratique contre l'intérêt des peuples, la décision cachée donc antidémocratique, l'accord commercial qui ferait la part belle aux banques, aux multinationales, aux lobbies, tous aussi coupables et malfaisants.

Pour Debout la République la cause est majeure car « Le TAFTA, accord de libre-échange UE-USA, est un danger pour nos démocraties et nos peuples ». Du coup, « @DLR_Officiel se bat depuis des mois contre #TAFTA » et « Nous, nous combattrons #TAFTA sans relâche au Parlement européen », ce qui n'est pas le cas des parlementaires français à Strasbourg car « Nos "élus" sont des traîtres ». Et l'heure est si grave qu'ils relaient un tweet d'un souverainiste marqué à gauche (blogueur vedette de la gauche opposé au Traité constitutionnel de 2005) : « RT @Etienne_Chouard: Grand marché transatlantique : des tribunaux privés pour détrousser les contribuables ! ». Et cette menace grave est avalisée par les forces de gouvernement de droite ou de gauche, propos qui permet de valoriser sa posture de parti antisystème. La gravité de l'enjeu est toute aussi exceptionnelle selon le Front National : « Le front national s'opposera avec force pour faire échouer le traité transatlantique en cours de négociation par l'UMPS ! » car « #TAFTA est un véritable choc de dérégulation ». En effet, « Le traité de libre échange transatlantique, c'est l'assujettissement définitif au droit des multinationales de 800 millions de consommateurs » ou encore : « Le traité de libre-échange transatlantique est révélateur d'une #UE fabriquée pour les multinationales, contre les peuples. #TTIP », et d'ailleurs attention aux parties cachées mises au jour par Etienne Chouard : « Des tribunaux pour détrousser les Etats. Les non- dits du traité transatlantique ». Même constat lugubre au Front de Gauche : « Les États-Unis véritable empire joue partout le jeu de la guerre économique » donc il faut « faire de cette élection un référendum contre le Grand Marché Transatlantique ». Car « Poulet à la javel, bœuf aux hormones, porc aux hormones ! Voilà ce qu'est le #GMT ! ». « Le grand marché transatlantique = les multinationales contre la démocratie ».

Il est intéressant dès lors de noter que la force de ce credo anti-américain explique sans doute qu'aucun de ces trois partis ne s'adonne à une virulente critique de l'Allemagne et d'Angela Merkel. On trouve certes des piques contre l'Allemagne, mais assez peu finalement, et souvent ramenées à d'autres enjeux. Chez DLR, quand Angela Merkel est convoquée c'est pour souligner par contraste la faiblesse politique du Président Hollande : « Hollande est nul. Élu par défaut, il est la marionnette parfaite de Merkel » ; « Ce qui apparente Hollande à Louis XVI c'est sa faiblesse. Il n'osera jamais être ferme face à Merkel ». Pour le FDG, l'Allemagne est surtout l'archétype d'un modèle économique rejeté : « Le modèle allemand, mirage libéral ! » (propos suivi de liens URL renvoyant vers des articles décrivant les difficiles conditions de vie des travailleurs précaires dans ce pays). On leur reproche aussi le fait que « les Allemands spéculent sur les dettes des autres pays ». Pour le Front national, le cas allemand est mobilisé pour dénoncer la grande coalition SPD-CDU qui est au gouvernement, afin de « prouver » qu'il en irait bien de même en France, avec l'alliance objective entre le PS et l'UMP : « Hollande avec Merkel sur l'Europe. Normal : en RFA c'est la coalition CDU-SPD ; ici c'est l'UMPS. Mais là-bas, au moins, c'est officiel !... ». Ce cas allemand sert donc à démonétiser la parole socialiste : « Le PS dénonce la mainmise des conservateurs sur l'UE mais s'allie avec Martin Schulz, dont le parti gouverne en Allemagne avec Merkel... ». L'histoire de la relation franco-allemande, faite de trois guerres destructrices en un siècle et de la volonté de ne plus jamais connaître ça, en construisant « l'amitié franco-allemande », explique aussi qu'une rhétorique très hostile à l'Allemagne est devenue inacceptable en France, contrairement à ce qu'on a pu observer en Italie durant cette même campagne.

On voit ici, une autre forme de convergence entre ces trois partis politiques positionnés pourtant très différemment sur l'échiquier politique : tous dénoncent les forces de gouvernement, et ce qui est censé être leurs collusions, leur impuissance, leur trahison face aux intérêts de la nation et/ou du peuple. Et l'échelon européen, où existe au Parlement une coopération entre les deux principaux groupes politiques, ne vient alors que conforter cette dénonciation au niveau national. Chacun a donc entonné sur Twitter l'air bien connu du « sortir les sortants », avec une petite musique spécifique pour chaque parti.

À Debout la République, la collusion est dénoncée avec constance, au deux échelons politiques : « 94 % des décisions ont été votées conjointement par le PPE et le PSE! », « Entendez-vous les leaders #UMP et #PS qui ne remettent RIEN en question? Il n'y a plus rien à attendre de ces gens » ; « Ils sont surtout ok pr se partager le pouvoir et ne rien changer. La preuve par les traités signés » ; « Les députés UE PS et UMP et associés ne disent rien des graves décisions qui sont votées par le Parlement ». Du coup, à l'instar de Bepe Grillo en Italie ou du parti Podemos en Espagne, Nicolas Dupont-Aignan appelle à renverser toute la classe politique : « Le grand ménage de la classe politique #UMP #PS est un devoir citoyen. Nous payons pour leurs incompétences et malversations. #STOP ! ». Et il se félicite d'ailleurs de la victoire de Nigel Farage tant pour ses positions eurosceptiques que pour ce qu'il représente de coup de balai contre les forces de gouvernement.

Même rhétorique au Front National où les futurs dirigeants de la Commission sont jugés interchangeables : « Débat ce soir Juncker-Schulz sur LCI/RTL. Deux voix pour un monologue européiste ». Mais le FN, fidèle à son héritage d'extrême-droite, y ajoute un couplet plus complotiste, sur la collusion de la « classe politico-médiatique » qui serait coupable à la fois de sous-représenter la voix du FN et de ne pas parler des « vrais enjeux » cachés du scrutin : « le black out des médias masque l'échec de l'UMPS ! », « Le complexe médiatico-politique a donné congé au peuple », « Ces atteintes à la liberté d'expression sont affligeantes ! Le peuple Français rompra ces chaînes par le vote ! ».

Le Front de Gauche, outre sa dénonciation de l'extrême-droite (« Face à l'extrême-droite Toute-s mobilisé-e-s pour l'égalité et la solidarité » ; « Cette femme [Marine Le Pen] n'a qu'un discours haineux et mortifère ! » ; « Je dis : soyez fâchés mais pas fachos.» #Mélenchon »), s'en prend aussi aux positions communes des deux grandes forces de gouvernement : « le #PS a vidé de son contenu la résolution #StopTTIP du #FdG, avec l'aval de l'#UMP » ; « Les partis socio-démocrates, la droite et les libéraux votent ensemble au Parlement européen dans 80 % des cas ». Et bien sûr les socialistes au pouvoir sont aussi une cible, on dénigre « L'hypocrisie du PS » ou « le mensonge du PS sur les travailleurs détachés », voilà pourquoi « Nous devons donner une bonne raclée à ceux qui ont oublié d'être de Gauche ! ».

On retrouve enfin dans les deux forces de la droite extrême, un discours ouvertement xénophobe, faisant de l'immigration un fléau à combattre et l'Europe une « passoire » ou pire un facteur d'encouragement à l'immigration.

Debout la République se plaint que « Le poste frontière ressemble à une ruine », dénonce « l'Europe passoire ». Le Front national préconise « la sortie de la France de l'espace #Schengen pour lutter contre l'#immigration de masse ! ». Les accords de Shengen deviennent l'archétype de ce contre quoi il faut lutter car « l'espace Schengen a détruit nos frontières nationales ». Donc « Le Pen dénonce «une immigration considérable» due à Schengen et propose une politique nataliste » selon un tweet relatant un de ses meetings. Pour DLR, la priorité est de « stopper toute nouvelle adhésion » et surtout de refuser à jamais la Turquie, au nom des racines chrétiennes de l'Europe.

Au Front national, on trouve des candidats avec des positions bien plus radicales qui n'hésitent d'ailleurs pas à recycler des tweets issus de mouvances ouvertement racistes et complotistes, venant notamment du mouvement dit « identitaire ». Ce mouvement dit défendre la race blanche et française contre les juifs, les musulmans et les immigrés, tous supposés être de mauvais Français. On voit ainsi circuler dans notre corpus des tweets venant du compte @francaisdesouche développant la thèse du « grand remplacement ». La population française (présentée comme de souche) serait en train d'être submergée par des vagues d'immigration qui la rendraient à terme minoritaire. Pareille menace justifie un appel au sursaut dans les urnes : « Enfants Issus de l'immigration : 1 naissances sur 3 en France entière; le grand remplacement est en marche ! le 25 votez pour des frontières » (FN). L'Europe qui s'est créée dès le Traité de Rome en 1957 pour abaisser les frontières (douanières) entre les peuples est donc un ennemi à combattre car elle empêcherait les États de se défendre contre les invasions en cours, faute de frontières nationales. Le hashtag #islamisation ou #immigrationmassive ont aussi circulé sur les comptes de candidats FN.

5.4 Des tweets-polémiques adossées à l'ironie et aux sarcasmes

La dérision politique se porte fort bien sur l'Internet, grâce aux vidéos diffusées sur les sites spécialisés, grâce à la circulation accélérée et massive de caricatures, blagues ou clips, comme la campagne *sarkostique* l'avait déjà en 2006–2007, bien montré. Grâce à l'effet d'archivage que ce support permet, il est devenu plus facile de proposer des montages mettant des élus en flagrant délit de contradictions entre des propos tenus un jour et les propos et actes d'aujourd'hui. De plus, la montée en puissance de l'usage politique des médias sociaux, en France, s'inscrit dans un contexte de forte contestation des dirigeants politiques et des partis traditionnels et d'installation de pratiques protestataires chez une partie des citoyens. Par ailleurs, les premières études sur l'usage des médias sociaux insistent sur la forte implication personnelle et émotionnelle des propos publiés. Et nous voyons que les forces politiques ont intégré les médias sociaux à leur répertoire d'action collective (Mercier, 2015), surtout lors des campagnes électorales, faisant des comptes Twitter, Facebook, Instagram et autres, un prolongement des technologies de « web campaigning ».

C'est en combinant l'ensemble de ces données que l'on doit appréhender la manière dont les citoyens utilisent les médias sociaux (Twitter et Facebook essentiellement, mais aussi parfois Tumblr ou Instagram) durant les campagnes, pour participer au processus électoral, de façon critique. Et on voit que ces espaces d'expression sont souvent utilisés à des fins polémiques, pour émettre une critique politique à au moins trois niveaux : déstabiliser un adversaire politique pour des raisons tactiques et idéologiques, critiquer le jeu politique et partisan tel qu'il se déroule dans son ensemble, associer à cette critique de la politique, les autres acteurs du jeu électoral que sont les médias et les journalistes. Le tout se faisant par des jeux de posture et des échanges d'arguments plus ou moins agressifs et radicaux, mais qui ont souvent pour caractéristiques communes de jouer de l'ironie, des attaques personnelles ridiculisantes, des photomontages sarcastiques, qui sapent la légitimité ou la crédibilité des personnes ciblées.

Mais les forces politiques ne sont pas en reste et adoptent elles aussi, ce style contestataire pour renouveler leur style de campagne sur les réseaux socionumériques. À l'occasion de ce traité, on a donc vu apparaître une figure symbolique inattendue des méfaits de la négociation entre l'Union européenne et les Etats-Unis : le poulet chloré. Dans beaucoup de tweets on évoque cette figure emblématique des traités commerciaux qui se feraient contre l'avis et l'intérêt des consommateurs. L'Europe devient le fourrier de la malbouffe contre les traditions culinaires françaises. Le Front de Gauche et Debout la République vont même en faire des clips de campagne, avec une séquence qui se veut ironiquement amère pour ce dernier (scène de repas familial où le père est critiqué par sa femme et ses enfants pour avoir cuisiné un poulet qui sent mauvais, arguant qu'on ne trouve plus que ça à acheter : du poulet américain lavé au chlore, les poulets français étant devenus hors de prix).

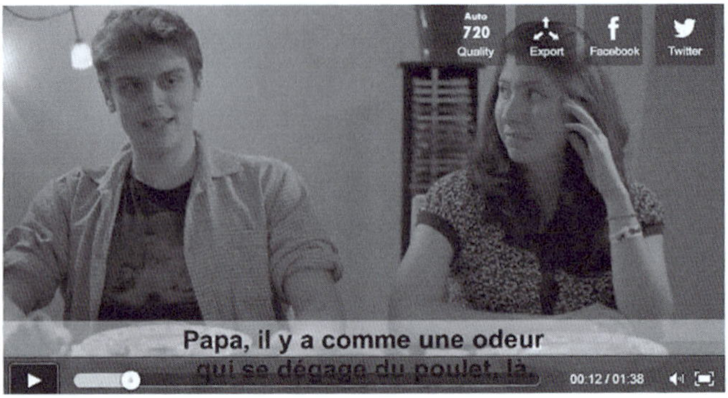

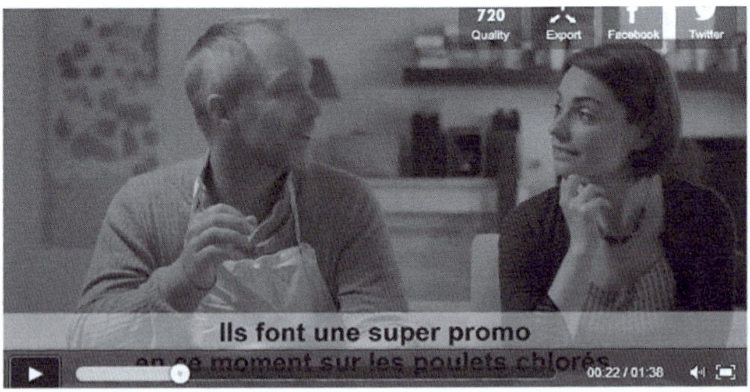

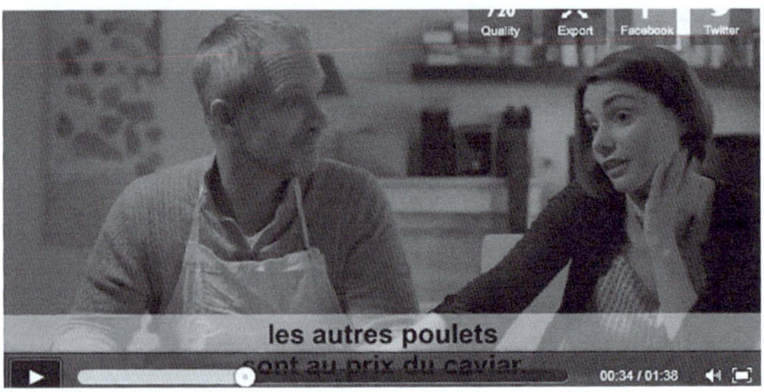

Au Front de Gauche, on joue des codes de la contestation sur Internet, en mettant en circulant sur Twitter le lien vers une vidéo où on voit un homme habillé en poulet se rouler à l'entrée d'une piscine, dans de l'eau chlorée donc. Le tout accompagné d'un message visant à frapper les esprits, à dénoncer l'absurdité d'un tel procédé pourtant toléré aux États-Unis.

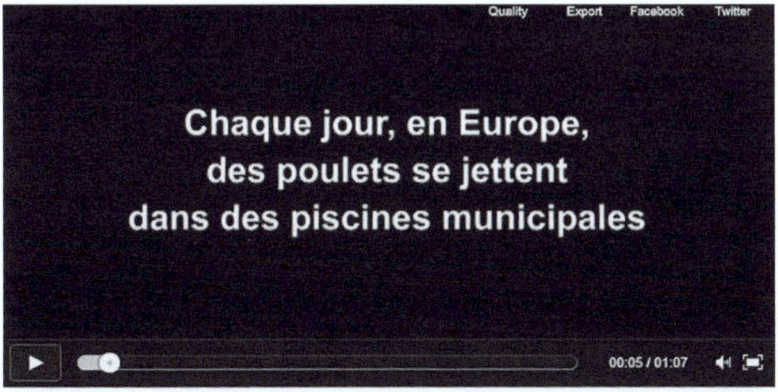

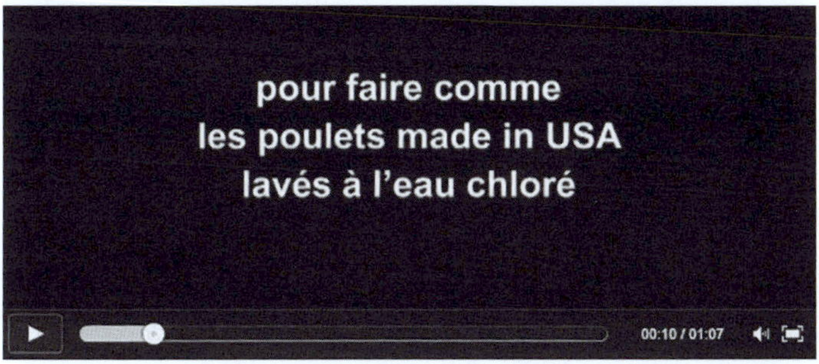

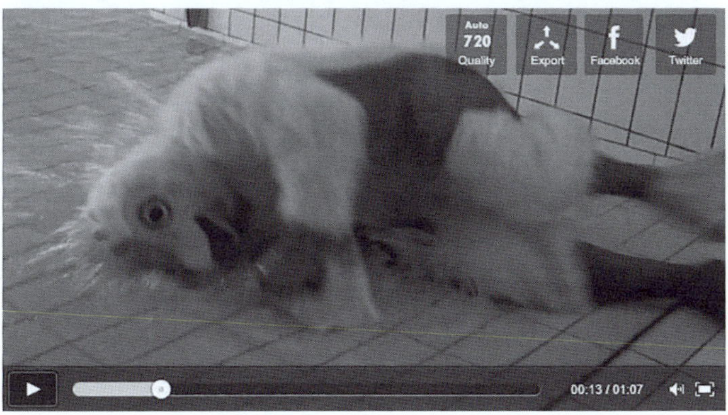

Par ailleurs, la contestation protestataire s'exprime à travers le recours à divers jeux de mots dont la force comique ou caustique semble devoir se suffire à elle-même et semble pouvoir remplacer un argumentaire élaboré. Le discours protestataire repose en effet souvent sur ce type d'effet rhétorique, où la pirouette lexicale, le mot qui frappe, la formule choc font office d'arguments.

En faisant un jeu de mot à base d'un préfixe en « euro » (ce que les candidats italiens ont utilisé bien plus que les Français), DLR se moque des pro-européens, qualifiés « d'euro-béats », alors même qu'il y aurait matière à se révolter vu ce qui nous est imposé : « L'Europe selon les euro-béats : le fouet autoritaire » (DLR).

L'habitude prise par les institutions et les entreprises de composer des mots commençant par le préfixe « euro » (Eurodéputés, Eurobaromètre, Eurostat, Europol, Euratom, Euronews, Eurostar, Eurovision…) sert aussi de modèle pour construire des noms ou des adjectifs désignant une qualité ou un défaut attribuable aux institutions ou aux citoyens européens (eurosceptiques, europhiles…). Grâce à ce préfixe court et facilement encastrable dans un adjectif ou un nom, on peut produire des mots composés, sur un mode spécifique, avec une productivité infinie. L'inventivité des locuteurs est dès lors sans limite pour créer des mots nouveaux associant l'Europe à un mot existant pour faire advenir une réalité, par sa simple nomination. Par le pouvoir performatif du langage, la construction euro+nom ou euro+adjectif permet de définir des catégories, d'essentialiser des pratiques, tout en introduisant une relation ambiguë entre les mots en présence, puisque « euro » peut juste dénoter une extension géographique et politique (à l'échelle de l'Europe) ou bien (dans la bouche des adversaires de l'Union) « euro » connote une caractéristique négative, faisant peu ou prou de l'Europe, la responsable, la coupable et entachant les personnes ou les qualités du terme qui suit, d'un biais, d'une tare irrémédiable. On trouve dans notre corpus de nombreux exemples : eurobéats ; euroPropagande ; euro-pompiers pyromanes ; eurocrates ; eurogagas ; euromondialisme ; autant de qualificatifs péjoratifs auxquels s'opposent des termes dont se parent les adversaires de l'Union : euro-refondateur ; eurocritique ; euro-lucide. Notons aussi ce tweet FN contre « le bombardement propagandiste €-phile par la caste politico-médiatique ».

On trouve aussi trace de cette inventivité au service de l'amalgame et de la dénonciation dans l'art de créer certains hashtags et de faire quelques jeux de mots. Le hashtag est aussi souvent l'opportunité de créer des mots composés ou des mots-valises, contractant deux mots pour en faire un troisième plus riche de signifiant, prenant valeur de slogan : #STOPTAFTA (FDG) ; #lobbytour (FDG) pour une série de liens militants ou de presse sur le travail des lobbies à Bruxelles. Les candidats ont créé de nombreux hashtags pour s'adapter à ce mode expressif né sur Twitter et donner la force d'une formule-slogan à un regroupement de deux mots et plus : #MéprisdeCaste (FN) ; Nogender (FN) ; Savefamilly (FN) ; OuiLaFranceNonBruxelles (FN) ; #Gauchetarée (FN) #droitetarée (FN) ; GéronthocratieBasta (FN) ; #JAiMalAMaFrance (FN). Debout la France Debout la République n'est pas en reste en matière d'inventivité verbale pour ses hashtags sous forme de contractions : #débacledelamorale (DLR) ; BygmalionThon, #Sarkothon ou #QuiVeutGagnerDesBygmalion (DLR) pour moquer l'aide demandée aux adhérents de l'UMP pour renflouer les caisses du parti ; #HollandeTouteLaFranceVeutTaDémission avec une variante plus simple #Hollandedémission ou #Taubiradémission (DLR) ou le plus brutal #Hollandedégage (DLR). Enfin, au Front de gauche également on utilise beaucoup de hashtags pour condenser du sens. Ces hashtags sont des cris de révolte : #bellecolère ; #çasuffit ; #placeaupeuple ; #enfumage ; #foutagedegueule ; #enviedevomir ; #nopasaran (intégrée à la mythologie révolutionnaire de gauche depuis la Guerre d'Espagne) ; #onlacherien ; #StopOligarchie ; #doublelangage (pour dénoncer l'action de F. Hollande et des socialistes au pouvoir, présentés comme des sociaux-traîtres) ; #lecampdupeupleestnotrecamp ; #jesaisvousvousenfichez (FDG). On trouve aussi quelques jeux de mot pour marquer les esprits par la force d'un bon mot : « La jeunesse Contre Le Pen de mort » (FDG) (jeu de mot avec la peine de mort) ; ou encore « Le @FDG mobilisé contre l'Europe méTAFTAsée ! » (jeu de mot avec la métastase qui compare donc le traité Europe-Amérique à un cancer).

5.5 Conclusion

On voit que l'appropriation des styles Twitter contestataires se fait dans chaque parti, avec des formules chocs, l'invention de hashtags mobilisateurs et de quasi slogans, des propos très ironiques et sarcastiques pour décrier les adversaires, et la mise en circulation de liens URL pointant vers des vidéos, des photomontages ou des blogs où une virulence plus forte et plus condamnable s'y exprime plus librement. Les réseaux socionumériques en général, sont perçus et vécus comme des technologies d'affirmation de soi, permettant de laisser libre cours à l'exposition de son intimité, de ses goûts, de sa personnalité, sans censure, au risque même de l'impudeur.

Sur les réseaux numériques, l'individualisme expressif suit souvent une logique de libération de certains cadres et conventions sociales qui régissent les interactions sociales ordinaires. Le succès de ces dispositifs technologiques de communication auprès de nombre d'usagers s'explique par son adéquation avec des aspirations sociales à ce que le sociologue néerlandais, Cas Wouters nomme « *informalization* ». Ce sociologue constate dans nos sociétés occidentales depuis

1945, une baisse tendancielle de la pompe rigide, des codes cérémoniels ancestraux, de l'autocontrainte chère à Norbert Elias dont il se veut le continuateur. Au contraire, monte un sentiment de liberté assumé pour vivre comme on l'entend. Il détecte donc « un accroissement des alternatives comportementales et émotionnelles, socialement acceptées » (Wouters, 2007 : 57). Cela correspond à une tendance lourde d'aspiration à ne pas être contraint, à s'affranchir des marques traditionnelles de déférence sociale.

Ici, les candidats des forces protestataires s'engouffrent dans ces formes d'usage, hésitant beaucoup moins que les candidats des forces dites de gouvernement à manier l'insulte, l'ironie méprisante, la formule choc, pour faire des soutiens à un processus de construction européenne transnationale des ennemis politiques contre lesquels tous les coups sont permis sur Twitter.

Références bibliographiques

Amossy R., Burger M., 2011, « Introduction : la polémique médiatisée », *Semen*, 31, p. 724.

Kerbrat-Orecchioni, C., 1980, *Le Discours Polémique*. Lyon : Presses universitaires de Lyon.

Mercier, A., 2015, « L'intégration de Twitter au répertoire d'action électorale des campagnes municipales françaises de 2014 », in : *La communication électronique : enjeux, stratégies et opportunités*, éditions Lambert-Lucas, p. 149–168.

Mercier A., 2002, « L'anti-américanisme, priorité des caricaturistes français », *Les Dossiers de l'audiovisuel* n°104, juillet-août, p. 44–48.

Micheli, R., 2011. « Quand l'affrontement porte sur les mots *en tant que mots* : polémique et réflexivité langagière », *Semen*, 31, p. 97–112.

Revel, J.-F., 2002, L'obsession anti-américaine. Son Fonctionnement, Ses Causes, Ses Inconséquences, Paris, Plon.

Small, T., 2010, « La politique canadienne en 140 caractères : la vie des partis dans l'univers Twitter », *Revue parlementaire canadienne*, 33 (3), p. 45–49.

Wouters C., 2007, Informalization. Manners and emotions since 1890, Londres, Sage.

Yanoshevsky, G., 2003. « De la Polémique à la Polémique Journalistique ». *Recherches en Communication,* 20, p. 37–52.

Marina Villa, UniCatt (Milan)

6. Les discours sur l'Europe dans la tweet-campagne en Italie

Abstract
The chapter studies the polemic discourses in the tweet-campaign for the European elections 2014: the arguments pro and against EU, the negative images of Europe, the common "enemies". The analysis of 70.549 tweets posted by candidates in 7 lists is quantitative (content) and qualitative (rhetorical strategies, argumentation, polemic issues).

6.1 Introduction

Twitter est un instrument important dans la communication politique en Italie. Plusieurs membres du Gouvernement et de l'opposition l'utilisent régulièrement (le Premier Ministre Matteo Renzi en particulier); en outre, les partis contestataires et antisystème, comme le Mouvement de Beppe Grillo et la Ligue du Nord, sont de plus en plus actifs sur Twitter.

Le tweet permet aux hommes politiques de communiquer avec les citoyens d'une façon simple, brève et rapide, mais surtout moins formelle, avec un effet d'intimité et de proximité ; une communication directe qui ne passe plus par les journalistes et les partis, dans une logique de désintermédiation (Boccia Artieri 2013). Twitter est aussi une occasion de se rendre visible pour les médias et de communiquer en leur direction (le tweet remplace le communiqué de presse). Pour les journalistes, qui sont très actifs sur Twitter et suivent constamment les leaders, cette plateforme est une source et un lieu d'échange avec la politique (Mancini et Mazzoni 2014).

Pendant les campagnes électorales, Twitter est un outil efficace en raison de ses spécificités : la versatilité ; l'hybridation des langages ; le potentiel de la plateforme pour le storytelling, l'interaction discursive de plusieurs acteurs qui crée une narration collective ; l'accessibilité totale à cette narration, la visibilité ample (Bentivegna 2015).

Twitter est donc un bon observatoire pour les discours de campagne, car la brièveté du texte est une contrainte mais aussi une opportunité pour être plus créatif et incisif (Bichard & Parmelee 2012) : le tweet favorise la diffusion de slogans et de petites phrases, mais aussi la focalisation sur les points essentiels du programme, la recherche de l'argument efficace et la répétition de mots-clés ;

et devient un support important pour la communication polémique contre les adversaires (*cf.* chapitre 5 dans ce volume).

Cette contribution se propose d'analyser la tweet-campagne pour les élections européennes de tous les candidats italiens présents dans les listes qui ont obtenu plus que 3 % des voix, c'est-à-dire 7 listes : Partito Democratico (PD) avec 40,81 % des voix; Movimento 5 Stelle – Beppe Grillo (M5S) : 21,16 % ; Forza Italia (FI) : 16,82 % ; Lega Nord-Basta Euro (LN) : 6,16 % ; Nuovo Centro Destra (NCD) : 4,38 %; L'altra Europa con Tsipras (LT) : 4,03 % ; Fratelli d'Italia-Alleanza nazionale (FDI) : 3,66 %.

L'analyse de notre corpus – 70.549 tweets – est quantitative et qualitative (portant sur les stratégies rhétoriques, l'argumentation, les propos polémiques) et se pose trois questions : quels sont les contenus de la tweet-campagne? Quels sont les arguments pro- et anti- Europe? Y-a-t-il des sujets polémiques et des « ennemis » communs à sept partis si différents?

Sur le fond, on cherchera aussi d'identifier des stratégies de communication spécifiques des partis et des candidats en campagne.

6.2 Les tweets des candidats

Notre corpus contient 315 comptes, pour 309 candidats (il y a des candidats avec plus qu'un compte).

Tableau 6–1: Nombre des tweets et des retweets des candidats dans les 7 listes

Liste	**Nombre de candidats**	**Nombre de tweets**	**dont RT**
FI	51	19592	10435
PD	62	14210	5176
FDI	35	9936	4386
M5S	57	8791	3243
LN	24	7907	3048
NCD	43	5433	2338
Tsipras	37	4680	1280
Total	**309**	**70549**	**29906**

La production des candidats n'est pas homogène, car en quatre semaines certains candidats tweetent plus que 2000 fois et d'autres n'ont que 2 ou 3 tweets[79].

79 Par exemple, Elisa Montemagni (LN) et Stefano Cobello (PD) avec 2 tweets chacun dans les 4 semaines.

En considérant les 6 premiers candidats par nombre de tweets dans les cinq listes qui ont plus de tweets, on voit qu'il y a des différences dans la distribution des tweets : le PD a seulement une candidate avec plus que 1000 tweets, tandis que pour FI il y en a 6.

Tableau 6–2: Les candidats qui tweetent le plus (dans les 5 listes qui ont plus de tweets)

FI (19592 tweets)	**PD (14210 tweets)**	**FDI (9936 tweets)**	**M5S (8791 tweets)**	**LN (7907 tweets)**
Lara Comi 2627	Elly Schlein 1607	Pino Galluzzo 1184	Beppe Grillo 2097	Claudio Borghi 2409
Ylenia Citino 2288	Gianni Pittella 877	Chiara Mengoli 1172	Marika Cassimatis 1068	Francesca Onorato 1740
Raffaele Fitto 2174	Mercedes Bresso 569	Lucia Arizzi 1146	Isabella Adinolfi 435	Claudia Bellocchi 1103
Licia Ronzulli 1601	Isabella del Monte 505	Guido Crosetto 1025	Antonella di Prima 428	Angelo Ciocca 559
Simone Furlan 1480	Paolo de Castro 504	Massimo Gianpieri 691	Alice Salvatore 373	Matteo Salvini 456
Alessandra Mussolini 1462	Luca Barbieri 496	Magdi Allam 592	Massimo Scabbia 318	Oscar Lancini 324

Parmi les leaders des trois partis dits « protestataires », qui utilisent fréquemment les médias socionumériques, le plus productif est Beppe Grillo (M5S), avec 2097 tweets, qui sont pour la plupart des retweets de ce que disent les citoyens ou les médias (1996 retweets). Il écrit seulement 101 tweets lui-même et il est peu retweeté par les candidats du M5S : 25 fois au total. Matteo Salvini (LN), au contraire, produit 456 tweets dont seulement 4 sont des retweets : il obtient 249 retweets des candidats de la LN. Giorgia Meloni, leader de FDI, produit 388 tweets (dont 103 retweet) et obtient 667 retweets, donc c'est la plus retweetée parmi ces trois leaders.

Les tweets des candidats aux européennes en Italie sont plus nombreux que dans les autres pays étudiés dans le corpus de la recherche TEE2014 (Compagno 2015). Nous cherchons alors d'indiquer les raisons d'une production de tweet si importante.

- Pour les élections européennes, beaucoup de candidats ont un compte Twitter. Plusieurs d'entre eux ont ouvert leur compte juste au début de la campagne ou même quand elle était déjà en cours, et utilisent ce compte seulement pour retweeter leur parti : cela donne au candidat de la visibilité et lui permet de se doter d'un outil « nouveau », même s'il reste peu suivi[80]. D'autres candidats qui se servent depuis longtemps de leur compte intensifient l'activité pendant la campagne. Certains leaders et têtes de liste ont plusieurs comptes (le compte officiel plus des comptes de campagne) et donc amplifient leurs messages : on dénombrait 3 comptes pendant la campagne, par exemple, pour la seule candidate de FI, Licia Ronzulli. Enfin, certains candidats sont assistés par une équipe de campagne qui tweete régulièrement à partir de leur compte pour rendre visibles leurs commentaires sur l'actualité et le récit de leur campagne[81].

- Twitter est utilisé pour retweeter, en amplifiant le message, les tweets d'autres figures politiques (du parti ou de la tête de liste, par exemple). Cette activité est rendue plus facile grâce à des applications pour le téléphone qui permettent de retweeter automatiquement les tweets du parti ou du leader : Matteo Salvini (LN) en promouvait une d'entre elles. Le corpus comprend de nombreux retweets et certains comptes de candidats n'incluent que des retweets.
- On a observé aussi des usages assez particuliers, moins conventionnels, de Twitter comme outil de diffusion de matériel « en série ». Par exemple, le même message tweeté plusieurs fois avec un @ différent (donc un message répété adressé à des personnes différentes) : à titre d'exemple, Camilla Sebezzi de LT tweete 50 fois le même message avec le lien à son interview dans un quotidien. De la même manière, Ilenia Citino (FI) produit 143 tweets pour annoncer l'événement de clôture de sa campagne électorale. Un autre usage particulier du tweet est la reproduction des matériaux électoraux : plusieurs tweets sont envoyés à des comptes différents avec la même image de propagande et le même slogan. Ainsi, Lara Comi de FI produit 47 tweets avec son affiche et son slogan. On voit donc l'usage d'un outil nouveau avec des logiques de diffusion typiques des vieux médias : dans le premier cas le tweet est diffusé à plusieurs destinataires, à l'image d'un communiqué de presse ou d'un e-mail, dans le deuxième cas, on parlera d'une utilisation en tant que « tweet-tract ».

80 Dans FDI, trois candidats produisent des tweets identiques – même texte et heure de production – pendant toute la campagne, donc écrits par la même personne ou avec le même outil de reproduction (ils sont les trois qui ont plus de tweets dans FDI).

81 La preuve que les candidats considèrent Twitter comme instrument stratégique et un signe de popularité est le nombre de citations des outils pour mesurer l'activité des candidats sur les réseaux sociaux (la « top dix » des candidats, les plus tweetés ou les plus « sociaux »). Les candidats de FI, par exemple, citent ces données 96 fois.

- Les médias utilisent fréquemment Twitter comme source de déclarations politiques et comme outil pour relancer des informations politiques qui sont déjà en circulation dans l'espace public. Donc pendant la campagne ils citent encore plus souvent les hommes politiques et les leaders d'opinion : et le candidat, avec une sorte d'effet miroir, cite les tweets des médias qui le citent[82]. De plus, comme on le verra plus loin, en Italie la télévision est un sujet important dans les tweets en campagne électorale, ce qui s'explique par la quantité et la popularité des *talk shows* politiques qui invitent les candidats : cela augmente la production de tweets, surtout quand il y a des leaders dans l'émission.

6.3 Les contenus de la tweet-campagne

L'analyse des tweets montre qu'il y a des contenus de campagne électorale communs, même s'il reste des spécificités remarquables dans la propagande de 7 partis si différents (*infra*). En particulier, nous nous focalisons sur quatre sujets traités par tous les partis.

6.3.1 Le récit de la campagne sur le terrain et sur les plateaux télévisés

Presque tous les candidats de notre corpus, même ceux qui tweetent rarement, parlent de leur campagne électorale et proposent des annonces, des images et des comptes rendus d'événements : un« récit » de l'activité de campagne comme occasion de rencontre avec les citoyens et de présence sur le terrain. Le résultat est une sorte de journal de bord, où chaque meeting et chaque rencontre (même la plus petite et familiale) est une étape dans un voyage réel et symbolique vers les électeurs de la circonscription : on donne le rendez-vous, on crée l'attente, on relate en direct – si possible avec des images – on commente après la fin (souvent avec des retweets des participants), on remercie pour la participation, on met des liens vers les articles sur la campagne. Et ainsi on donne même à ceux qui n'ont pas pu participer les informations sur l'événement. Twitter est l'instrument idéal pour suivre ce genre d'activité de campagne sur le terrain, car il permet des mises à jour continues et une description « live », une communication immédiate et

---

82 Par exemple le tweet de A. Cecchi Paone qui retweete l'émission « Agora » qui cite son intervention : « *RT @agorarai : "Pourquoi ceux qui contestent l'Europe veulent aller en Europe?" @ACP_CecchiPaone #agorarai* ».

personnalisée, un lien aux documents (articles, photos) qui expliquent le sens de l'événement et en amplifient les effets.

Cette attention sur les événements de campagne dans les tweets semble avoir quatre buts.

a) Avant tout, pour certains candidats c'est une simple publicité pour se rendre visibles et accessibles aux sympathisants (« venez à l'apéritif électoral», « à 20h suivez-moi en live streaming ») et pour souligner l'élan vers l'objectif final, les élections : « *Bonjour à tous, le count down continue, -12…et je continue mon voyage #versEU2014 en direction Brindisi* » (NCD). b) Dans certains cas, le récit de la campagne a aussi la fonction de témoigner du succès des événements, la popularité du parti, et de faire une « contre-information » : le M5S publie les photos des foules qui écoutent Beppe Grillo pour contraster les informations relayées par les médias, qui seraient peu objectifs en parlant du mouvement. c) Pour d'autres candidats, les tweets suivent les étapes d'une véritable tournée électorale organisée pour visiter la circonscription et arriver dans des lieux symboliques (« la tournée des entreprises », « la tournée de la dégradation urbaine» ou simplement « la tournée du candidat en caravane » dans son territoire). d) Enfin, l'événement de campagne peut être l'occasion de faire participer les *followers* à la vie du candidat et écrire quelque chose de personnel.

Pour quatre listes, ces contenus qu'on pourrait appeler « *campaign issues* » (événements de campagne, activité sur le terrain, lien aux articles qui parlent de la campagne du candidat, écrits du candidat sur la campagne) représentent plus que 22 % du total des tweets[83].

En parallèle, il y a le récit de la campagne sur les plateaux télévisés : dans un pays où les rapports entre télévision et politique sont étroits, et les *talk-shows* politiques ont une bonne audience, les candidats parlent souvent de télévision. Et les interventions télévisées des leaders sont un sujet important dans les tweets. Le récit de la campagne des 7 listes étudiées s'enrichit ainsi de 5884 tweets consacrés à la télévision : annonces de la présence télévisée des candidats et des leaders, commentaires en direct sur les émissions politiques, liens aux vidéos des interventions. En particulier, les interviews de Berlusconi (qui avait des restrictions dans la communication électorale sur le terrain) et de Grillo (qui d'habitude évite les plateaux télévisés) ont créé un flux de communication important (cf. chapitre 10 dans ce volume).

---

83 Les tweets sur les *campaign issues* sont 27.74 % sur le total de tweets pour PD, 27.72 % pour NCD, 22.90 % pour M5S, 22.74 % pour Tsipras.

Tableau 6–3: Nombre des tweets sur les événements et le récit de la campagne (campagne sur le terrain et à la TV)

Liste	tweets sur la campagne de terrain (a)	tweets sur la campagne à la TV (b)	tweets sur la campagne de terrain + campagne à la TV (c)	% de (c) sur le total des tweets
FI	2859	1401	4260	21,74
PD	3942	475	4417	31,08
M5S	2013	699	2712	30,85
FDI	753	2046	2799	28,17
LN	1120	697	1817	22,98
NCD	1506	318	1824	33,57
Tsipras	1064	248	1312	28,03
Total	13257	5884	19141	27,13

6.3.2 L'émergence du thème de l'immigration

Suite aux débarquements continus sur les côtes italiennes et à l'absence d'une réponse jugée adéquate de la part des institutions européennes dans ce domaine (nonobstant la requête d'aide provenant de l'Italie), la question de l'immigration est sensible pour l'opinion publique italienne et tous les candidats en parlent. C'est ce sujet qui provoque les propos les plus conflictuels dans les tweets.

Tableau 6–4: Nombre des tweets sur l'immigration

Liste	tweets sur l'immigration	% sur total de tweets
FI	274	1,40
PD	146	1,03
M5S	19	0,22
FDI	556	5,60
LN	448	5,67
NCD	118	2,17
Tsipras	58	1,24
Total	1619	

Pour les partis d'opposition et eurocritiques, le sujet « immigration, débarquements, clandestins » est crucial, car il permet : d'agiter le phantasme d'une invasion des migrants; de critiquer le gouvernement pour son (in)action; et d'accuser l'Europe de désintérêt et d'incapacité.

Pour LN, FDI et FI, le ton et les arguments sont semblables, quand ils attaquent l'Europe et dramatisent (même si FI n'a pas les déclinaisons xénophobes des deux autres) :

> *« Désastreuse absence UE, l'Italie abandonnée et trahie » (FDI);*
> *«Immigration, l'Italie élève la voix mais l'Europe fait semblant de ne pas entendre» (LN) ;*
> *« #immigration : nous n'en pouvons plus ! L'#Europe DOIT aider l'#Italie » (FI)*
> *« On ne peut pas accepter une Europe qui tourne la tête de l'autre côté tandis que les bateaux coulent » (LN) ;*
> *« L'UE myope nous fait subir le problème des migrants sans se préoccuper des politiques d'accueil »* (FDI) *;*
> *« #Berlusconi : Bruxelles est rapide quand elle doit imposer des contraintes et est lente quand elle doit nous aider à résoudre le problème de l'immigration » (FI).*

La critique est adressée à l'action même du gouvernement, et spécifiquement du Ministre de l'Intérieur Alfano : « *Encore 1.600 CLANDESTINS arrivent en Sicile. Bastaaaaa! Renzi et Alfano, vous êtes COMPLICES!'* » (LN) ; « *@angealfa*[84] *en évidente difficulté sur l'immigration, il a fait le taxi de clandestins avec Mare Nostrum au service du PD* » (FI) ; « *#Immigration : #Alfano élève la voix mais c'est lui qui a signé les mises à jour des Accords de Dublin* » (FDI).

Un des arguments les plus fréquents dénonce les hauts coûts de l'accueil des migrants et insiste sur la priorité donnée aux Italiens dans la distribution des ressources.

> *« Un autre échec d'#Alfano, l'opération #Mare Nostrum a attiré 30.000 immigrés et coûte 9,3 millions par mois »* (LN) ; *« Aux clandestins 40 euros par jour, aux handicapés même pas 10. Etat raciste »* (FDI)
> *« #Salvini : personnes âgées sous-alimentées, 4Mde chômeurs (1 sur 3 parmi les jeunes) : IL N'Y A PAS TOUT POUR TOUS, les ITALIENS premiers» (LN) ; « L'Italie et les Italiens viennent en premier, l'Europe et les immigrés après »* (FI).*« Immigrés? Que la solidarité s'exerce auprès des Italiens en premier. Qu'est-ce qu'on dira à nos chômeurs qui n'ont aucun droit alors que les clandestins oui ? »* (FDI).

Les tweets les plus alarmistes inspirés par l'immigration tournent autour des concepts d'invasion et de clandestinité :

84 Compte de Alfano.

> « *400 #clandestins arrivent à Catane, 800 à Trapani : c'est #INVASION!* » (LN), « *DEBARQUEMENTS augmentés de 800 % par rapport à l'année dernière. C'est l'#INVASION programmée!* » (LN), « *Il faut arrêter ces débarquements. On est désormais la poubelle d'Europe* » (LN). « *L'#Italie est envahie par les #immigrés, l'Europe nous laisse seuls.*» (FI). « *Il y a 4 millions d'italiens qui crèvent la faim et nous dépensons 10 millions d'euros pour nous faire auto-envahir. Basta !* » (FDI) ; « *Toute cette fausse bonté et ce style bon garçon pour les clandestins qui débarquent sur nos côtes me font vomir. Prenez-les chez vous* » (LN)

Parmi les eurosceptiques, le M5S se différencie, car il attaque souvent l'action du gouvernement, mais jamais sur le sujet de l'« immigration » : il fait peu d'interventions sur les migrants, surtout concernant le désintérêt de l'Europe et la « solitude italienne en face de l'UE ». Le M5S préfère suggérer des actions concrètes, ou même répondre aux proclamations de la Ligue (« *@matteosalvinimi les immigrés ne veulent pas l'Italie, nous sommes seulement la frontière la plus proche #europe* » – M5S).

Enfin, les partis de gauche ou au gouvernement parlent moins des débarquements et de l'immigration, mais partagent avec les partis de l'opposition la préoccupation pour la distance de l'Europe sur ce problème (avec des accents plus modérés) : « *L'Europe ne peut pas sauver les États, les banques et puis laisser mourir les mères avec les infants » (PD).*

Quand les arguments sont si controversés, les hashtags sont importants.

Le NDC, parti du ministre Alfano, fait un discours modéré, de soutien au gouvernement et lance « #NousNeLaissonsMourirLesPersonnesDansLaMer"

La Ligue, qui a profité de l'émergence débarquements pour renforcer sa campagne contre l'accueil des migrants « économiques » et pour la réintroduction du délit d'immigration clandestine (en appelant les italiens à signer pour un référendum sur ce sujet), utilise souvent #clandestinoèreato (clandestin est délit).

6.3.3 L'ennemi allemand

Une thématique distinctive de la campagne italienne est la polémique contre l'Allemagne, et en particulier contre Mme Merkel. C'est un conflit personnalisé et dramatisé, qui montre un ressentiment anti-allemand et risque parfois de déraper vers de discutables attaques personnelles.

L'argument le plus fréquent accuse l'Allemagne d'imposer sa volonté en Europe au détriment des intérêts des autres pays, de vouloir gouverner et soumettre ses concurrents, en profitant de la faiblesse des pays en crise.

> « Le *25 mai pourrait être la dernière fois que nous votons en tant qu'État national. Ils veulent nous réduire à une colonie allemande* » ;
> « *Nous risquons de devenir un protectorat allemand » (FDI).*

> *« Nous ne voulons pas être les majordomes de Mme Merkel. En avant il y a les intérêts de chez nous. » (FDI)*
> *« Sortons de l'Europe, l'Italie est une madrague et l'Allemagne est le pêcheur » (LN)*
> *« Arrêtez de faire révérences à l'Allemagne ! »*
> *« Suivre les ordres de l'#Allemagne c'est suivre les ordres de notre concurrent principal »* (FDI).

Un autre argument attaque soit l'euro soit l'Allemagne, car c'est à celle-ci que la monnaie unique profiterait. *« #euro n'aide aucun pays, excepté l'Allemagne »« En Europe seul l'Allemagne croit »*(FDI);*« GiorgiaMeloni : L'Euro est un marc allemand qui renforce l'Allemagne »* (FDI); *« #Salvini : l'Euro est une monnaie étrangère, allemande, mauvaise »* (LN); *« Il y a 15 ans, sans euro, nous n'étions pas un paillasson soumis à Berlin comme aujourd'hui #Salvini »* (LN).

> *« RT @GiorgiaMeloni : '#Euro monnaie faite pour renforcer quelqu'un et affaiblir autres, nous tirons le chariot pour les Allemands' »* (FDI)
> *« L'Allemagne nous a harcelés. C'est autoritaire, d'utiliser l'euro pour croitre au détriment de tous les autres pays, comme la #Grèce ».*

Pour les partis d'opposition italiens le contraste est très personnalisé, parce que la critique de l'Allemagne sert pour se différencier des adversaires internes : Mme Merkel devient une menace, l'épouvantail, et on argumente que voter pour les partis qui ne s'opposent pas au pouvoir allemand, c'est comme voter pour Mme Merkel. *« Celui qui vote PD vote Berlin »* ; *« Quand les Italiens votent Renzi, Berlusconi, Alfano font les intérêts de l'Allemagne »* (FDI).

> *« Si tu votes pour eux [FI, NCD, PD], tu votes pour Merkel »* (LN) ; *« #ForzaItalia est un vote utile à #Merkel. #FDI le seul #voteutile à l'Italie »* (FDI).[85]

Les partis qui parlent le plus de l'Allemagne sont les deux qui s'opposent fortement à l'euro : FDI (221 tweets pour les candidats de la liste) et LN (138 tweets).

6.3.4 Les ennemis internes

La campagne électorale européenne est souvent l'occasion de se mesurer aux autres partis italiens sur des sujets nationaux. Les candidats semblent avoir identifié des adversaires internes, qui sont les cibles d'une communication polémique : des adversaires politiques directs en tant que candidats dans la circonscription ; les adversaires de toujours, comme le maire de Rome, Marino, pour FDI ; des

85 Le tweets contre l'Allemagne proposent souvent des images et des articles polémiques ou dérisoires envers les autres partis et leaders italiens. Par exemple, Forza Italia tweete des photomontages avec le corps de Angela Merkel et le visage à la fois de Renzi, de Alfano, de Verdini (FI)... et le slogan : "Se voti loro, voti lei" (si tu votes pour eux tu votes pour elle).

adversaires qui représentent une bataille du parti (par exemple l'ancienne ministre Fornero contre laquelle la LN a fait une campagne à cause d'une reforme sur les retraites controversée) ; et enfin des adversaires occasionnels, qui deviennent des ennemis dans le déroulement de la campagne. L'exemple de ces derniers est Alessandra Moretti, qui a accusé le M5S d'un manque de transparence dans la gestion de l'argent et pour cela devient la cible de 215 tweets des candidats M5S, avec de dures attaques personnelles et parfois sexistes (on l'appelle poule, soubrette, parasite) et des hashtags comme #Morettimenteuse, #morettioùestlargent : « *RT @MSimone93JSC : Moretti représente totalement le flétrissement et la fausseté de cette classe dirigeante. #MorettiMenteuse* ». Les attaques ad hominem et sexistes ne sont pas rares : on pourrait aussi citer Cécile Kyenge, candidate congolaise du PD, comparée à un singe (comme la ministre guyannaise Christiane Taubira en France) par son adversaire de la LN Borghezio et objet de 52 tweets de la liste LN.

Les partis protestataires sont les plus polémiques vis-à-vis de leurs adversaires : des candidats de la LN émettent 341 tweets contre des adversaires ; le M5S en émet 934.

Dans le cas des adversaires internes, les stratégies de construction de l'ennemi se basent souvent sur l'ironie et la dérision : Alfano devient « Alfango » (Al-bue) pour FI et « Alfanano » (Alfanain) pour le M5S. Un faux compte M5S contre Pina Picierno était @pin-up icierno. Le M5S en particulier, utilise les noms tournés en jeux de mot et les surnoms offensifs : Renzi est nommé par le mouvement depuis longtemps Renzie, ou même « ebetino » (petit idiot). Pendant la campagne il est appelé aussi Renziegnoccofritto (Renziegnocchifrits), qui devient un hashtag assez cité (94 fois dans nos tweets). En étant des concurrents directs, Renzi et les membres du PD (appelés les « pidiots » ou « les PD moins L ») sont une des cibles préférées des candidats M5S : le seul Renzi est cité 303 fois dans des hashtags dérisoires (comme par exemple #renziement, #renziezérolois, #renzipagliaccio, #renzi raconte mensonges, #renziemangebananes…).

Pour tous les partis les hashtags servent pour fixer et répéter le jeu de mot contre les adversaires, avec inventivité. La dérision s'exerce aussi sur les slogans des adversaires : par exemple le slogan du PD « lasvoltabuona » (le virage bon) devient «lastoltabuona » (l'imbécile bonne).

Il s'agit de « jeux de mots dont la force comique ou caustique semble devoir se suffire à elle-même et semble pouvoir remplacer un argumentaire élaboré. Le discours protestataire repose en effet souvent sur ce type d'effet rhétorique, où la pirouette lexicale, le mot qui frappe, la formule choc font office d'arguments » (Mercier, 2015, *infra*).

6.4 Les tweets sur l'Europe : un discours conflictuel

Les tweets des candidats sur L'Europe reflètent le débat critique sur l'action de l'UE et sur la monnaie unique, très animé en Italie. La propagande sur Twitter est influencée, en particulier, par une campagne d'opinion menée par des mouvements « NOeuro » et par les partis LN et FDI, qui dans leurs listes ont présenté des candidats connus pour leurs positions anti-monnaie unique (des économistes, par exemple).

6.4.1 Contre l'euro

Les sept partis ont des positions très différentes sur l'Europe et en particulier sur la monnaie unique : LN et FDI proposent de sortir de l'eurozone (« no euro » ou « basta euro » sont leurs slogans de campagne et leurs hashtags préférés); ils contrastent aussi les politiques d'austérité et l'(in)action des institutions européennes. Par rapport à ces partis le PD, le centre-droite NCD et la liste de gauche Tsipras sont plutôt « optimistes », bien que conscients des limites de l'euro : ils se définissent« réalistes », « euro-impatients », « euro propositifs ». FI a une position pas si claire et parfois très critique sur les politiques européennes et l'euro. Plusieurs anciens députés européens de FI tiennent un discours modéré sur l'Europe, mais quand les nouveaux candidats et le leader de Fi parlent de l'euro, ils semblent utiliser les mêmes expressions des contestataires : « *#Berlusconi : basta avec l'euro monnaie étrangère* » (la même phrase tweetée par Salvini) « *Basta avec #Europe marâtre* » [mot utilisé aussi par FDI, comme on verra].

Les partis qui s'expriment officiellement contre l'euro se définissent « Noeuro » ou « euro-critiques »[86] et pendant la campagne organisent plusieurs événements anti-euro pour obtenir l'attention des électeurs : le « Bastaeuro tour » (LN), qui a touché toute l'Italie avec Matteo Salvini sur une caravane; la collecte de signatures pour demander un référendum sur l'euro (LN); le tour des marchés pour parler des prix augmentés avec l'euro et les avantages du retour à la monnaie nationale (FDI) ; la diffusion d'un livret contre l'euro (LN).

86 Parfois ils se définissent aussi « populistes », en donnant à ce terme le sens de « proche du peuple » et « antisystème », pour contraster les critiques de populisme qu'on leur fait et pour se distinguer des autres partis : « Je suis un populiste de fer contre les euro-bureaucrates » (M. Borghezio, LN), « Je préfère être populiste qu'esclave [de l'Europe] » (G. Meloni, FDI)

Le M5S a une attitude particulière : le mouvement était parfois critique sur l'Union Européenne et l'euro, mais jamais contre explicitement. C'est au moment de la campagne que l'euroscepticisme du M5S se montre, avec des déclarations clairement anti-euro de certains candidats et avec la proposition d'un referendum sur la monnaie unique[87].

Les tons des tweets contre l'euro sont très forts : « *L'euro est la continuation du nazisme avec d'autres méthodes » (LN) « À #Bolzano. L'euro n'est pas une monnaie, c'est un système de contrôle des peuples auquel nous devons nous soustraire #électionseuropéennes »*

La LN produit 584 tweets (7,4 % du total) sur ce sujet et utilise beaucoup d'hashtags polémiques contre l'euro (#basteuro, #noeuro, #euroexit, etc. : 413 occurrences).

6.4.2 Contre l'Europe

Les arguments contre l'Europe sont multiples.

- Beaucoup des candidats de tous les partis (pas seulement NOeuro) critiquent l'Europe des banques et de la finance, qu'ils opposent à l'Europe des peuples :

> *« Nous voulons l'Europe des peuples, pas celle des banques et de la rigueur! » (FDI)*
> *« #jevoteTsipras parce que je veux une Europe des personnes en non des banques » (LT)*
> *« Renversons l'#Europe des banques, construisons l'Europe des droits » (M5S)*
> *« Je veux une Europe où la finance est au service de la production et de la société et pas vice-versa.... » (FI)*
> *« Après sauve-banques, l'UE doit devenir sauve-familles et sauve-entreprises #europechangedirection » (PD)*
> *« LE SME ET L'EURO c'est un système POUR GARANTIR AUX MULTINATIONALES ET BANQUIERS une LIBERTE' ABSOLUE, su la PEAU DES CITOYENS #M5S »*

En particulier, les « bureaucrates »sont une cible constante, un ennemi commun à tous les partis :

> *« Basta de subir les choix de banquiers et bureaucrates, il est temps que les citoyens DECIDENT! #Salvini » (LN)*
> *« #Outre l'Europe de banquiers et bureaucrates @forza_italia l'unique alternative » (FI)*
> *« Nous ne voulons plus être gouvernés par banquiers et bureaucrates de l'UE qui utilisent les premiers ministres comme laquais et serviteurs. #vinciamonoi #M5S »*
> *« Contre l'Europe des bureaucrates vote NCD »*

---

87 Selon quelques chercheurs (Franzosi, Marone, Salvati 2015) l'euroscepticisme que le M5S a montré en campagne électorale semble plus stratégique qu'idéologique, car il ne correspond pas souvent à un comportement de vote anti-EU dans le parlement européen.

- Les institutions européennes elles-mêmes sont critiquées, parce qu'elles apparaissent distantes et elles ne s'occuperaient pas des problèmes des États membres : l'Europe est vue comme « aveugle »/ « sourde », « pas intéressée », traîtresse, surtout sur le problème de l'immigration :

« En Italie- et pas seulement ici – cette Europe semble lointaine et marâtre » #FdiAn (FDI)
« @Corriere, #DellaLoggia : la surdité de l'Europe sur les immigrés trahit l'absence d'un espace politique commun des Pays UE. Intéressant #eurosalini » (NCD)
« L'indifférence européenne sur le sujet immigration à Lampedusa doit finir » (NCD)

Une déclinaison de cet argument est l'opposition entre États du Nord (avantagés) et du Sud de l'Europe (exploités, ignorés et laissés seuls face au problème de l'immigration)

« UE égoïste, ce n'est pas une union mais un supermarché où les Pays du Nord prennent ce qui leur convient et se déchargent des problèmes » (FDI)
@OlivieroAlotto a @confcommerciomi : européistes convaincus, nous ne voulons pas l'austérité. Le Sud de l'Europe est en souffrance, non à l'UE à deux vitesses » (PD)
« EU plus méditerranéenne et moins nordique! » (FI)

- L'Europe est accusée de n'être pas démocratique (et on arrive à la comparer aux pires régimes, notamment au fascisme) :

« L'Union Européenne a un déficit de démocratie, parce qu'elle n'est pas née d'en bas » (PD)
« @robfratt @Ingestibile79 @ladyonorato l'euro est l'instrument de la BCE pour gouverner hors de la démocratie au profit des capitaux ». (LN)
« RT @matteosalvinimi : #Lega ne propose pas son candidat à la présidence de la Commission Européenne, car c'est un organisme antidémocratique » (LN)
« La Ligue avec Salvini tente de conquérir Rome contre "l'Union soviétique européenne" » (LN)
« L'eurozone est un régime fasciste » (LN), une« *dictature relativiste et financière* » (FDI).
@Crisi_Finanza @ladyonorato Et encore avec la dictature du spread? Est-ce que vous comprenez, chers fascistes, que nous voulons décider sans la matraque? (LN)

- L'Europe est perçue comme un organisme qui enlève (vole) la souveraineté aux États membres :

« BASTA DES SERVITEURS A L'EUROPARLEMENT. Cette fois qui seulement peut nous redonner la Souveraineté volée » (LN)
« Maria Cristina Saija, Allons en Europe pour reprendre nos souverainetés » (M5S)
« L'Italie doit cesser d'être un pays à souveraineté limitée. @FidanzaCarlo #agorarai » (FDI)

- A propos de l'activité du Parlement, on l'accuse de ne pas s'occuper des problèmes réels et des personnes, mais des petites questions et des lois absurdes, surtout en matière d'alimentation :

« Hier on a vu comment l'Europe aborde l'important problème des.... Légumes », « La Troika veut même expliquer aux Grecs comment produire le yaourt » (FDI).

De la même façon, on reproche à l'Europe de ne pas défendre les produits nationaux :

« RT @MarcoScurria : Pour la pêche, l'agriculture et pour le #madeinitaly la situation est tragique, à cause de la concurrence déloyale #Rainews24 » (FDI) ; « #Salvini : oranges de Sicile, notre lait, sont aussi bons, l'Italie ne défend plus sa production, et on donne des mld à la Turquie! #portaaporta » (LN)

- Certains traités européens sont critiqués parce qu'ils ne protègent pas les intérêts des citoyens, donc on demande leur abolition ; Le TTIP (TAFTA), en particulier, est la cible principale :

« Fiscal Compact, Mes, ERF, TTIP sont des armes de destruction de souveraineté » (M5S)
« La EU-Goebbels production présente : 'le merveilleux TTIP'! » (LN).
« TTIP, ERF, Fiscal compact...ils jouent avec les mots, mais ils sont tous des cordes au cou des citoyens, des entreprises.... »
« dans le silence le plus absolu et avec la complicité de Renzi, l'Europe lance le 'monstre' L'EUROPEAN REDEMPTION FUND » (FDI)
« Nous devons renégocier certaines règles que l'Europe nous a imposées, par exemple modifiant le Fiscal Compact et le Pacte de Stabilité » (FI).

- Enfin, la conséquence de l'euro et de la (mauvaise) action de l'UE est la pauvreté des Européens :

« # FdIAn @GiorgiaMeloni : «C'est un fait : cette Europe affame les peuples pour favoriser les #pouvoirsforts » (FDI)
« RT @MarcoScurria : Nous demandons des règles égales pour tous en Europe, nous ne pouvons pas continuer à nous appauvrir à cause des autres #FdiAn »
« #Salvini : l'Euro est la monnaie de la FAIM et du CHOMAGE » (LN)

6.4.3 Contre les europtimistes et les "terroristes pro-euro"

Les partis « eurosceptiques » critiquent et considèrent comme des ennemis ceux qui soutiennent le projet européen et l'euro, et ils se moquent d'eux. Il s'agit de trois genres d'ennemis : la première cible sont les défenseurs de l'euro en général, méprisés avec les termes « euristes » « euro-menteurs », «euro-crétins » (*« Les euro-menteurs ne savent plus quoi dire pour défendre une monnaie morte. Basta Euro : reprenons notre futur »*– LN). Le deuxième ennemi regroupe ceux qui craignent une sortie de l'eurozone, en montrent les conséquences négatives et diffusent l'alarme, et pour cela sont accusés de « terrorisme » : « DEMENTIR *publiquement l'Euroterrorisme. Il y a l'embarras du choix* »; « *Le terrorisme pro-euro se propage* » (LN). Enfin, très critiqués sont les médias, qui selon les eurocritiques lancent des messages pro-euro :

« Contre la guerre terroriste médiatique aux # européennes vote @FratellidItalia ». « @RaiTv @SkyNews @Agenzia_Ansa lancent une guerre médiatique contre ceux qui veulent sortir de l'#euro et sont contre la #troika » ; « la désinformation bolchevique sur l'euro est commencée #stravinciamonoi ». « #euroexit #noeuro avec @magdicristiano contre une TV d'Etat à côté de la dictature financière de l'UE »

6.4.4 Pour l'Europe

Dans notre corpus, on trouve néanmoins différents arguments favorables à l'Europe, même si ceux-ci n'ont pas la force et la virulence des arguments « contre ». Les tweets pro-Europe des candidats ont des objectifs différents :

a) répondre aux polémiques des partis protestataires contre l'Europe et ses institutions, mais surtout contrer la campagne intensive contre l'euro ; b) faire des propositions pour changer l'Europe et résoudre ses problèmes, en particulier pour améliorer son rapport avec les citoyens ; c) mettre en évidence les aspects positifs (et la nécessité) de notre appartenance à la communauté européenne ; d) informer sur l'activité (et l'efficacité) du Parlement et des institutions européennes ; e) enfin, plus rarement, la dérision et la polémique sur les « eurosceptiques ».

Trois partis en particulier, NCD, PD et Tsipras, tweetent avec des tons positifs sur l'Europe.

Plusieurs candidats du PD diffusent les matériaux de la campagne nationale européiste du PD, dans lesquels le parti a voulu répondre aux objections des « eurosceptiques » avec des contre-arguments. Sur la monnaie unique, par exemple, la campagne « Toute la vérité sur l'euro » est une sorte de *fact-checking* : les affiches mettaient en avant une phrase, barrée, des anti-euro (« Sans l'€ les prix ne seraient pas doublés ») et une réponse avec des explications. Les jeunes démocrates à Bruxelles, de plus, ont préparé un « argumentaire » avec toutes les critiques fréquentes sur l'Europe et les réponses possibles. Certains candidats du PD ont repris ces arguments dans leurs tweets[88] : « *Italie, sortir de l'euro ? Seulement ceux*

88 Par exemple, Andrea Cozzolino :
« Ce que @beppe_grillo et @matteosalvinimi ne disent pas : On peut sortir de l'l'Euro dans un week-end. FAUX! »
« Ce que @beppe_grillo et @matteosalvinimi ne disent pas : L'euro est un projet économique failli. FAUX! »
« Ce que @beppe_grillo et @matteosalvinimi ne disent pas : La sortie de l'Euro favorise la production et l'occupation parce que la compétitivité augmente. FAUX! »
« Ce que @beppe_grillo et @matteosalvinimi ne disent pas : La conversion des bons publics dans la nouvelle lira allège la dette publique. FAUX! »

qui ont de l'argent à l'étranger en gagneront, ici on perdrait la valeur des salaires #l'EuropeSociale » (PD)

Le même discours est fait avec les hashtags : '#Europachenondicono' ("l'Europe qu'ils ne disent pas", utilisé par Elly Schlein) et les slogans de la campagne nationale #celochiediitu ("c'est toi qui le demande") ou #Europacambiaverso ("l'Europe change de direction").

Forza Italia insiste sur les opportunités d'un changement en Europe et critique les positions anti-européistes (surtout de Grillo, son ennemi numéro un), en faisant des efforts pour expliquer les avantages de l'appartenance à la UE.

Mais quand les candidats parlent de l'euro les messages ne sont pas univoques, comme on l'a déjà écrit.

« L'altra Europa con Tsipras » utilise une stratégie qui correspond aux cas b) et c), et souligne la nécessité d'un changement, d'une Europe « autre » (reprenant le nom du mouvement). Ses candidats se proposent comme une alternative au PD et au M5S : *« politique par le bas pour changer l'Europe #sansdemanderpermission », « #EU2014 derby italien entre la rage #grillo et l'espoir #Renzi. @altraeuropa est l'alternative pour un vrai changement ».*

Plusieurs arguments visent à montrer les aspects positifs de l'appartenance à l'UE : le PD propose d'imaginer ce que serait l'Italie sans l'Europe : #senzaeuropa[89] ; PD et Tsipras soulignent des sentiments positifs liés aux élections et à l'Europe, en particulier l'espoir et l'attente d'un changement comme promesse pour l'avenir.

> *« RT @GBugaro : Nous sommes eurodéçus mais pas eurorepentis! Nous travaillons pour une #Europe meilleure et plus forte! @NCD_tweet @PPE_IT @angealfa »*

6.5 Quelques représentations négatives et positives de l'Europe

Dans les tweets des candidats, l'Europe et l'euro sont associés à beaucoup d'images négatives, avec des métaphores efficaces. On peut reconnaitre, en particulier, des mots et des champs sémantiques assez singuliers.

Les premiers termes et images associés à l'Europe décrivent une situation de privation de liberté et d'asservissement. L'Europe est présentée comme une prison, une cage, et c'est un risque d'esclavage pour les citoyens :

> *« L'euro crée une cage de règles qui empêche à notre économie de croître »* (FDI)

« Ce que @beppe_grillo et @matteosalvinimi ne disent pas : Politique monétaire à la Banque d'Italie pour monétiser la dette publique. VRAI, MAIS... »

89 *#sansEurope la nourriture que tu donne à tes enfant serait un risque et sans contrôle. #sansEurope aucune certitude de paix dans un continent qui pour des siècles était marqué par les guerres.*

> *« Se libérer de la cage Euro et arrêter l'invasion clandestine. A Rome une salle pleine de gens » (LN)*
> *« #FdIAn pour dire basta à la cage de l'euro qui étrangle notre économie. Jamais plus esclaves de Bruxelles »! (FDI)*
> *« #25mai choisissons d'être libre et souverains ou esclaves de #Merkel. Nous avons choisi le premier chemin! » (FDI)*
> *« Bientôt à San Bonifacio : Sauvons les Italiens de l'esclavage de l'euro ! »*

Un deuxième champ sémantique important, le plus significatif à notre avis, est celui de la mort. La LN est le parti qui utilise le plus d'images de ce genre. L'euro, en particulier, est représenté comme une force mortifère, comme une arme fatale ou un vrai suicide. Et Mme Merkel, encore, est associée à ces images de mort.

> *« on a une monnaie qui nous assassine ».*
> *« #Salvini : Je ne veux pas mourir d'euro »* (LN).
> *« RT @TW_laPadania : L'Euro est mort et il risque de tuer l'Europe aussi #Salvini #Lega »* (LN)
> *« Euroexit n'est pas sans douleur mais – douloureux que ce suicide »* (LN)
> *« Mieux les risques de #euroexit qu'une mort CERTAINE! »*
> *« L'€ est le poison, l'éliminer désarme ceux qui l'utilisent pour empoisonner. Les coupables de son introduction en répondront »*
> *« RT @doranapolitano : @LanciniOscar euro et Allemagne sont en train de nous tuer. bastaaa!!! »*
> *« On ne peut pas mourir de suicide assisté (par Merkel) »*
> *« Nos gouverneurs on fait les intérêts de merkel. Europe médecin qui nous a donné du poison au lieux d'un médicament »*
> *« Mais pourquoi continuons-nous à rester en Europe avec nos bourreaux du ppe? @forza_italia @gasparripdl @Storace @msgelmini… »* (FI)
> *« @Ale_Mussolini_ @forza_italia le problème est que le gouvernement veut réanimer les immigrés et ne s'aperçoit pas que son peuple est en train de mourir »* (FI).
> *« Les contraintes budgétaires européennes tuent la démocratie et dévastent l'état social » #elezionieuropee #tsipras #altraeuropa #notriv »* (LT)

Les images positives de l'Europe sont moins présentes, mais constantes dans les discours des europtimistes.

L'association qui prévaut est celle avec l'espoir : on peut encore espérer et se battre pour une Europe différente. *« Pour une nouvelle #Europe qui donne espoir aux peoples#EP2014 @altraeuropa »* (LT);

> *« nous misons sur l'espoir, contre le populisme anti-européiste. #celochieditu #europachecambia » (PD) ;*
> *« Alfano : 'Nous sommes l'espoir contre la rage' »* (NCD).
> *« Nous avons espoir. Nous changeons l'Europe. @matteorenzi @simonabonafe »* (PD)
> *« RT @claudiamdd : Dimanche 25 mai allez voter, n'ayez pas peur, choisissez l'espoir »*

On arrive même à parler de renaissance. « *#enplace avec les #idées non pas avec les #insultes, nous sommes pour une* #renaissanceeuropéenne» (PD). « *RT @ragnofelice : #vinciamonoi, nous traversons la nouvelle renaissance italienne et l'Europe nous suivra* » (M5S).

En parallèle avec l'espoir, il y a le futur.

> « *RT @cescverducci : #enplace @pdnetwork ensemble nous changeons l'Europe, du coté de ceux qui réclament futur. #no à ceux qui profitent du désespoir» (PD) ;*
> « *Spoleto @altraeuropa Il n'y a pas de futur hors de l'Europe » (LT)*
> « *#salvini : l'Etat et Bruxelles nous ont volé le futur, avec ces enfants, mères et pères nous le reprenons ! ».*

Un champ sémantique efficace (et attendu) est celui de la construction/destruction. On pourrait dire que c'est le vrai enjeu, même dans le discours :

> « *RT @riccardogarella : @alessiamosca «Le vote aux Européennes sera historique : Destruction contre Construction. Nous voulons construire!» » (PD)*
> « *Le choix est entre destruction ou réponses données avec responsabilité, courage et pragmatisme #européennes2014 (NCD)*
> *RT @VivecaAnna : @LiciaRonzulli @forza_italia L'œuvre de Grillo est détruire, mais au contraire il faut reconstruire.* (FI)
> « *RT @intelligonews : @Fabio_Armeni : "Nous sommes l'unique alternative aux euro-démolisseurs de Grillo "* » (FI)

Enfin, il y a beaucoup de métaphores associées au changement : à la fois rassurant, à la fois bouleversant. Une image intéressante est celle du vent, que certains partis utilisent pour représenter la force du changement (« Ne confondons pas le vent du changement avec le vent de l'anti-européisme» – PD) , mais que le M5S associe au tornade qui éliminera les vieux bureaucrates et politiques : « Beppe Grillo à Pavie : nous ne sommes pas un souffle de vent… nous serons la tornade qui les anéantit ! », « Le vents se lève et il deviendra un ouragan, Merkel se tient fort #Schulzsoyezserein » (c'est la réponse à Martin Schultz, qui avait qualifié le M5S de « vent sans substance »).

Pour conclure ce paragraphe sur la représentation positive et négative de l'Europe il faut rappeler qu'une des stratégies les plus utilisées est l'opposition, le conflit entre visions alternatives, pour invoquer le choix décisif.

Le conflit, avant tout, est un derby :

> « *Européennes seront un derby entre banques et travail, entre technocraties et peuples #rachèteItalie* » (FDI)
> « *Ces européennes 2014 sont un derby entre #rage et espoir. Il y a qui hurle et hait et il y a qui dialogue et construit le futur* » (PD)

C'est aussi un choix contre la proteste et la rage :

> *« Nous sommes le futur, eux ils sont la rage #europequichange »* (PD)
>
> *« L'alternative est claire : faire vaincre la protestation et l'extrémisme ou récompenser la responsabilité et le changement»* (NCD)

Parfois le choix est sur les idées, les idéaux. Et tout cas, c'est toujours un choix décisif.

> *« L''Europe de Machiavel ou celle de l'Illuminisme et de Gramsci »*
>
> *« L'Europe des différences ou celle des inégalité »*
>
> *« Le futur ou les ruines »*
>
> *« Nous travaillons pour la gauche ou pour l'austérité »*

6.6 Discours polémiques et traces d'un débat sur l'Europe

En conclusion, rappelons que les propositions pro et anti Europe dans notre corpus ont représenté une sorte d'échange/débat conflictuel via Twitter, qui reprend, et peut être amplifie, le débat sur ce sujet présent en Italie. Et les tweets ont été un instrument immédiat (et parfois créatif) pour proposer un discours polémique contre les adversaires sur des sujets européens. Cette persistance des positions dialectiques et l'importance du sujet « Europe » dans notre corpus sont une donnée importante.

Plusieurs chercheurs ont souligné qu'en Italie les élections européennes sont assez souvent une occasion pour discuter des enjeux nationaux, pour mesurer le rapport de force entre les partis. Les sujets européens sont peu traités, soit par les partis soit par les médias. Et, comme partout en Europe, pour ces élections les partis investissent moins d'argent, moins d'énergies organisationnelles et peu de ressources en termes de personnalisation (Negrine 2006). On a donc parlé d'élection « de second ordre » (Reif et Schmitt 1980), même si plusieurs chercheurs italiens ont remis en cause ce paradigme en cherchant de sortir de la dichotomie premier/second ordre et de trouver des nouvelles donnes (Marletti et Mouchon 2005, Bobba 2010, Roncarolo 2010). En particulier, ils ont observé que dans les campagnes électorales récentes l'Europe est redevenue un sujet de la propagande, surtout au niveau local, grâce à l'activité des candidats, tandis que les partis restent dans une logique de « nationalisation » des enjeux. Dans les élections de 2009, les candidats (qui demandent un vote de préférence et s'adressent aux électeurs sur le terrain) parlent de l'Europe comme opportunité, des bénéfices obtenus grâce à l'UE, de leur engagement passé et futur pour représenter le territoire en Europe : il y a des « *policies communities* faites par des *incumbents* qui – au-delà des appartenances partisanes, et parfois en opposition à celles-ci – revendiquent les mérites d'une action menée dans le domaine communautaire et ancrent leur candidature aux résultats visibles de l'"intégration positive' largement fondée sur les incitations au développement des zones les plus désavantagées (Scharpf, 1999) » (Roncarolo 2010 : 11).

De plus, l'analyse du contenu de l'actualité sur les élections européennes a montré que « la presse et les contenus réunis sur le net créent un espace d'échange d'informations sur l'Europe qui pourrait impliquer des audiences plus larges » (Belluati et Bobba 2010).

Notre analyse des tweets des candidats confirme cette tendance : les candidats tweetent souvent sur l'Europe, soit du point de vue des actions positives, des *policies* et de l'intégration, soit du point de vue des critiques et des problèmes. Et cela dans un moment où les partis fatiguent à se concentrer sur les sujets transnationaux : l'analyse de la campagne sur Twitter faite par l'Observatoire de la communication politique de Turin montre que les comptes des partis italiens en 2014 « ont présenté seulement d'une façon marginale l'Europe comme cadre de sens en campagne électorale, en attribuant peu d'importance et pertinence aux hashtags dénotatifs d'événements, sujets et acteurs avec valence continentale » (Cepernich 2015).

Donc c'est dans les comptes Twitter des candidats (plus que dans ceux des partis et des médias) que les sujets européens sont parfois traités. Et c'est dans ces mêmes comptes qu'une sorte de débat sur l'Europe et l'euro émerge, bien que d'une façon critique et conflictuelle, parfois avec un langage virulent. On a vu le développement d'une dialectique entre des visions différentes de l'Europe, où il y a des prises de positions très fortes contre les concrétisations actuelles du projet européen, mais où rarement il y a une négation des principes de l'Europe ou une requête d'en sortir (la sortie qu'on propose est plutôt d'un des dispositifs supranationaux : la zone Euro, Schengen, les traités internationaux…). Et on a vu que, nonobstant les différences entre les partis italiens regardant l'Europe, on peut retrouver parfois des ennemis communs, des cibles récurrents.

La comparaison avec les données de l'analyse de la tweet-campagne française suggère que certains enjeux et même certains ennemis sont communs entre les deux pays : au-delà des frontières nationales, des spécificités de parti et de système politique, « on commence à posséder en commun des arguments de refus, qui structurent donc un espace public partagé à l'échelle européenne » (Mercier, 2015, infra).

Références bibliographiques

Belluati M., Caraffini P. (eds) (2015), L'Unione Europea tra istituzioni e opinione pubblica, Roma : Carocci

Bentivegna S. (2015), A colpi di tweet. La politica in prima persona, Bologna : Il Mulino

Bentivegna S., (ed.) (2014), La politica in 140 caratteri. Twitter e spazio pubblico, Milano : ANgeli

Bobba G. (2010), Più locale che nazionale. La comunicazione elettorale dei partiti per le europee del 2009 in Italia, *Comunicazione politica*, I

Bobba G., Belluati M. (2010), "European elections in Italian media : between second order campaign and the construction of a European public sphere", CEU Political Sciènce Journal (CEU Political Science Journal), issue : 02 / 2010

Castelli Gattinara P., Froio C. (2014). "Opposition in the EU and Opposition to the EU : Soft and Hard Euroscepticism in Italy in the Time of Austerity", *Rising Populism and the European Elections*. IED, Brussels, Spring.

Cepernich C. (2015), "L'Europa nella comunicazione dei partiti su Twitter alle europee 2014", in M. Belluati, P. Caraffini (eds)

Chadwick A (2013), The Hybrid Media System : Politics and Power, Oxford University press

Franzosi P., Marone F., Salvati E. (2015), "Populism and Euroscepticism in the Italian Five Star Movement", International Spectator, Number 2, 3 April 2015, pp. 109–124

Gerstlé J., Semetko H., Schoenbach K., Villa M. (2000), L'éuropeanisation défaillante des campagnes nationales, en Grunberg G., Perrineau P., Ysmal C., Le vote des Quinze, Paris : Presses de Sciences Po

Maier M., Strömbäck J. et Kaid L. (eds) (2011),. Political Communication in European Parliamentary Elections. I. England/USA : Ashgate Publishing Limited

Mancini P., Mazzoni M. (2014), "Politici e social network : un trampolino per i media *mainstream*. Un sistema ibrido (tutto) italiano", in Bentivegna 2014

Marletti, C. & Mouchon, J. (eds) (2005), La costruzione mediatica dell'Europa. Milano : Angeli.

Mazzoleni G. (2012), La comunicazione politica. Milano : Il Mulino

Mercier A. (ed.), 2003, *Vers un espace public européen ?*, Paris, L'Harmattan.

Murru M. F. (2016), *The performative role of hashtags in the politicization of Europe. 2014 European elections on Twitter*. In I. Vobič, T. Deželan, (R)evolutionizing Political Communication through Social Media, Pennsylvania : IGI Global

Negrine, R. (2006). The long road to professionalization. Campaigning in Europe vs. campaigning for Europe, in M. Maier e J. Tenscher (a cura di) *Campaigning in Europe, campaigning for Europe* (pp. 31–44). Berlino : Lit Verlag.

Parmelee John, Bichard Shannon, 2012, *Politics and the Twitter Revolution*, Lanham, Lexingtn Books.

Reif, K. e Schmitt, H. (1980). Nine second-order national elections : A conceptual framework for the analysis of European election results. *European Journal of Political Research*, 8 (1), 3–45.

Roncarolo F., Media, partiti e *second order elections*, Comunicazione Politica 1/2010, pp. 5–14.

Roncarolo, F. (2000). L'Europa in agenda. Campagna permanente ed elezioni di secondo ordine. *Comunicazione politica*, I (2), 181–203.

Scharpf, F. (1999). *Governing in Europe : Effective and democratic?* Oxford : Oxford University Press. Trad. it. : *Governare l'Europa*. Bologna : Il Mulino, 1999.

Weber, T. (2009). When the cat is away the mice will play : Why elections to the European parliament are about Europe after all. *Politique européenne*, 28 (2), 53–71.

Elena Albu, Univ. of Geneva

7. Love Britain? Vote UKIP! The Pragmatics of Electoral Tweets during the European Elections 2014

Abstract
This chapter discusses the linguistic strategies the UKIP candidates used in "call for action" tweets sent during the 2014 European Elections. Form and content analysis suggests that the tweets are built on the implicit premise that the UKIP is the solution, and a contrastive context of interpretation that generates a conditional type of reasoning is created.

7.1 Introduction

Launched in 2006, Twitter has rapidly become an important communication platform worldwide. If it was initially meant to send real-time news updates, Twitter is now used for numerous reasons in a variety of contexts. The use of Twitter in politics, in general, and during election times, in particular, is one illustration of the multifarious character this micro-blogging service has.

The 2014 European elections are considered to be "the Twitter elections" due to the extensive use of the on-line platform by the political candidates in all 28 member states. The features and constrains of the platform, on the one hand, and the political orientation and ideology, on the other, have led to the emergence of a particular type of political discourse during these European elections. Although the political activity on Twitter has received a lot of attention, the language the politicians use and the impact it has on the electorate's cognitive environment are still under-explored areas of study. The aim of this paper is to discuss the specificity of the electoral tweets the United Kingdom Independence Party (UKIP) political candidates sent before the elections. The *call for action* tweets represent a form of strategic and goal-oriented discourse meant to persuade the electorate to vote for them. Particular attention will be paid to the various cognitive and discursive strategies used and to the role they play during the interpretation process. Shedding light on the mechanisms which direct the hearer towards a certain interpretation and the extent to which the linguistic details influence people's attitudes about political candidates is essential to understanding the process of decision-making. To this end, a corpus-based and a corpus-driven analysis is suggested. Starting from the *vote UKIP* collocation, a relevant corpus of data has been gathered and further analysis using the *AntConc* software has been conducted in order to discuss the content of the selected tweets. The corpus-based analysis concentrates on a formal analysis of the *vote UKIP* collocation while the content investigation aims at identifying what linguistic strategies are used and at discussing whether they are productive and how they function at the cognitive level.

The results indicate that the *vote UKIP* collocation is a very powerful and direct phrase whose role is to persuade the electorate to vote for the mentioned party. The candidates use it alone as a slogan or in different combinations with various operators in order to draw the voters' attention and to make their tweet visible. A particular function of the hashtags #VoteUKIP and vote#UKIP is also suggested, i.e. to create a contrastive context of interpretation which generates a conditional type of reasoning. The content analysis brings forward two main types of tweets: informative and argumentative. The analysis of the latter reveals that the argumentative tweets are built around the implicit premise *UKIP is the solution* and generate a contrastive negative campaigning argumentative orientation which allows the political candidates to foster a negative image of the opponents and a positive image of UKIP at the same time.

For the purposes of our argument, the paper is organised as follows. Section (2) discusses the main features of the tweets as particular samples of language use. The discussion is organised around the particularity of the the tweets in comparison with face-to-face communication and with other forms of digital interactions. To set the frame for the analysis of the political tweets during the 2014 European elections, the reasons for which Twitter has been embraced worldwide as an important communication tool during electoral campaigns are indicated. The next section is dedicated to the linguistics of the tweets. After briefly indicating the specificity of the electoral call for action tweets and indicating the corpus and the method of analysis, a formal analysis of the *vote UKIP* collocation and a content analysis are suggested. The paper end with conclusions.

7.2 The Political Discourse on Twitter

7.2.1 Twitter as a Communication Tool

Initially created as a way to provide personal status updates and to discover the latest news related to subjects one cares about, Twitter has rapidly become an extremely efficient communication medium worldwide. According to the Help Center, Twitter is "an information network made up of 140-character messages called Tweets"[90]. One of the most popular micro-blogging services, it is used for a variety of reasons in various societal and political contexts.

Twitter is a form of computer-mediated communication that shapes a particular type of discourse. In the attempt to compare digital media and face-to-face communication, on the one hand, and to differentiate between different media, on the other hand, Baym (2010) suggests seven key concepts. They are represented by: interactivity, temporal structure, social cues, storage, replicability, reach and mobility (Baym 2010: 7). Considered the main features of the discourse on social media, the seven concepts characterise all forms of computer-mediated communication, such as SMS, chat, email, blogs and others. Nevertheless, there are variations between the different types of digital media, which grant them unique and individual styles.

Displayed in different degrees, *interactivity* is said to characterize the mode of communication on the internet. The interactivity on Twitter is represented by different types, such as: social, technical and textual. The social interactivity enables social interaction between groups and individuals, the technical interactivity represents the medium's capability of letting human users manipulate the machine via its interface while the textual interactivity refers to the creative and interpretive interaction between users and texts (Baym 2010: 7–8).

In terms of the *temporal structure* of the communication medium, Twitter displays features of both synchronous and asynchronous communication. Among the features of synchronous media the following can be mentioned: the rapid transmission of messages, despite the physical distance between the participants, and the sense of placelesness (Baym 2010: 8), which enables virtual closeness between participants. In contrast, the advantage of also having features specific to asynchronous communication is represented by the fact that the tweeters are allowed to manage their self presentation more strategically.

The *social cues* refer to the context, the meanings of messages and the identities of the people interacting. The Twitter platform displays no physical context as well as no verbal, non-verbal nor para-verbal elements. The next feature is represented by *storage and replicability*, as the tweets can be stored on the platform, replicated, retrieved and edited prior to sending. The *reach* refers to the size of the audience Twitter can attain: it has huge potential, depending on the topic, to reach local and global audiences. Twitter is also characterised by increased *mobility*, as people can send and receive tweets regardless of their location.

90 https://support.twitter.com/articles/215585?lang=en

In terms of main features, the tweets are characterised by brevity constraint and the absence of the verbal component and of any prosodic items. As there are no contextual, visual (no body movement, facial expressions nor eye gaze) and auditory (pitch of the voice) cues available, which are important elements in the interpretation process of face-to-face communication, different techniques have been developed that have a great impact on the linguistics of the tweets, such as: the creative use of punctuation, visual interaction, special orthography, abbreviations, acronyms, to name but a few.

A tweet is limited to no more than 140 characters in length. A direct consequence of this brevity constraint is that the tweets may not necessarily contain well-formed ideas or a very developed context. Additionally, the body of the tweet is accompanied by four operators: @-mentions, retweets (RT), hashtags (#) and hyperlinks (http://). By using the @-mention the user addresses and mentions other users, the retweet allows the users to re-send other tweets while the hashtag marks the topic of the tweet and makes it searchable. As a result of the constant references to other users and topics, the conversation on Twitter is said to be "multiparty, temporarily fluid and highly intertextual" (Zappavigna 2012: 195). The tweet may also contain hyperlinks sending to various newspaper articles and documents supporting and exemplifying the claims made in the body of the tweet. A functional operator model (Einspanner-Pflock, Anastasiadis and Thimm 2016: 45) has been suggested in order to indicate the impact the operators have in creating the interaction on Twitter.

The tweets represent particular samples of language use pointing towards novel techniques in the process of *meaning derivation and interpretation*. The length limitation imposes important constrains in creating the tweet. As a consequence, the tweets can be more or less explicit and sometimes the tweeter is expecting his audience to undergo some inferential work in order to reach the intended interpretation. Nevertheless, the background and contextual assumptions the participants share play an important role in guiding the interpretation process.

7.2.2 The Use of Micro-blogging in Political Communication

The Twitter platform was extensively used in the political campaign of Barack Obama in 2008. The main function of the tweets was to send campaign updates and provide the people with the opportunity to volunteer and get involved in the campaign (Abroms and Lefebvre 2009). Ever since Twitter has been embraced by politicians worldwide as it offers real-time access to the public sphere allowing them to create a direct and fruitful relationship and on-line interaction both with the citizens and the journalists in a networked environment (Bruns and Burgess 2011, Graham et al. 2013).

The extensive use of Twitter as the channel of choice for diplomacy and communication between world leaders, governments, foreign ministries and diplomats has led to the emergence of digital diplomacy. *Twiplomacy* is the leading global study of world leaders on Twitter, conducted by leading global public relations and communications firm Burson-Marsteller[91]. Federica Mogherini, the Vice President of the European Commission, considers Twitter to be "a revolutionary social network even in politics. [...] but not all Twitter exchanges are diplomatic, real world differences are playing out on Twitter and sometimes end up in hashtag wars between embassies and foreign ministries"[92].

Becoming aware of the huge potential Twitter has, many politicians have used it as an important communication tool during parliamentary, presidential, congressional, federal and local elections in numerous countries. Politicians choose to use Twitter, in general, and during election time, in particular, for several reasons. First, it grants them the opportunity to address a wider and collective audience. They seek to interact with other political members but also with media and journalists and especially with the large mass of voters. Furthermore, a tweet offers the possibility of constant switching between multiple roles and fragmented audiences (Broersma and Graham 2012). This does not only raise the level of participation in public debate (Bruns and Burgess 2011, Graham et al. 2013, Vergeer et al. 2013) but also raises people's awareness and encourages them to vote.

Second, Twitter allows the politicians to personally get involved in the political campaign. It grants them the opportunity to take individual initiatives and to shape the conversation about elections, to set the news agendas and send their messages to the public directly, being "un-touched by journalists" (Broersma and Graham 2012). The tweets are said to represent important news source, and they are sometimes quoted entirely. A well-chosen utterance can reach the electorate without being mediated by journalists and, therefore, generate a lot of publicity (Thorsen 2014).

7.2.3 Literature Overview

Various investigations were dedicated to how Twitter was used and what purposes it served. For instance, Golbeck, Grimes and Rogers (2010) focused on the Twitter use during the US Congress elections. The analysis revealed that the tweets

91 http://twiplomacy.com/blog/twiplomacy-study-2015/#section-22
92 http://twiplomacy.com/blog/twiplomacy-study-2015/

were used rather like "vehicles for self-promotion" (Golbeck, Grimes, and Rogers 2010: 1620), as the members of the Congress tweeted primarily to disseminate information and to report on their daily activities. Conway et al. (2012) looked at the number of tweets posted, the followers gained and the followers added, the occurrence of hashtags, user mentions, hyperlinks and content categories within tweets during the 2012 US presidential campaign. It resulted that the candidates used Twitter to broadcast information about issues they wanted people to know and to self-promote as opposed to transparency.

Although many studies concentrate on the American elections, there are also studies bringing forward how Twitter was used elsewhere. For instance, Gaffney (2010) studied Twitter use during the 2009 Iran elections by tracking the use of the Iran Election hashtag. Tumasjan et al. (2010) studied tweets related to the 2009 German federal election in terms of their content as a reflection of the offline political landscape. Larsson (2012) discussed the Swedish elections in 2010 by presenting a rationale for data collection and analysis of Twitter users with an emphasis on the practice of civic microblogging.

In sum, the accent is placed on how the Twitter networking is created, on the number of tweets posted, the followers gained, the various occurrences of hashtags, user mentions and different content categories within tweets. Nevertheless, little has been said about the content and the language of the tweets, how politicians use Twitter and how efficient their tweets are in communicating their message and persuading the citizens to vote for a particular candidate or party.

2014 European Elections on Twitter

Electoral campaigns are complex and organized political events meant to influence the decision-making process. The campaign teams resort to different channels and techniques to make the message of the campaign visible and to communicate with the electorate. Successfully used in the political campaign of Barack Obama in the USA in 2008, social media, in general, and Twitter, in particular, have become key communication tools during election times, being embraced by politicians across Western democracies. If the main function of the tweets in Obama's campaign was to send updates and provide the public with the opportunity to volunteer and get involved in the campaign (Abroms and Lefebvre 2009), the 2014 European elections proved to be a turning point which led to the confirmation of what has been called the "institutionalization" of Twitter (Smyrnaios 2014). Many institutions like the European Parliament, the Commission or certain European parties have used Twitter as their main communicational tool during the campaigns by creating official hashtags and having special companies provide analytics and promote Twitter accounts and hashtags on other media (Smyrnaios 2014). If the 2009 elections were considered to be the Facebook elections[93], the extensive use of Twitter during the 2014 elections by public institutions, political parties and candidates, media and journalists and citizens led to the conclusion that the 2014 elections were "shaping up to be the Twitter elections".

There are important differences that lead to variations on the linguistics of Twitter as a result of the different contexts in which it is used, the purposes it serves and the audiences it addresses. The context shapes the discourse type and its features and plays an important role in the process of meaning derivation and interpretation. In comparison with other situations where the context in not defined by a particular event, the participants do not share many contextual assumptions and the tweeter has little control on the type and size of the audience, 2014 European elections set a particular social and discourse context. Even if some information may be left implicit due to the brevity constraint, it may be easily recovered due to the contextual assumptions available represented by the approaching elections and existing political landscape. The political candidates engage with large audiences and target mainly their supporters but they are also trying to make other citizens adhere to their ideology and set of beliefs.

The use of Twitter during the 2014 European elections has led to the emergence of a particular political discourse, shaped in accordance with the characteristics and constraints imposed by the online platform. The specificity of the electoral tweets is also influenced by the ideology and beliefs of the political party the candidates are part of. They play an important role in choosing different linguistic strategies meant to emphasize their political views, on the one hand, and to make the electorate take action, on the other hand.

7.3 The Linguistics of the Call for Action Tweets

7.3.1 General Description

Tweets can be classified in relation to the Election Day in tweets sent *before* and *after* the elections. In the first category the following types of tweets are included: (a.) informative tweets used in order to broadcast information about the politicians' daily activities and their media appearance, (b.) messages as position taking, (c.) direct replies to other tweets, (d.) call for action tweets, i.e. tweets usually inviting people to vote, (e.) tweets promoting negative campaigning and

93 Tony Lockett's blog *European Union 2.0*: https://tonylbxl.wordpress.com/2014/02/16/will-2014-be-europes-twitter-election/

(f.) positive campaigning. In the second category the following types can be mentioned: (g.) thanking their supporters, (h.) posting the official results, (i.) making reference to the efforts of the campaign, (j.) acknowledging their political role.

In this paper particular attention is paid to the *call for action tweets*, i.e. to the way in which the UKIP political candidates reach out to the audience and try to persuade them in order to get their vote. The language politicians use plays an important role in the processes of persuasion and decision-making. Depending on what linguistic strategies are used, the tweets can have different cognitive impacts and, therefore, be more or less efficient in convincing the electorate to vote for them.

The common elements of any political campaign, regardless of the election type, are usually represented by information and news sharing, information about the campaign, location and activity sharing, direct interaction with citizens, personal messages and messages targeting campaigns and mobilization support (Ikiz et al. 2014). Political campaigns are complex events with important stakes consisting of more phases relative to particular key moments. This leads to a dynamics of the tweets content, as the political candidates resort to different linguistic strategies that serve their communicative purposes in different moments during the campaign. If at the beginning of the campaign the politicians are often engaged in conversations with the electorate, answering their questions and addressing them directly, towards the end of the campaign and around the election day the discourse becomes asymmetrical, a one-way transfer of information, from the politicians to the audience. The call for action tweets under investigation in this paper characterize the end of the political campaign.

7.3.2 Corpus and Method of Analysis

The corpus of data is represented by the tweets sent by the UKIP political candidates within the time span of two weeks prior to the 2014 European elections. The analysis is partly corpus-based as the word search represented the analytical starting point and partly corpus-driven as the findings were used for further analysis, i.e. to establish more categories of tweets sent by politicians in order to reach out to the audience and persuade them to vote for them.

The analysis consists of more steps. First, the tweets have been selected by word search: *vote UKIP*, including the combination of the collocation with hashtags and @ mentions. Second, the tweets have been coded by hand and only the relevant tweets have been selected, i.e. those concerning the elections and expressing the politicians' intentions towards the approaching vote. No retweets have been included in the analysis as the interest lies in the candidates' way of approaching the electorate in their attempt to create a connection with them. The software used for concordancing and text analysis is AntConc (Anthony 2014).

As a result of the corpus-based analysis, a formal analysis of the *vote Ukip* collocation is suggested while as a result of the corpus-driven analysis a content investigation is put forward.

7.3.3 Vote UKIP

In terms of strategies, the *vote UKIP* structure, with the variation *vote for UKIP* or *voting UKIP*, is by far the most frequently used. The message it conveys is simple, clear, direct and does not require any inferential work in order to be understood by the audience. It is a memorable structure which quickly draws the voters' attention. These features have an immediate effect on the voters' cognitive environment, making this linguistic strategy a very efficient one.

As expected, most of the *vote UKIP* tweets were sent closer to the election day. The collocation appears 107 times in the investigated corpus of data under all its forms: used alone, in combination with the operators (32 instances of *vote #ukip* and 4 instances of *vote @ukip*), in upper or in lower case.

The orthography of this collocation can vary from one tweet to another. An interplay between upper and lower case has been noticed: either the verb *to vote* or the name of the party is emphasized. There are also instances when the first letter of the verb *vote* is written in upper case followed by the name of the party in capital letters (*Vote UKIP*), even if it is inserted in the body of the tweet:

(1) Alan Stevens: Remember to Vote UKIP tomorrow. Polls are open from 7am until 10pm. http://t.co/EBGWJddXxA

This message was tweeted under the exact form by more politicians from different regions. The hyperlink at the end of the tweet sends the reader to the UKIP's website where the photo of Nigel Farage together with some other party members is displayed. The picture is accompanied by the following message: *Vote UKIP tomorrow. Polls are open from 7am until 10pm*. The insertion of this message in the body of the tweets explains the upper case used for the verb *vote* even if it is not signalled accordingly.

There are also instances when only the first letter of the name of the party is in upper case (*vote Ukip*) or the entire name of the party is written in lower case as part of the informal style that characterizes sometimes Twitter (*vote ukip*). As there are no prosodic elements available, the orthographic interplay creates a visual impact important in drawing people's attention and making the message memorable.

Vote UKIP can be followed by different adverbs with an informative purpose like *today*, *tonight* or *tomorrow*, depending on the time frame of the tweeter and the date of the elections. Sometimes there are semantic alternatives used for the *Vote UKIP* phrase, such as: *look for the ukip logo, look out for our famous pound logo, Look for the "£" logo*!:

(2) Jill Seymour: Everyone remember to go out and vote @UKIP Look out for our famous pound logo

The *vote UKIP* structure can occupy different places in the tweet which leads to different cognitive and emotional impacts. It is not used on the first position at the beginning of the tweet very frequently but rather at the end. It is usually part of the body of the tweet when the tweet is informative as shown in (1). If the tweet is argumentative it can follow an argument offered by the politician, being directly related to its content or it is simply added at the end of the tweet in order to categorize it and to draw attention to it. In the latter situation, the *Vote UKIP* collocation functions like a slogan having a greater emotional impact on people's cognitive environment, as shown in (3) and (4):

(3) Bill Etheridge: Stand up to the mindless thugs and chants of the hard left. Stand up for freedom. Vote ukip!
(4) Michael Heaver; UKIP; East of England; 4; Make history. Vote UKIP.

The *vote UKIP* structure is used in different semantic combinations with the same role of recalling the vote and encouraging the electorate to give them their vote. Different semantic categories have been identified, ranging from telling the citizens to urging them to vote for their party in particular: *remember to vote, don't forget to vote, please vote, please remember to vote*. These tweets have mainly an informative role, being used to broadcast general information about the vote, position on the ballot paper, the location and time of the vote, etc.:

(5) Jonathan Arnott;UKIP;UKIP;North East;1;UKIP supporters are the most certain to vote, so I'm confident that a bit of rain won't hurt our chances. Don't forget to vote #UKIP today!
(6) Paul Nuttall;UKIP; North West;1; Don't forget to vote @UKIP today for the European and Local council elections. Every vote matters. Let's cause a political earthquake.
(7) Louise Bours;UKIP;UKIP;North West;2; Today is the day where we can cause this political earthquake! Thanks for your continued support. Please vote #UKIP!
(8) Roger Helmer;UKIP;UKIP;East Midlands;1; Tomorrow: Please remember to vote #UKIP. Bottom of the ballot paper. Top of the poll!

While many tweets are directive speech acts, meant to recall the vote and invite the citizens to vote for them, the *vote UKIP* structure can also be part of a rhetorical question. In this case the accent is not placed on the interrogative part, as the politician is not seeking for information, but his tweet functions like a confirmation, being followed by details regarding the ballot paper and the place the party occupies on it. By using the imperatives *make sure* and *complain* he draws the people's attention regarding the good functioning of the election:

(9) Paul Oakley; UKIP; London;2; Voting UKIP tonight? Make sure your ballot paper's unfolded. We're at the bottom. Complain to staff if you can't see us.

There are also tweets where a mix of strategies can be noticed. In the following example the candidate used a combination of *do not forget*, followed by the location on the ballot paper and the semantic alternative for the name of the party *Look for the "£" logo*:

(10) Louise Bours;UKIP;UKIP;North West;2; Do NOT forget that #UKIP is at the bottom of the ballot paper. Vote very carefully! Look for the "£" logo! We can do this #Chester!

The *vote UKIP* structure can be inserted in the body of the tweet or can be used in combination with different *operators*, such as hashtags or @ mentions. Different combinations between the *vote UKIP* structure and the operators have been identified in the corpus of data. For instance, the *vote UKIP* can be used as a hashtag (*#VoteUKIP*) or the operators, the hashtag or the @ mention, can be used before the name of the party (*vote #UKIP, vote @UKIP, vote for #UKIP, voting #UKIP*[94]). The latter situation is the predominant one in our corpus of data, as shown in the following examples:

(11) Jonathan Arnott; UKIP; North East; 1; UKIP supporters are the most certain to vote, so I'm confident that a bit of rain won't hurt our chances. Don't forget to **vote #UKIP** today!

(12) Jill Seymour; UKIP; WestMidlands; 1; Everyone remember to go out and **vote @ UKIP** Look out for our famous pound logo.

The analysis revealed that there is a correlation between the place of the hashtag in the tweet and the function it has. The hashtag can be integrated in the body of the tweet and be used on middle or final position as in (13) or can be unrelated to the body of the tweet, being used at the end, as in (14):

(13) Donna Edmunds; UKIP; UKIP; South East; 5; @State_Control maybe by 'our country' he means 'Europe'. Anyway, he can't hear their voices either. If he could, **he'd #voteUKIP** @Ed_Miliband

94 Although only the second part represents a proper hashtag, *vote #UKIP* will be analysed like a collocation, as it seems to form a complex unit in the corpus of data.

(14) Gawain Towler; UKIP; UKIP; South West; 3; for years the legacy parties and media have demonised a the 'feckless young' to justify mass immigration. It's a disgrace **#VoteUKIP**

While in (13), the hashtag is part of the conditional clause replacing the predicate and the direct object, in (14) it is added at the end of the tweet, without any apparent connection to the content. In both cases, the hashtags are used to make the tweet visible, to organise the election conversation, to draw attention to it and make it user-friendly.

Apart from their main functions, the *#VoteUKIP* and *vote #UKIP* hashtags serve other purposes, contributing differently to the process of meaning derivation and interpretation. In (14), the hashtag goes beyond search functionality: without the hashtag, the content would have been incomplete and fragmentary and the reader would not have been able to reach the intended interpretation. With respect to it, Scott considers the hashtags to be "highlighting devices", as they guide the hearer towards the intended overall interpretation (Scott 2015: 14). In other words, the hashtags create a particular context of interpretation by making certain background and contextual assumptions highly accessible to the readers. For instance, the #VoteUKIP and vote #UKIP hashtags activate the background assumptions which situate the tweet in the context of the approaching elections and function like reminders of the party running for the European elections.

The role the hashtag plays is even more complex. Without the hashtag, the tweet seems to express the politician's attitude towards a description of a long lasting situation. The political candidate criticizes and expresses his disagreement to the way in which the mass immigration problem has been dealt with. By using the hashtag, he suggests that the party he is representing has different views and beliefs and is, therefore, the solution to the mentioned problem.

Scott (2015) identifies more categories of hashtags that serve different functions in the discourse and play different roles in the process of meaning derivation and interpretation. In relevance-theoretic terms (Sperber and Wilson 1995), the hashtags can contribute to the derivation of the proposition expressed by the tweet, i.e. explicature and higher-order explicature, or to the implicitly communicated meaning, i.e. implicated premises and implicated conclusions.

By activating certain contextual assumptions the hashtag creates a contrastive context of interpretation which facilitates the following conditional type of reasoning: *if you vote UKIP, the mass immigration problem will be solved*. In other words, the intended interpretation is arrived at inferentially, i.e. the reader has to take an inferential route in order to derive the *implicated premise*: *UKIP is the solution to the mentioned problem*. In sum, the hashtag is used to create a contrast between the negative image of the political opponents and the solution represented by the mentioned party. By using the hashtag, the politician obeys the brevity constraint and manages to send a powerful message meant to discredit his opponents at the same time.

There are cases when more operators are used, such as: the hashtag #VoteUKIP, the mention @UKIP and the hashtag #UKIP, in the attempt to make their tweets visible and easy to find:

(15) Jason Smith; UKIP; UKIP; Yorkshire and the Humber; 5; Immigrants do lots of jobs in public sector because they're cheap labour – less jobs for Brits and drive down wages **#VoteUKIP @UKIP #UKIP**

(16) Jason Smith;UKIP;UKIP;Yorkshire and the Humber;5; Tories support Turkey joining the EU!! Tories are EU puppets **#VoteUKIP @UKIP #UKIP**

At first sight, this overuse of operators may seem redundant, all of them serving the same purpose: making the tweet searchable and highlighting a trending topic. In line with the suggested analysis, the #VoteUKIP hashtag is more complex, playing an important role in guiding the reader's inferential process. The #VoteUKIP creates a contrastive context of interpretation, in the attempt to discredit the political opponents and promote their own image. Furthermore, voting their party is equalled with the solution of the mentioned problems as they have the exactly opposite values and beliefs.

On balance, depending on their position and whether they are part of the body of the tweet, the hashtags fulfil distinct roles, leading to a reinterpretation of the hashtags in terms of the roles and functions they perform. Apart from the search functionality, as a consequence of the brevity constraint, the hashtags are used to create a particular context of interpretation, i.e. they make certain contextual and background assumptions available to the audience. The #VoteUKIP hashtags contribute to the derivation of the implicitly communicated meaning and generate a conditional type of reasoning in a contrastive context of interpretation: *if you vote UKIP, the problem, whatever that is, will be solved.*

7.3.4 Content analysis

In this section particular attention is paid to the content of the call for action tweets. Although all the tweets under investigation have the same topic, i.e. the approaching elections, and are part of the same category, i.e. call for action tweets, further analysis is necessary in order to discuss the functions they perform within this category and to identify what linguistic strategies are used by the political candidates in order to reach their communicative goals. Furthermore, particular attention will be paid to whether the linguistic strategies are productive, on the one hand, and to the way in which they function at the cognitive level, on the other. A content analysis of the call for action tweets is important to see how the speaker's meaning is created and how the intended interpretation is reached by the hearer.

Two main types of the call for action tweets predominate in the corpus of data: informative tweets and argumentative tweets. The first category is meant to offer general information about the vote, such as the date and the location of the vote, as well as the position UKIP has on the ballot paper. It is a limited category, the tweets being used mostly to recall the vote and to invite the electorate to vote for their party, as indicated in the previous section. The political candidates adopt different styles, ranging from impersonal messages, as shown in (17) and (18) to personal tweets in which they kindly ask the electorate to vote for their party, as shown in (19) and (20). The message is usually direct and the interpretation is easily reached, as no information seems to be left implicit:

(17) Bill Etheridge;UKIP;UKIP;West Midlands;3; Voting for the euro and local elections is on Thursday may 22nd. Please look for the ukip logo on your ballot… http://t.co/WMNcuKfaUs
(18) Alan Stevens;UKIP;UKIP;South East;8;Remember to Vote UKIP tomorrow. Polls are open from 7am until 10pm. http://t.co/EBGWJddXxA
(19) Margot Parker;UKIP;UKIP;East Midlands;2; #UKIP Team East Mids MEP candidates in Newark campaigning today. Please Vote#UKIP May 22nd
(20) Andrew McNeilis;UKIP;UKIP;London;6; Please vote on Thursday. And I would be honoured if you voted for us http://t.co/8gyItp9Q7L

While in the first three examples, the audience is addressed collectively, the last tweet brings forward the politician's voice. Apart from the interjection *please*, used to politely ask the electorate for their vote, the first-person personal pronoun *I* indicates that the speaker is committed and assumes what he is saying. Furthermore, the candidate grants more expressive force to his message by choosing to express his attitude towards voting for their party *(I would be honoured)*, referred to by the inclusive first-person plural pronoun *us*.

The second category is represented by the argumentative tweets. In comparison with the informative tweets, this category is broader, the accent being placed on answering the question *why the electorate should vote UKIP*. The analysis of the tweets indicates that the answers provided are built around general arguments and anti-EU arguments, which shape a negative campaigning argumentative orientation to the politicians' discourse.

Considered to be an important part of a politician's campaign arsenal, negative campaigning focuses on fostering a negative image of the opponents with reference to their personality, record and opinions. Negativity is considered to be valuable to voters, as well. Mattes and Redlawsk (2014) suggest a theoretical model and carry out experiments which show that voters need more than the arguments provided by the candidates for why they should be elected. It appears that negativity assures more attention from voters, on the one hand, and the voters are more likely to incorporate the negative information into their evaluation, on the other (Mattes and Redlawsk 2014: 4–5).

The politicians can choose to attack their opponents directly, without mentioning any of their their views and actions, or they can compare and contrast themselves with their opponents. In the latter situation, they usually provide positive information about their own record while the information about the opponents is negative. The call for action tweets under investigation in this paper fall into the second category, i.e. the contrastive negative campaigning argumentative orientation characterizes the discourse of the UKIP political candidates. They choose to always juxtapose themselves with their opponents as it allows them to create a negative image of the opponents and a positive image of UKIP at the same time. In what follows, particular attention is paid to the way in which the contrastive negative campaigning argumentative orientation is realised and to the linguistic strategies used by politicians in contrasting and comparing themselves with their opponents. To this end, the following aspects will be discussed: how the question *why UKIP should be voted for* is addressed, how the premise (*UKIP is the solution to the problem x*) is expressed, how the negativity is expressed and what type of reasoning is activated. All the tweets under investigation are meant to answer the question *why the electorate should vote UKIP* and they are all based on the same premise *UKIP is the solution*. However, what is different about them is the way in which the question is addressed and what linguistic strategies are used. They can range from being explicitly expressed to being left implicit for the reader to infer, situation in which more cognitive effort is required.

Based on the combination between how the question is addressed and how the premise is expressed, different categories of tweets have been identified: (a.) the question is expressed directly and the premise is identified with a minimum of cognitive effort; (b.) the question is indirectly addressed and identifying the premise does not require a great deal of cognitive effort; (c.) the question is in the background and the premise is left implicit and therefore more cognitive effort is required in order to reach the intended interpretation.

(a.) The first category of tweets is represented by the situation when the question is directly addressed and the premise follows naturally, as in the following examples:

(21) Michael Heaver;UKIP;UKIP;East of England;4; *Why the City should vote UKIP in the EU elections* http://t.co/Vf13XsLgqE

(22) Donna Edmunds;UKIP;UKIP;South East;5; "Ukip hold dear the true and honest views of the Great British people". *Why are you voting UKIP on May 22nd?* http://t.co/cC5p7WT4ho"
(23) Paul Nuttall; UKIP; UKIP; North West; 1; EU migrant figures up again with 7 % increase in foreign workers. *Another reason to vote @UKIP today.* http://t.co/bYoTruNJmw

In all three cases, the arguments are given in the newspaper articles the hyperlinks at the end of the tweet are pointing to. The body of the tweet can be interpreted to be an introduction to the arguments provided at length in the newspaper articles and are marked at the linguistic level accordingly. The second tweet is represented by the actual background question: *Why are you voting UKIP on May 22*[nd]*?* while the first one is a report of the same question. The difference between the two, apart from the direct vs. reported style, is to be found at the way in which the electorate is addressed: *the City* vs. *you*, respectively. The second person pronoun *you* adds more expressive force to the message, by addressing the electorate directly in comparison with the general, impersonal *the city.* If the first two tweets offered general arguments, the last one focuses on a particular one, represented by the mass immigration, explicitly introduced by *another reason to vote @UKIP today*. Although at first sight the tweets seems to address the question without expressing any negativity, at a closer look it can be noticed that the negativity is found in the newspaper articles the hyperlinks send to and not in the body of the tweets.

Another example of a direct way of presenting the reasons why the electorate should vote UKIP is represented by the tweets sent by Jonathan Arnott. Unlike his colleagues, he compiled a list of reasons he labelled *7 reasons to vote UKIP on Thursday* and presented them the week before the elections. Similarly to the previous category, the negativity is expressed contrastively in the hyperlinks:

(24) Jonathan Arnott;UKIP;UKIP;North East;1; In the week up to the election, I'm doing **'7 reasons to vote UKIP on Thursday'**. To kick things off, reason #7 here: http://t.co/WpTd6RoKIt
(25) Jonathan Arnott;UKIP;UKIP;North East;1; The fourth in my week-long series of reasons to vote UKIP on Thursday. Reason #4: EU money is OUR money http://t.co/MYimQDdah1

The structure and the argumentative pattern of this politician's tweets are similar: an introductory remark about his series of reasons, the argument itself, followed usually by a hyperlink sending to a newspaper article, which provides more information to support his opinion. In spite of the length of the tweets, the arguments are concise and presented more as campaign messages. This makes them memorable, directly influencing the citizens' evaluations and the process of decision-making.

The hashtag *#WhyIvotedUKIP* was also created in order to address the background question and indicate why anyone should vote UKIP. Its structure consists of the wh- word *why*, the first-person pronoun *I*, the past tense of the verb *to vote* and the name of the party. It is based on the interplay between lower and upper case, meant to create a strong visual impact, which makes it easy to remember.

In terms of content, it is inherently argumentative. The wh- word *why* forms a correlative pair with *because*, as part of the questions – answer pattern, the tweeter being expected to give arguments to support his statement. Mainly used by Barry Cooper, the hashtag is placed on initial position in order to categorize the tweet and make it visible. It is usually followed by *I want* and *I think*, *because* being mostly left implicit:

(26) Barry Cooper;UKIP;UKIP;South East;10;#WhyIvotedUKIP I think it is ridiculous that we spend more on foreign aid than we do on policing our streets and keeping communities safe

(27) Barry Cooper;UKIP;UKIP;South East;10;#WhyIvotedUKIP I want politics to be more about politicians asking people what they want and not telling them want they need

(28) Barry Cooper;UKIP;UKIP;South East;10;#WhyIvotedUKIP I want our armed forces properly supported, our veterans cared for and the military covenant taken seriously

By using the first-person singular pronoun *I* both in the hashtag and in the body of the tweet, the candidate expresses high commitment to what he is stating and personal involvement in the issues he is describing. It also helps the politician to distance himself from the other political candidates, fostering a positive image of himself, as being someone who has principles, takes responsibility and who is not afraid to take action when necessary.

Apart from the first-person singular pronoun *I* to mark his own voice, the inclusive plural form *we/us* is also used in the attempt to present himself as being part of the same group as the electorate and having shared values. By establishing an *us vs. them* dichotomy the speaker creates an image of the group he belongs to in a positive way and the other group in a negative way. At the same time, he is making his opponents responsible for all the issues he is mentioning.

A pretty similar hashtag is also used: *#WhyImVotingUKIP*. Apart from the aspectual difference, i.e. perfective *(voted)* vs. imperfective (*am voting*), *#WhyImVotingUKIP* is used mostly on final position and the tweet usually begins with *because*. In comparison with the subjective stance adopted by the tweeter in the case of the previous hashtag, there is a combination between a subjective approach, marked by the use of the first-person *I*, as in (29), and an impersonal and general tone, depicting a particular situation, as in (30):

(29) Donna Edmunds;UKIP;UKIP;South East;5; Because I want my daughter to grow up in a free country #WhyImVotingUkip

(30) Donna Edmunds;UKIP;UKIP;South East;5; Because democracy only works when our representatives are directly accountable to us. End the democratic deficit. #WhyImVotingUkip

(b.) The second category of tweets is represented by instances where the question *why the electorate should vote UKIP* and the premise *UKIP is the solution* are addressed indirectly but they are easily inferred by the reader and therefore little cognitive effort is required in reaching the intended interpretation. In contrast, UKIP's beliefs and position towards particular problems are directly expressed (*Only UKIP is unequivocally opposed to them* and *that's what UKIP voters believe in and vote for)*, as in the following examples:

(31) Roger Helmer;UKIP;UKIP;East Midlands;1; The Telegraph reports there are now 30,000 on-shore wind turbines in the UK. **Only UKIP is unequivocally opposed to them**. Vote #UKIP.

(32) Michael Heaver;UKIP;UKIP;East of England;4; Getting out of the EU, proper border controls, creating new grammar schools: **that's what UKIP voters believe in and vote for.**

Although similar in the message they convey, the argumentative patterns of the two tweets are different. The first pattern is built, as follows: the problem is highlighted, Ukip's position to the problem is stated (*Only UKIP is unequivocally opposed to them)* and the solution to the problem is offered (Vote #UKIP). In terms of argumentation, the following set of explicit and implicit premises can be identified: *the UK has a lot of wind turbines; the wind turbines are bad* (implicit); *UKIP is against them; UKIP wants, can or will do something about them* (implicit). And the reasoning behind this pattern is represented by the following inference: *if you want less // no on-shore wind turbines in the UK, then vote UKIP.* UKIP is, therefore, implicitly presented as being the solution to the on-shore wind turbines problem.

In the second pattern the solutions to more problems are first offered, followed by an emphasis (*that's what UKIP voters believe in and vote for*) on the implicit premise represented by UKIP is the solution to the mentioned problem. In this case, the interpretation is based on the following reasoning: *if you want these problems solved, then vote UKIP*. In sum, an explicit image of UKIP as having opposite values, of being different from the other parties is created in both cases. The negativity is explicitly represented by the dichotomy *us* vs. *them*, i.e. UKIP vs. the opponents.

The reasoning behind the tweets is conditional and has the following form: *if you want the problem x solved, then vote UKIP.* The interpretation is reached by undergoing the same type of conditional reasoning that was activated in the interpretation of the hashtags, discussed in the previous section. In contrast with the consequent which is always the same (*vote UKIP*), the antecedent of the *if... then* construction varies corresponding to different factual aspects. Therefore, the interpretation of the *if...then* construction is not based on truth-conditions but the accent is rather placed on how persuasion is arrived at. To this end, the context and people's knowledge are important factors that influence the derivation of of this structure.

Based on pragmatic inference, the conditional reasoning is a rich source of context and content effects. Unlike deductive inferences, where the conclusion is a logical result, always derived from the stated premises, pragmatic inferences yield probable conclusions which are only likely to be true. Additional premises that represent relevant factual information may be added to the initial premises which increase the semantic information. Looking at the tweets, it can be noticed that the conditional reasoning is activated by the vote UKIP collocation used at the end of the tweet. In other words, the *vote UKIP* structure plays an important role in the interpretation process as it helps the reader to retrieve the implicit premise.

(c.) The third category of tweets is represented by the instances where the premise *UKIP is the solution* is left implicit. It is a complex category, the tweets focusing on complex arguments built mainly around anti-Europe. Therefore, UKIP is presented as being and standing for the opposite values and policies in comparison with the unfavourable depicted reality. The question *why the electorate should vote UKIP* is usually left implicit and the degree of negativity in these tweets is high. A dichotomy between an unfavourable, negative reality and the solution to those problems expressed by *vote UKIP* is created. The following examples are representative for this category:

(33) Andrew McNeilis;UKIP;UKIP;London;6; Check out low EMPLOYMENT rates of EU economic miracle. Spain, Italy Romania would you want that for uk! Vote UKIP http://t.co/ZR1C3SeuTy

(34) Jonathan Arnott;UKIP;UKIP;North East;1; 10,000 EU officials earn more than our Prime Minister. What a waste of our taxes. Vote #UKIP today http://t.co/HntjJ8p2qu

The same pattern can be identified in these tweets: a fact is presented, followed by a personal comment and the solution (*Vote UKIP*) is presented at the end of the tweet. Although personal, the comment is presented under a general form. Without explicitly committing and assuming his remarks as there is no first-person singular pronoun used, by presenting negative information the political candidate appeals to the electorate's emotions in the attempt to capture their attention. Moreover, negative items are said to be remembered with more detail and for longer periods in comparison with positive and neutral items (Mickley and Kensinger 2008).

The *vote UKIP* collocation used at the end of the tweet is rich in content as it fosters a positive image of the party the politician is representing, on the one hand, and guides the readers towards the intended interpretation by encouraging them to undergo a conditional reasoning, on the other.

Although at first sight the following tweet seems fragmentary and incomplete, its logical form and argumentative orientation can be easily retraced:

(35) Michael Heaver;UKIP;UKIP;East of England;4; Of course, you can only control immigration by leaving the EU. So vote UKIP today.

The reasoning behind the tweet suggesting the solution to the immigration problem seems to be based on the following premises: *the UK has an immigration problem*; *the immigration problem can be controlled contrary to what others say; leaving the EU solves the immigration problem; Ukip wants to leave the EU*; which lead to the following conclusion: *if you want the immigration problem solved, then vote for Ukip*.

Some inferential work is needed in order to reach the intended interpretation. There are some discursive clues which guide the interpretation process. The discursive markers *of course* and *so* play key roles in providing the necessary contextual information. *Of course* is highly conversational and emphasizes the fact that the tweet was sent in response to a previous message debating the immigration problem and the UK leaving the EU. Therefore, this tweet is part of a larger conversation built around some key topics addressed during the 2014 European elections, such as the immigration problem and the UK leaving the EU. The discursive marker also emphasizes the existence of more opposing points of view, the tweet representing a counter argument in the debate regarding immigration. The second discursive marker *so*, functions as a conclusion: *So vote UKIP today.* In other words the solution to the immigration problem is represented by leaving the EU, action that is fully supported by UKIP.

The same type of conditional reasoning can be identified in the following examples as well:

(36) Andrew McNeilis;UKIP;UKIP;London;6; More from the ministry of fear – don't forget the govt funds this think tank. **Love Britain? Vote UKIP** http://t.co/Py0jBNp38g

(37) Andrew McNeilis;UKIP;UKIP;London;6; Ok. Imagine the media over last 5 weeks played the ball (issue) not the man (Farage etc) **the truth is do you love the uk? Then vote UKIP**

The *if...then* structure has a different form in these tweets. While the consequent is represented by the *vote UKIP* collocation, the antecedent is represented by the question: *Love Britain?* which leads to the following recreated structure: *if you love Britain, then vote UKIP*. The same pattern with a small variation at the level of the antecedent can be noticed in the next example:

(38) Tim Aker;UKIP;UKIP;East of England;3;Tory change in the EU = £55 m a day to the EU, more EU immigration, more EU laws. Love Britain, Vote #UKIP

The content of the tweet makes reference to the newspaper article which considers the UK leaving the EU not to be an appropriate measure. The political candidate holds different views and accuses the party in office of supporting the issues discussed in the article. By calling the party in office *ministry of fear*, the political candidate attempts to create a negative image of his opponents and, implicitly, promotes his own image and that of his party.

At first sight, the reasoning line is represented by the following premises: *UKIP disagrees with the current opinion of the government; UKIP thinks they are playing EU's interests and not Britain's* which lead to the conclusion: *If you love Britain, then vote UKIP*. Therefore, in the attempt to recreate the premises of this argument, a transition between political aspects to loving UK correlated with voting UKIP can be noticed. In other words, the antecedent built around *loving UK* encompasses more layers of meaning: being against the current government and political aspects, on the one hand, and supporting UKIP which represents a change in the political landscape, on the other. At a closer look, based on the following premises: *leaving the EU means loving Britain; UKIP wants Britain to leave the EU; UKIP loves Britain* more embedded *if...then* constructions can be identified, as follows: *if you love Britain, then you want the UK to leave the EU; if UKIP is elected, then Britain will leave the EU*; to culminate with: *if you love Britain, then vote UKIP.*

Looking at the argumentative line, a strong appeal to emotion can be noticed in comparison to a logical argumentation. The lexical markers focusing on feelings *(ministry of) fear* and *love*, accompanied by the urging advice *don't forget* are meant to manipulate the electorate's emotions, influencing them in the process of decision making. It is a fallacious argumentation, based on *argumentum ad passiones*, because inciting emotions in people does not serve as evidence for a claim. The same pattern and the same argumentative line can be noticed in (37) as well. The consequent is explicitly expressed by *then vote UKIP* and the antecedent is represented by the same question *do you love the uk?*. In this example, UKIP is equalled to the combination expressed by values of truth and love. The appeal to the electorate's patriotism and feelings of belongingness leads to a fallacious type of argumentation.

In conclusion, all three categories of tweets are built on the same cognitive pattern, based on the premise according to which UKIP is presented as being the solution to the problems depicted more or less explicitly. The conclusion is reached inferentially, only some clues being given that lead to the intended interpretation. Negativity is an inherent property of all the call for action tweets under investigation. It is displayed in various degrees and can be found in the grammatical forms used, in the hashtags and in the hyperlinks accompanying the tweets. To reach the intended speaker's meaning, the reader has to undergo an inferential route represented by the conditional type of reasoning, derived in a contrastive context of interpretation.

Conclusions

This paper aimed at discussing the specificity of the call for action tweets sent by the UKIP political candidates during the 2014 European Elections. The call for action tweets are the political messages sent usually towards the end of the electoral campaign when the discourse becomes asymmetrical, as a one-way transfer of information from the politicians to the electorate. Based on the premise that they have different impacts on the people's cognitive environment and they can influence the electorate's opinions about certain candidates and political parties, particular attention is paid to the linguistic strategies and grammatical forms the politicians use.

A general description based on Baym's seven key concepts is suggested in order to highlight Twitter's individuality in comparison with face-to-face communication, on the one hand, and with other forms of computer-mediated communication, on the other. As a result of the main linguistic features, such the brevity constraint and the absence of any verbal, non-verbal and para-verbal components, the tweets represent particular samples of language use whose derivation and interpretation led to the development of novel techniques.

Twitter has been used in politics on a daily basis, as a channel of choice in diplomacy and during election times. The politicians choose Twitter as an important communication tool during the electoral campaign for several reasons: they can address wider and collective audiences, it offers them real-time access to the public sphere, it grants a new dimension to the public debate, and it allows the politicians to get personally involved and take individual initiatives as the message is un-mediated by the media. Due to the extensive use of the platform in all 28 member states, the 2104 EE are considered the "Twitter elections".

The analysis is two-fold, organised around the *vote UKIP* collocation and around the content of the tweets. A formal analysis of the *vote UKIP* collocation is provided with an emphasis on the following aspects: the orthography, the importance of the different positions it occupies in the tweet, the semantic alternatives used for the collocation as well as the combination between *vote UKIP* and different semantic categories. The *vote UKIP* collocation is also used in combination with the # hashtag and @-mention operators, as follows: *#VoteUKIP*, *vote #UKIP*, *vote @UKIP*, *vote for #UKIP*, *voting #UKIP*. A correlation between the place of the hashtag in the tweet and the role it fulfils has been identified: when it is added at the end of the tweet without any apparent relation with the body of the tweet, it functions like a slogan and has a strong cognitive impact on the electorate.

Special emphasis is put on the functions the hashtags have. Apart from making the tweet visible, organising the election conversation, drawing attention to it and making it user-friendly, the hashtags have developed a special function which plays an important role in the process of meaning derivation and interpretation. The *#VoteUKIP* hashtag creates a contrastive context of interpretation which generates a conditional *if…then* type of reasoning.

The content analysis concentrates on two main types of tweets: informative and argumentative. While the informative ones are meant to recall the vote and to invite the electorate to vote for their party, the argumentative ones seek to provide various arguments to the question *why the electorate should vote UKIP.* The analysis reveals that the argumentative tweets are characterised by a contrastive negative campaigning argumentative orientation, as the political candidate choose to always compare and contrast themselves with the opponents. Consequently, a constant dichotomy between the negative image of the opponents and the positive image of UKIP presented as being the solution to the mentioned problems is created.

In the attempt to indicate how the contrastive negative campaigning argumentative orientation is realised a set of criteria has been suggested based on the following points of discussion: how the question *why UKIP should be voted for* is addressed, how the premise (*UKIP is the solution to the problem x*) is expressed, how the negativity is expressed and what type of reasoning is activated.

Based on these criteria, three categories of tweets have been identified, as follows: (a.) the question is expressed directly and the premise is identified with a minimum of cognitive effort; (b.) the question is indirectly addressed and identifying the premise does not require a great deal of cognitive effort; (c.) the question is in the background and the premise is left implicit and therefore more cognitive effort is required in order to reach the intended interpretation. All the tweets are built on the implicit premise *Ukip is the solution* and a contrastive context of interpretation that generates a conditional type of reasoning is created.

The results cannot be taken as representative of the entire behaviour of Twitter during the 2014 European elections and are best regarded as a selective snapshot of the political activity of the UKIP political candidates. Further comparative analysis between other parties in the UK but also between different European countries is required in order to have a more comprehensive picture of the Twitter use during the 2014 European elections.

References

Abroms L., and Lefebvre C. (2009). Obama's Wired Campaign: Lessons for Public Health Communication. Journal of Health Communication, vol. 14, p. 415–423.

Anthony L. (2014). AntConc (Version 3.4.3) [Computer Software]. Tokyo, Japan: Waseda University. Available from http://www.laurenceanthony.net/.

Baym N. (2010). *Personal Connections in the Digital Age*, Polity Press, Cambridge.

Broersma M. and Graham T. (2012). Social media as beat: tweets as news source during the 2010 British and Dutch elections. Journalism Practice, vol. 6(3), p. 403–419.

Bruns A. and Burgess J. (2011). #ausvotes: how Twitter covered the 2010 Australian federal election. Communication, Politics & Culture,vol. 44(2), p. 37–56.

Conway et al. (2012). Twitter Use by Presidential Primary Candidates During the 2012 Campaign. American Behavioral Scientist, vol. 57(11), p. 1596–1610.

Einspanner-Pflock J., Anastasiadis M., and Thimm C. (2016). Ad Hoc Mini-Publics on Twitter: Citizen Participation or Politicical Communication? Examples from the German National Election 2013. Citizen Participation and Political Communication in a Digital World, New York, Routledge, p. 42–59.

Gaffney D. (2010). #iranElection: quantifying online activism. Paper presented at WebSci10: Extending the Frontiers of Society On-Line, Raleigh, NC: US.

Golbeck J., Grimes J.M. and Rogers A. (2010). Twitter Use by the US Congress. Journal of the American Society for Information Science and Technology, vol. 61(8), p. 1612–1621.

Graham T., Broersma M. and Hazelhoff K. (2013). Closing the gap? Twitter as an instrument for connected representation. The Media, Political Participation and Empowerment. Routledge, London, p. 71–88.

Ikiz et al. (2014). Political Use of Twitter: The Case of Metropolitan Mayor Candidates in 2014 Local Elections in Turkey. ICEGOV '14 Proceedings of the

8th International Conference on Theory and Practice of Electronic Governance, ACM, New York, p. 41–50.

Larsson, O. (2012). Studying political microblogging: Twitter users in the 2010 Swedish election campaign. New Media & Society, vol.4, p. 729–747.

Mattes K. and Redlawsk D. (2014) *The Positive Case for Negative Campaigning*, University of Chicago Press, London and Chicago.

Smyrnaios N. (2014): *#EP2014: the European election through the lens of Twitter*, http://ephemeron.eu/1219.

Scott K. (2015). The pragmatics of hashtags: Inference and conversational style on Twitter. Journal of Pragmatics, vol. 81, p. 8–20.

Sperber D. and Wilson D. (1995). *Relevance: communication and cognition*, Wiley-Blackwell, Oxford.

Thorsen E. (2014). *Online Reporting of Elections*. Routledge, New York.

Tumasjan et al. (2010). Predicting Elections with Twitter: What 140 Characters Reveal about Political Sentiment. Paper presented at the Fourth International AAAI Conference on Weblogs and Social Media, George Washington University, Washington, DC.

Vergeer M., Hermans L. and Sams S. (2013). Online social networks and microblogging in political campaigning: the exploration of a new campaign tool and a new campaign style. Party Politics, vol. 19(3), p. 477–501.

Zappavigna M. (2012). Ambient affiliation: A linguistic perspective on Twitter. SAGE Internet Research Methods, Vol. 4: Research 'On' and 'In' the Internet – Investigating the Online World. London SAGE Publications Ltd, p. 193–215.

Part 3:
Integration of Twitter in political strategies in different national contexts

Frédéric Junger & Gilles Brachotte, Univ. de Bourgogne

8. Élections européennes de mai 2014 : étude des données du corpus français de TEE 2014 afin d'appréhender les usages des candidats et la circulation de l'information sur Twitter

Abstract

Cet article interroge et présente les pratiques sur Twitter des candidats et des partis aux élections européennes en France. Il s'intéresse aux codes de ce dispositif sociotechnique qui permettent une mise en relation des différents acteurs (candidats, citoyens, ...). De plus, sur la base d'une analyse quantitative des indicateurs d'interactions (tweets, RT, #), nos résultats mettent en exergue des différences dans l'usage selon le statut des partis et selon les caractéristiques des candidats.

8.1 Introduction

Ce chapitre[95] est ancré dans l'analyse des usages sociaux et en particulier l'utilisation et l'appropriation par les partis et les candidats politiques français de l'outil de microblogging, Twitter. Ce dispositif sociotechnique n'a pas actuellement, en France, la même popularité et la même notoriété que d'autres réseaux socio-numériques comme Facebook. En effet, selon un sondage réalisé par IPSOS en 2013, seul 5 % de la population détenait un compte Twitter et 61 % avait moins de 35 ans[96]. Cela ne permet pas à l'outil d'être considéré comme réellement représentatif de la société, mais il offre un terrain propice aux études et aux analyses sur la participation politique « on-line » et l'usage d'un dispositif socionumérique. De plus, de par ses caractéristiques d'interactivité et de discussion, *Twitter* est un objet d'étude qui soulève des problèmes intéressant le champ des Sciences de l'Information et de la Communication en particulier dans la compréhension de

95 Le chapitre s'inscrit dans un travail de thèse en Sciences de l'Information et de la Communication à l'Université de Bourgogne, intitulé « *La mise en scène des élus politiques sur les réseaux sociaux, relations et interactions dans les communautés d'administrés* ». Dirigée par P. Lardellier et co-encadrée par G. Brachotte.

96 Usages et pratiques de *Twitter* en France. (n.d.). Consulté le 7 octobre 2015, URL : http://www.ipsos.fr/decrypter-societe/2013-04-25-usages-et-pratiques-Twitter-en-france

la construction des relations entre les acteurs, de leurs pratiques et de leurs usages mais également dans l'analyse des mécanismes de diffusion de l'information/désinformation. En effet, Twitter repose sur une promesse : proposer un outil supplémentaire permettant et facilitant les échanges sur Internet, ceci au travers d'une solution instantanée et interactive. *In fine*, l'utilisation d'Internet et des services associés s'organisent autour de la notion d'interactivité avec « *l'idée [...] que la parole circule mieux, plus vite et de façon plus conviviale, si les normes oratoires qui en organisent la distribution incitent chacun, d'une part à parler librement, quand il veut, et d'autre part à choisir de préférence un propos en rapport, en réaction, avec ce qui vient d'être dit, afin de nouer le lien social le plus étroit possible* » (Breton, 2007 : 28). Les enjeux sont multiples et s'articulent donc autour des notions d'instantanéité, de communication permanente et de présence connectée (Licoppe, 2011) propres à ce qui définit les échanges et les prises de parole au travers des outils de communication apparus parallèlement au développement d'Internet.

Plus globalement cette recherche s'attache à étudier et à comprendre les caractéristiques de la participation « on-line » des politiques dans l'espace public numérique[97]. Aussi, comme le souligne P. Flichy, « *Internet, contrairement à la radio ou à la télévision, met en situation d'égalité l'émetteur et le récepteur, c'est donc à première vue, l'outil idéal pour une démocratie participative où le citoyen pourrait intervenir très régulièrement dans le débat public* »[98]. Il constituerait ainsi un nouvel outil de participation du citoyen à la vie politique, ce qui est d'autant plus intéressant à observer dans un contexte où les médias connaissent une importante crise de crédibilité et où les partis politiques cherchent à remobiliser les foules autour des grandes questions de société dans l'objectif de faire chuter les taux d'abstention observés aux dernières élections françaises.

Pour mener à bien notre étude, nous prenons comme corpus[99] les données issues d'une recherche transversale et interdisciplinaire mise en œuvre lors du

---

97 Voir à ce propos, « *Espace public numérique et participation politique* », Les cahiers du numérique, vol 11, N°4/2015, dir. G. Brachotte & A. Frame, Lavoisier, Paris.

98 « *Internet, un outil de la démocratie* », www.laviedesidees.fr, janvier 2008. Consulté le 24 avril 2016.

99 Nous considérons notre corpus comme appartenant à ce que l'on nomme le « Big Data ». Cependant il est important de noter que ce terme ne revêt pas la même signification en fonction des disciplines. A titre d'exemple, les sciences informatiques considèrent le « Big Data » pour un volume de données de plusieurs téraoctets par jour (dimension relative). Dans notre cas, ce sont, sur la période considérée, plus de 4 millions de tweets capturés et donc nécessaires à analyser. Cela nécessite pour un chercheur en sciences humaines et sociales de reconsidérer sa manière de travailler à la fois dans son approche quantitative que qualitative.

scrutin des élections Européennes de 2014. Celui-ci est constitué des tweets de tous les candidats français ayant un compte Twitter, actif ou non[100]. En France, ce sont 49 partis et courants qui ont déposés 193 listes pour un total de 3754 candidats[101]. La période de collecte des données est comprise entre les trois semaines précédant le scrutin du 25 mai 2014 et la semaine suivante. Ainsi, l'analyse porte sur 2 137 128 tweets, exclusivement en langue française[102].

Les questions centrales qui sous-tendent notre analyse sont celles de la relation et de la circulation de l'information entre les acteurs présents sur Twitter (candidats, citoyens, partis, médias). A cette fin, nous nous sommes intéressés à la fois à l'aspect fonctionnel du dispositif (usage des RT, #, @) mais également à son aspect technique (nombre de tweets, partis qui twittent le plus, etc…). Dans une approche globale de notre corpus, nous avons posé comme hypothèse que les principaux partis avaient intégré la puissance du canal de communication des réseaux socionumériques dans leur stratégie de communication plurimédia alors que les « petits » partis, dont la présence sur les médias traditionnels est plus difficile, s'en servent prioritairement comme un moyen de visibilité, de diffusion du message politique et de contact avec le citoyen. Par extension, nous pensons que le degré de popularité des candidats influe sur leur présence sociale sur Twitter. Ainsi, plus le candidat est populaire, plus il l'utilise comme une nécessité d'occuper la totalité de la sphère des supports de communication. Les candidats à plus faible notoriété sont, quant à eux, dans un objectif d'existence au sein de la campagne avec une volonté prioritaire de s'afficher et de s'affirmer dans le monde politique. Enfin, notre dernière hypothèse résulte des caractéristiques intrinsèques et fonctionnelles de Twitter qui font que les échanges

---

100 Concernant les comptes des candidats, nous soulignons le fait que nous avons observé l'activité de ces comptes indépendamment du fait qu'ils peuvent être gérés soit par des équipes de communication, soit par les candidats eux-mêmes – voire par les deux dans certains cas. C'est ainsi l'activité du compte du candidat qui fait l'objet de notre analyse plus que l'activité du candidat

101 « Il y aura 193 listes aux élections européennes ». *L'Obs*. Consulté le 11 août 2015. http://tempsreel.nouvelobs.com/politique/elections-europeennes-2014/20140505.OBS6141/il-y-aura-193-listes-aux-elections-europeennes.html

102 Il est important d'évoquer l'existence de biais pouvant être présents au sein du corpus. En effet la collecte massive de données ne peut s'effectuer sans que soient capturés des comptes ou des tweets qui ne cadrent pas avec les critères que nous avions définis. Ceci, par exemple, au travers de comptes supposés en lien avec l'élection, mais qui ne le sont finalement pas. A titre d'exemple, nous avons capturé des comptes qui ont partagé le même hashtag sans que celui-ci ait une signification identique, ce qui est notamment le cas pour le hashtag #ff. Celui-ci a été utilisé durant la campagne pour François Fillon et parfois dans des sens différents (par exemple : follow friday).

sont définis comme y étant horizontaux, c'est-à-dire que l'on s'extrait des formes de communication verticale et hiérarchique (Cardon/Granjon, 2013) qui étaient les plus courantes dans la diffusion d'informations et de paroles politiques jusqu'à l'apparition d'Internet, puis des médias sociaux. Dans ce cadre, les indicateurs d'interactions peuvent expliquer la circulation des informations et de la parole politique et faire émerger des tendances, en termes de popularité, de partis ou de candidats lors des scrutins électoraux.

Cet article présente les principales données quantitatives de la tweet-campagne française. Nous mettons en exergue les activités des partis et des têtes de liste dans le but de dégager des indices pertinents de l'usage qui est fait de Twitter. Enfin, à la suite des premiers résultats obtenus sur l'usage, nous concluons cet article par la présentation d'éléments en lien avec la question de la circulation de l'information.

8.2 Quelques données sur la tweet-campagne

Dans cette partie, nous présentons les résultats issus de requêtes[103] informatiques qui illustrent l'usage du dispositif par les partis politiques et par les candidats. Notons que pour simplifier la présentation et la lecture, et puisqu'il s'agit d'illustrer les possibilités offertes par notre recherche, nous avons choisi de présenter uniquement les dix premiers résultats issus de l'exécution des requêtes. De plus, nous avons circonscrit notre démarche autour des tweets publiés sur les comptes des candidats et des partis. De ce fait, notre étude porte sur une observation effective de 150 464 tweets, publiée par l'intermédiaire des comptes de 616 candidats et de 47 partis et mouvements politiques. Le tableau ci-dessous expose les données globales suivant les indicateurs d'interactions.

Tableau 8–1 – Nombre d'indicateurs observés pour les candidats et les partis

	Données des candidats (616)	**Données des partis (47)**
Nombre de tweets	75203	75261
Nombre de #	75619	75007
Nombre de RT	39689	75203

103 Le terme « requête » désigne la commande en langage informatique nécessaire à l'exploitation des informations que nous cherchons à atteindre dans la base de données. Ceci dans le but de faire ressortir des réponses à nos questions dans la multitude de tweets qui ont été collectés. Les requêtes permettent donc d'extraire les données selon différents critères et de les ordonner pour en faciliter la lecture et l'exploitation.

Ce tableau résume nos observations au travers du nombre d'indicateurs présentés et permet d'ores et déjà de faire ressortir des pistes de réflexion et d'analyse quant à l'utilisation faite de *Twitter* par les protagonistes de l'élection de 2014. On constate tout d'abord, aussi bien pour les candidats que pour les partis, une appropriation et une maîtrise des règles et des codes du dispositif. A titre d'exemple, les niveaux d'usage fonctionnel des indicateurs d'interaction, comme la proportion de hashtags utilisés par rapport au nombre de tweets, sont presque équivalents. Le hashtag qui est l'indicateur le plus intégré, sert de signal d'interaction, mais il est également un potentiel générateur de nouvelles via sa logique de diffusion dans le réseau social.

L'autre indication intéressante est la fréquence du retweet. Pour les partis, on observe qu'ils correspondent au nombre de tweets publiés par les candidats. Nous pouvons ainsi supposer que les partis ont principalement servi de relais aux messages émis par les candidats, en agissant comme une sorte d'amplificateur de la parole émise par leurs favoris-candidats dans les différentes circonscriptions. Quant aux candidats, les RT sont moins importants et laissent supposer qu'ils ont davantage utilisé *Twitter* comme un outil d'expression directe envers les autres utilisateurs. Leur usage est donc plus dans une logique de production que de relayeurs d'informations. Il faut également noter qu'en mai 2014, l'indication « a retweeté » suivant le nom d'utilisateur n'était pas encore mise en place par *Twitter*. Il était donc difficile de pouvoir précisément différencier les tweets des RT. Les outils informatiques ont permis de faire cette différenciation dans notre corpus.

1.1.1 Résultats sur les partis politiques

(i) Partis les plus actifs

Nous avons ici entrepris de connaître le nombre de tweets global par parti politique ayant soumis au moins une liste à cette élection. Cette requête nous a permis de mettre en avant les partis qui ont le plus twitté et qui, en conséquence, ont été les plus actifs sur la plateforme *Twitter* durant la période où s'est opérée notre collecte.

Tableau 8–2 – Extrait : Nombre de tweets global par parti

Nom du parti	**Nombre de tweets**
EELV	9725
UDI-MODEM	9335
PS – PRG	6791
UMP	6683

Nom du parti	**Nombre de tweets**
Parti Pirate	5536
Nous Citoyens	5280
Front de Gauche	4242
Nouvelle Donne	4065
FN	3381
Parti Européen	2634

Les résultats montrent qu'EELV (Europe Écologie Les Verts) a été le parti le plus actif avec 9725 tweets durant cette période. Les listes rassemblant l'UDI et le Modem ont des données sensiblement équivalentes. Plus globalement, dans les dix premiers résultats de ce tableau, nous retrouvons les partis majeurs de la vie politique en France, mais également des formations moins connues qui ont su saisir le scrutin et la puissance du canal de communication pour étendre leur notoriété. C'est notamment le cas de « Nous Citoyens », de « Nouvelle Donne » ou encore du « Parti Pirate ».

Concernant les deux « leaders » du tableau, nous avons corrélé nos résultats avec la « vie des partis ». Cette nécessaire contextualisation de l'environnement permet de mieux analyser la plasticité des frontières entre vie réelle et présence virtuelle. Concernant EELV, la forte mobilisation sur *Twitter* peut s'expliquer comme une réaction à une situation délicate pour le parti écologiste[104]. En effet, le mois précédent cette élection, de fortes divergences ont miné les rapports entre les chefs de file du parti où s'opposaient alors une ligne portée par Cécile Duflot (qui a quitté ses fonctions de ministre et recherche une autonomie par rapport au PS) et une autre défendue par Jean Vincent Placé, partisan du maintien du lien avec le parti vainqueur des élections présidentielles de 2012. Twitter a servi de chambre d'écho et de sphère d'interaction et de débat.

Concernant l'UDI-Modem, une explication résulte de la naissance récente (novembre 2013) de l'alliance entre les deux partis représentés par François Bayrou (Modem) et Jean-Louis Borloo (UDI). L'objectif clairement affiché était de mettre en œuvre un partenariat politique pour les Européennes de 2014 devant

104 Desmoulières, R. B. (2014, June 14). Les chemins de Duflot et Placé se séparent. *Le Monde.fr*. Consulté le 15 octobre 2015, URL : http://www.lemonde.fr/politique/article/2014/06/14/les-chemins-de-duflot-et-place-se-separent_4438226_823448.html

se poursuivre pour les Régionales, voire les échéances nationales[105]. Ainsi, la forte participation sur *Twitter* peut s'expliquer, par la recherche d'une reconnaissance en tant que formation politique majeure en regard de l'expérience des deux formations sur la scène politique nationale.

Concernant l'usage des tweets par les partis, le graphique suivant représente le pourcentage de tweets publiés par chacun des dix partis observés durant la période d'observation.

Figure 8.1 – Nombre de tweets par parti

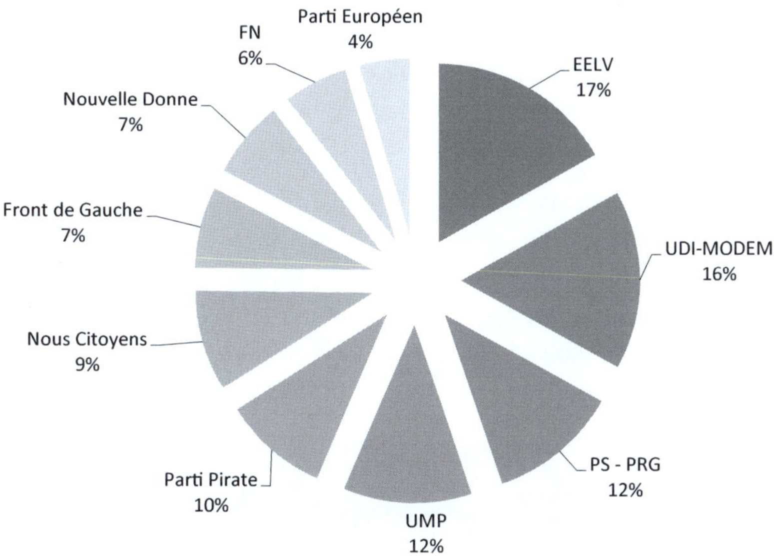

Au travers de cette illustration, nous pouvons constater que deux partis se détachent dans la fréquence d'usage, EELV et l'UDI-Modem. Les partis traditionnels de la vie politique française (PS et UMP) suivent ce duo dans une proportion équivalente. Ces deux partis disposent d'une organisation et d'une structure établie et ont été parmi les premiers à s'engager sur les réseaux sociaux, à l'image de la campagne de Ségolène Royal en 2007. Puis, nous pouvons voir que le Parti Pirate, jeune mouvement politique (fondé en 2009) reposant en large partie sur

105 Borloo et Bayrou alliés dans L'Alternative. (2013, November 5). Consulté le 15 octobre 2015 : http://www.lefigaro.fr/politique/2013/11/05/01002-20131105ARTFIG00597-borloo-et-bayrou-allies-dans-l-alternative.php

les problématiques soulevées à la suite du développement d'Internet, arrive en cinquième position. Ensuite, viennent d'autres formations, dont deux fondées en 2013 et issues de différents débats à gauche et à droite de l'échiquier politique que sont Nouvelle Donne et Nous Citoyens. Concernant ces trois derniers partis (Parti Pirate, Nouvelle Donne et Nous Citoyens), nous supposons qu'ils ont saisi l'opportunité d'une prise de parole dans l'espace public que constituent les dispositifs sociotechniques. Les partis plus importants et traditionnels ayant eux un accès plus aisé aux grands médias, dont la télévision, pour faire entendre leur voix et servir de mégaphone.

Enfin, il est intéressant d'observer que le Front National a publié près de trois fois moins de tweets que les partis les plus actifs. Pourtant, celui-ci, nous le savons à présent, a réalisé un excellent résultat électoral. *De facto*, la seule présence ou l'usage intensif d'un dispositif comme *Twitter* ne suffit pas à remporter des élections.

(ii) Partis ayant fait le plus de retweets

Au travers de cette requête, nous avons cherché à quantifier le nombre de RT réalisé par les comptes des différents partis présents à l'élection. D'une certaine façon, nous avons ici interrogé les usages des partis. En effet, l'utilisation d'un RT est tributaire d'une certaine maîtrise des codes et normes en vigueur sur le dispositif et démontre également une certaine forme d'appropriation du dispositif.

Tableau 8–3 – Extrait : Nombre de retweets par parti

Nom du parti	**Nombre de retweets (RT)**
EELV	9720
UDI-MODEM	9330
UMP	6981
PS – PRG	6679
Parti Pirate	5528
Nous Citoyens	5272
Front de Gauche	4239
Nouvelle Donne	4056
FN	3381
Parti Européen	2634

Les résultats montrent qu'à l'image des requêtes sur le nombre de tweets, c'est le parti EELV qui a été le plus actif dans les RT, suivi par l'UDI-Modem. L'UMP et l'alliance PS –PRG se partageant la troisième place avec sensiblement le même nombre de RT.

L'élément intéressant dans cette observation est le constat que nous avons pu faire en comparant le nombre de tweets (voir le tableau 1) et de RT. Nous observons qu'une grande partie des tweets émis par chaque parti sont en réalité des RT. Ceci est d'autant plus visible lorsque l'on compare les tweets et les RT du compte officiel du Front National et du Parti Européen, car le nombre de chacun d'entre eux est identique.

En complément de notre analyse, le graphique suivant illustre les proportions du nombre de RT de chaque parti au cours la période observée.

Figure 8.2 – Répartition des retweets sur les 10 premiers partis du corpus

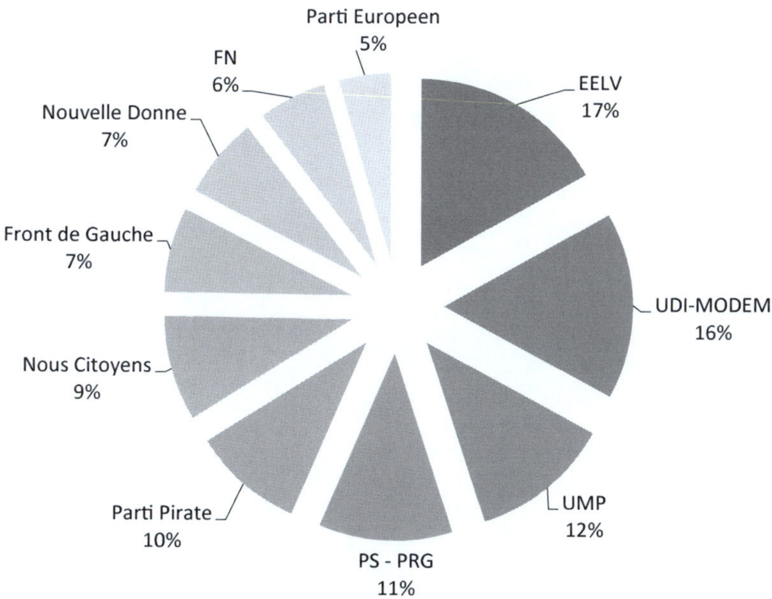

Au travers de ce graphique, nous constatons que la répartition des formations politiques est identique à celle précédemment présentée concernant le nombre de tweets. De la même manière, les proportions d'utilisation de RT correspondent également. La différence entre le nombre total de tweets et de RT étant proche, cela explique que les proportions ne changent pas.

Ainsi, les comptes officiels des partis sur *Twitter* serviraient principalement à soutenir les publications de leurs candidats. Nous supposons qu'ils agissent comme des comptes servant à fédérer les utilisateurs/citoyens afin de leur permettre de retrouver les comptes des candidats qu'ils ne suivent pas forcément et, comme nous l'avons indiqué précédemment, de servir de relais afin de faire écho aux messages de leurs candidats.

(iii) Hashtags les plus utilisés par les partis

Cette requête vise à connaître le nombre de hashtags que les partis représentés ont utilisés durant la collecte de tweets. Ainsi, nous nous sommes intéressés à une intégration plus générale de *Twitter* comme élément incontournable de la communication politique en fonction de la valeur ajoutée que peut constituer l'ajout d'un hashtag dans la publication d'un tweet.

Tableau 8–4 – Extrait : Popularité des hashtags par parti

Nom du parti	**Hashtag le plus utilisé**	**Nombre d'occurrences du hashtag**
EELV	#ee2014	3403
PS – PRG	#notreeurope	1990
EELV	#eelv	1488
UDI-MODEM	#ep2014	1271
Nouvelle Donne	#reprendrelamain	1090
Nous citoyens	#ee2014	1020
PS – PRG	#ep2014	944
UDI-MODEM	#leseuropeens	933
UMP	#ump	743
UMP	#europeennes2014	743

Le tableau *supra*, nous indique que le hashtag le plus utilisé par le parti EELV est « ee2014 » (3403 fois au cours de l'observation). Ce même parti se retrouve également en troisième position avec le hashtag de la formation « eelv », utilisé 1488 fois.

On constate que les principales formations politiques ont utilisé plusieurs hashtags durant notre période d'observation, c'est le cas pour le PS-PRG, l'UMP et l'UDI-Modem, qui trustent ainsi les premières places du nombre de placements de hashtags dans leurs tweets. Nous pouvons également voir comment des formations moins importantes de prime abord ont su efficacement utiliser cet outil offert par le dispositif pour accroître leur visibilité sur *Twitter*. C'est le cas pour Nouvelle Donne et Nous Citoyens.

8.3 Les résultats concernant les candidats

(i) Candidats les plus actifs sur Twitter

À la suite de ces premiers résultats, nous avons recentré notre attention sur les candidats. La requête suivante a consisté à mettre en lumière la participation effective de chacun des candidats observés. Nous avons extrait le nombre exact de tweets postés par chaque candidat dans l'objectif d'établir une hiérarchie dans la présence et la participation de chacun d'entre eux. Cela nous a permis de répondre à la question : quel compte de candidats est le plus actif durant la période observée ? Et donc, quel est celui qui a le plus tweeté ? Nous avons ainsi obtenu un classement complet de la participation des candidats dont les dix plus importants sont présentés dans le tableau suivant.

Tableau 8–5 – Extrait : Nombre de tweets envoyés par chaque candidat

Identifiant du candidat	**Nombre de tweets**
Louisdegouyon (Parti Européen)	2028
Jsherpin (EELV)	1827
Bdelgendre (Nous Citoyens)	1823
Relf_PP (Parti Pirate)	1270
M_GHISALBERTI (UMP)	941
JoelRoman75 (EELV)	926
Nrosenberg (Parti Pirate)	898
JulienAyoun (UDI-Modem)	864
DominiqueRiquet (UDI-Modem)	848
JB_COUTELIS (Nouvelle Donne)	833

On observe que c'est Louis de Gouyon Matignon, candidat de 23 ans, président du parti européen et considéré comme le porte-parole des gens du voyage qui a émis le plus de tweets, soit 2028 tweets durant la période observée. Notons que cet utilisateur est également tête de liste d'une formation présentant une unique liste en Ile-de-France.

Le second est Jean Sébastien Herpin, candidat de 45 ans, ingénieur en informatique et membre d'EELV, se définissant lui-même comme un « geek »[106] et candidat dans sur la liste de Clarisse Heusquin dans la circonscription Massif Central-Centre.

Béatrice Delgendre, candidate de 46 ans, de la formation Nous Citoyens, placée 17ème sur la liste conduite par Isabelle Bordry en Ile-de-France est la troisième candidate ayant le plus tweeté durant cette période. Ainsi, si nous considérons brièvement les trois candidats ayant le plus tweeté au cours de cette période, on constate qu'il existe différents profils d'utilisateurs. Ceci ne nous permet pas de typologiser un profil type d'utilisateur. Il apparaît, cependant, une caractéristique commune, qui est que ceux qui ont le plus tweeté ne sont pas des « personnalités » à forte notoriété et plutôt de générations acculturées au numérique et aux réseaux sociaux.

C'est pour cette raison, que nous nous sommes ensuite concentrés sur la participation des têtes de liste dans l'objectif de connaître leur place dans la liste des candidats ayant le plus tweeté au cours de la période. Le tableau ci-dessous présente les résultats que nous avons obtenus pour les dix premières têtes de liste.

Tableau 8-6 – Nombre de tweets envoyés par les dix candidats têtes de liste les plus actifs

Identifiant du candidat	**Nombre de tweets**
christineboutin (Force Vie)	703
Corinnelepage (Europe Citoyenne)	637
Josebove (EELV)	424
nadine__morano (UMP)	381
MLP_officiel (FN)	138
f_philippot (FN)	132
JLMelenchon (FdG)	129
Harlemdesir (PS-PRG)	85
BriceHortefeux (UMP)	85
MAlliotMarie (UMP)	39

106 http://jsherpin.fr/, consulté le 14 août 2015

Le premier élément, en comparaison avec ce qui a été précédemment énoncé, est que le nombre total de tweets publiés par le premier candidat tête de liste, ici Christine Boutin, est inférieur au nombre de tweets publié par le dixième candidat du tableau 5. Ce qui indique une utilisation plus importante de l'outil par les candidats non tête de liste. Ainsi, si l'on compare les deux premiers de chaque tableau, on constate qu'il y a une différence proche du triple dans la publication de tweets. Ceci nous permet de mettre en évidence le fait que les candidats disposant d'une faible notoriété utilisent *Twitter* au service de cette dernière. Le graphique présenté ci-dessous illustre cette différence dans la production de tweets, où l'on constate la faible production des candidats têtes de liste par rapport à l'ensemble des tweets observés.

Figure 8.3 – Proportion des tweets publiés par les candidats et les têtes de liste, par rapport au nombre de tweets observé

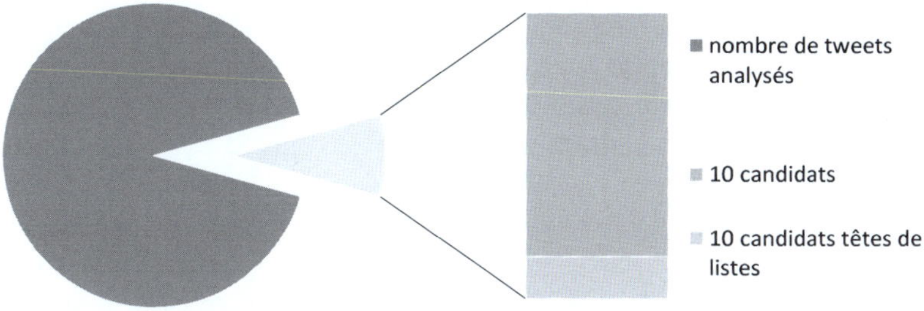

(ii) Candidats ayant fait le plus de retweets

Par l'intermédiaire de cette requête, nous avons cherché à connaître la fréquence de RT des différents candidats. Ceci permet de comprendre l'usage que font les candidats de l'outil *Twitter*, et principalement de l'un des indicateurs permettant d'introduire une relation avec d'autres utilisateurs, le retweet. Le RT étant une manière de faire « écho » à un message précédemment publié. Le croisement de ces données peut également s'avérer efficace puisqu'une mise en lien avec le nombre total de tweets de l'utilisateur nous permet de savoir quelle est la part de sa production personnelle d'information et le relais qu'il peut faire à d'autres. Notons toutefois que le RT peut être agrémenté d'un commentaire prenant différentes formes (critique, précision, etc.) et devenir à son tour une source d'information. Le tableau, ci-dessous, présente les résultats pour les dix candidats ayant fait le plus de RT.

Tableau 8-7 – Extrait : Nombre de retweets par candidat avec son parti

Identifiant du candidat	Nom du parti	Nombre de RT
bdelgendre	Nous Citoyens	1557
Relf_PP	Parti Pirate	788
DianVatlo	Nouvelle Donne	714
JulienAyoun	UDI-MODEM	708
DominiqueRiquet	UDI-MODEM	670
JoelRoman75	EELV	646
CecileMonnier	Nouvelle Donne	590
JB_COUTELIS	Nouvelle donne	568
louisdegouyon	Parti Europeen	549
M_GHISALBERTI	UMP	538

Nous pouvons observer que l'utilisation du RT représente une part plus ou moins importante de la participation sur *Twitter* selon les candidats. Ainsi, on peut constater que l'utilisateur bdelgendre a plus de 80 % de ses publications qui sont en fait des RT là où le candidat louisdeguyon a un peu plus de 25 % de ses publications qui sont des RT. Cependant, comme nous l'avons précisé précédemment, les profils de ces deux candidats sont différents, puisque louisdeguyon est également tête de liste du Parti Européen dont il est le principal acteur. De plus, nous pouvons constater, par rapport aux résultats précédents, l'apparition de nouveaux comptes de candidats, comme celui de DianVatlo, qui souligne le fait que certains candidats ont utilisé le dispositif *Twitter* principalement en soutien et en relais de messages d'autres utilisateurs.

Puis sur le même modèle que pour les autres requêtes, nous avons recherché le nombre de RT de chaque candidat tête de liste, dont les résultats sont présentés dans le tableau suivant. Nous précisons que nous n'avons pas pu obtenir les résultats concernant Harlem Désir et Brice Hortefeux pour cette requête.

Tableau 8-8 – Nombre de tweets par candidat tête de liste avec son parti

Identifiant du candidat	Nom du parti	Nombre de RT
christineboutin	Force Vie	520
corinnelepage	Europe Citoyenne	328
nadine__morano	UMP	326
josebove	EELV	255

Identifiant du candidat	Nom du parti	Nombre de RT
JLMelenchon	FDG	27
MAlliotMarie	FN	10
MLP_officiel	FN	9
f_philippot	UMP	8
Vincent_Peillon	PS	1

Au travers de ces résultats, nous retrouvons un classement de participation sensiblement identique au classement obtenu lorsque nous avons recherché le nombre de tweets de chaque candidat. Cependant, il convient de mettre en relation les deux résultats (nombre de tweets et de retweets) pour donner du sens à ces derniers. Nous constatons ainsi que la proportion d'utilisation de RT n'est pas la même pour tous les candidats, ce qu'illustre le graphique ci-dessous. Ainsi, les quatre premiers présentent une proportion de RT par rapport à leurs tweets de plus de 50 %, jusqu'à 85 % pour Nadine Morano. Ces résultats rejoignent nos remarques précédentes sur les RT. Pour les autres candidats, les proportions ne sont pas aussi importantes, ce qui de notre point de vue révèle une utilisation particulière de *Twitter*, compte tenu de leur qualité de tête de liste. En effet, cela montre qu'ils ont principalement utilisé le dispositif pour transmettre à leurs *followers* des informations, des avis, des remarques, etc. d'une manière à être, à leur tour, retweeté par les autres utilisateurs.

Figure 8.4 – Nombre de tweets comparé au nombre de RT pour les candidats tête de liste

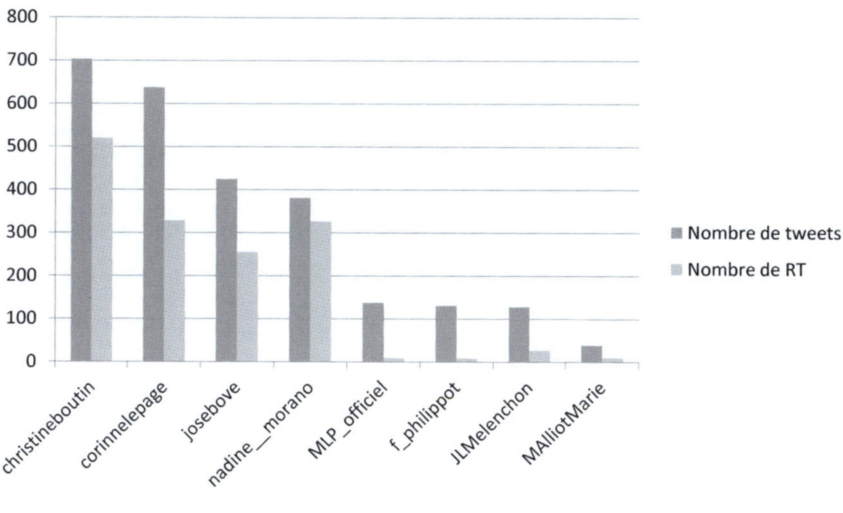

Pour cette observation, nous pouvons donc considérer qu'il existe différentes logiques à l'œuvre dans la production de tweets. En effet, si certains candidats sont dans une logique de production, c'est-à-dire que leur nombre de tweets est supérieur à leurs nombres de RT, d'autres candidats s'inscrivent dans une logique de reproduction, lorsque le nombre de RT est supérieur au nombre de tweets. De la même manière, on peut observer que les candidats ayant le plus tweetés au cours de la période, sont ceux qui font un usage assez important du RT.

8.4 Appréhender la circulation de l'information sur Twitter, exemple et perspectives

L'étude de l'usage qui est fait du dispositif par les candidats et les partis nous permet de mieux mesurer leur implication, leur intégration et leur appropriation des réseaux socionumériques. Pour compléter notre étude, nous avons souhaité présenter les prémisses d'une étude élargie en complément de l'analyse des utilisateurs et qui concerne les messages et leur circulation. Avant de présenter ces résultats, nous tenons à rappeler qu'il s'agit ici d'une expérience dont les résultats restent hypothétiques dans leur interprétation. En effet, bien que nous ayons suivi une méthodologie stricte dans la recherche sur les données, leur signification reste à éprouver dans la durée. Ainsi, l'exploitation de la base de données nous offre la possibilité de faire ressortir des variables concernant – comme dans le cas présenté dans les lignes suivantes – le nombre de RT de tweets de chaque candidat et des partis qu'ils représentent. Ainsi, après avoir observé l'activité des candidats et des partis, nous nous sommes interrogés sur le nombre de fois où un tweet de candidat avait été retweeté. L'objectif étant de voir, en fonction d'une production initiale et mesurée dans les résultats précédents, comment ces messages sont repris par les utilisateurs, et donc quels étaient les candidats têtes de listes, puis les partis, qui avaient été les plus retweetés.

Tableau 8–9 – Nombre de RT de tweets de chaque candidat tête de liste

Nom du candidat	**Parti**	**Nombre total de RT de tweets**
Marine Le Pen	FN	14678
Florian Philippot	FN	10917
Jean-Luc MELENCHON	Front de Gauche	6846
Aymeric Chauprade	FN	4490
François Asselineau	UPR	3379

Nom du candidat	**Parti**	**Nombre total de RT de tweets**
Corinne Morel-Darleux	Front de Gauche	3045
Nicolas Dupont-Aignan	Debout la République	2958
Louis ALIOT	FN	2578
Denis Payre	Nous citoyens	2444
Yannick JADOT	EELV	2290

On constate ici qu'en ce qui concerne les dix premiers candidats têtes de liste, quatre d'entre eux appartiennent au FN. Les deux premiers de cette liste étant respectivement Marine Le Pen, présidente du FN et son vice-président, Florian Philippot. On retrouve en troisième position Jean-Luc Mélenchon qui présente néanmoins un écart assez important en nombre de RT par rapport aux deux premiers candidats cités. Cette place importante occupée par les deux premiers candidats du FN s'illustre plus nettement dans le graphique ci-dessous (figure 9).

Figure 8.5 – Pourcentage de RT de tweets de chaque candidat tête de liste

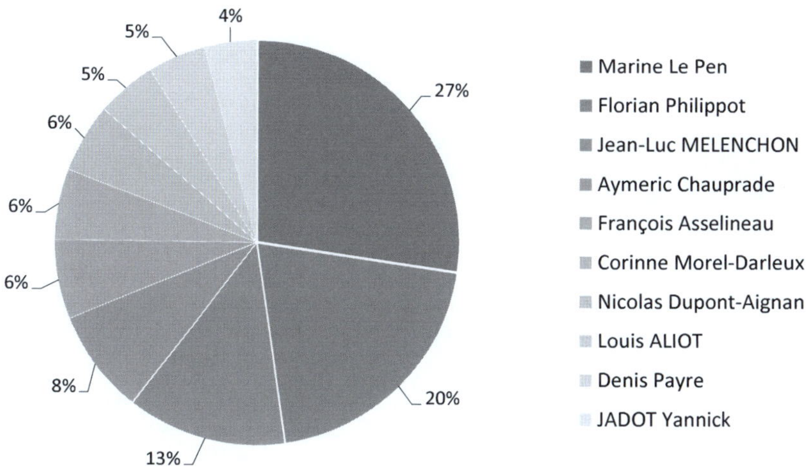

Concernant les trois premiers résultats de cette liste, nous pouvons mettre en rapport ce résultat avec les résultats précédents qui portaient sur la part de RT dans la production de tweets (cf, tableau 8 et figure 8). On peut ainsi constater que, si l'on croise ces deux résultats, les candidats qui s'inscrivent dans une logique de production de tweets semblent correspondre à ceux qui sont le plus retweetés sur *Twitter*. De plus, nous pouvons ici constater deux éléments. L'un concerne la forte représentation de candidats du FN, quatre sur dix, ce qui souligne le fort écho dont leurs tweets ont bénéficié sur *Twitter*. L'autre est l'absence de candidats issus des partis tels que l'UMP ou le PS.

De la même manière, nous avons voulu faire ressortir le nombre de RT de tweets des partis politiques. Comme nous l'avons vu précédemment, les tweets des partis sont principalement effectués dans le but de soutenir les prises de parole des candidats sur le terrain. Ils ont en effet réalisé un nombre de RT qui couvre sensiblement la totalité de leur publication.

Tableau 8–10 – Nombre de RT de tweets de chaque parti

Partis	**Nombre total de RT de tweets**
FN	47169
Front de Gauche	16934
UMP	12629
EELV	12520
UDI-MODEM	12224
PS – PRG	8422
Nous citoyens	5020
UPR	4234
Debout La Republique	4001
Force vie	3483

De ce fait, si nous prenons l'exemple du FN et que nous croisons les différents résultats obtenus, nous pouvons constater qu'ils ont publié 3381 tweets dont l'intégralité était des RT de leurs candidats. Ces 3381 tweets ont, à leur tour, été retweetés 47169 fois. Ce qui nous permet de constater la forte mobilisation de relais d'opinion, d'adhérents ou de sympathisants concernant ce parti. Comme nous pouvons le remarquer dans le graphique ci-dessous, le pourcentage obtenu par le FN sous cet angle est considérable.

Figure 8.6 – Pourcentage de RT de tweets de chaque parti

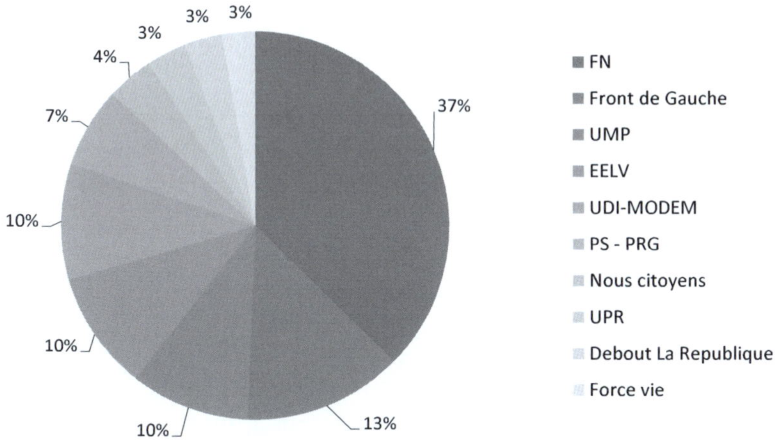

Pourtant, si la chambre d'écho produite par *Twitter* est importante, il n'en est pas de même pour les autres partis. Si nous considérons EELV, qui est le parti ayant produit le plus de tweets sur la période (9725), on constate que le pourcentage de RT s'inscrit dans la moyenne des dix premiers partis les plus retweetés. Ceci nous permet de considérer qu'il n'existe pas de relations entre une production importante de tweets et le relais qui peut en être fait sur *Twitter*.

8.5 Conclusion

Un des enjeux de notre recherche a été de comprendre et de mesurer le niveau des relations entre les acteurs et d'offrir des interprétations permettant de comprendre et de définir les mécanismes mis en œuvre sur les dispositifs socionumériques qui font que la communication prend forme entre les élus, les citoyens et les médias. Dans une perspective parallèle, au travers d'un article portant sur l'usage de *Twitter* par les journalistes, G. Brachotte et A. Frame (2015) notaient que : « *même si l'usage et le "style Twitter" (Thimm/Dang-Anh/Einspänner ; 2011, 2012) semblent plutôt passifs qu'actifs, les journalistes maîtrisent les codes du dispositif sociotechnique et l'utilisent à la fois comme outil de veille, de diffusion et d'interaction, mais à des degrés différents* ».

Figure 8.7 – Correspondance entre l'activité déclarée sur Twitter et les fonctions principales du dispositif (Brachotte/Frame, 2015)

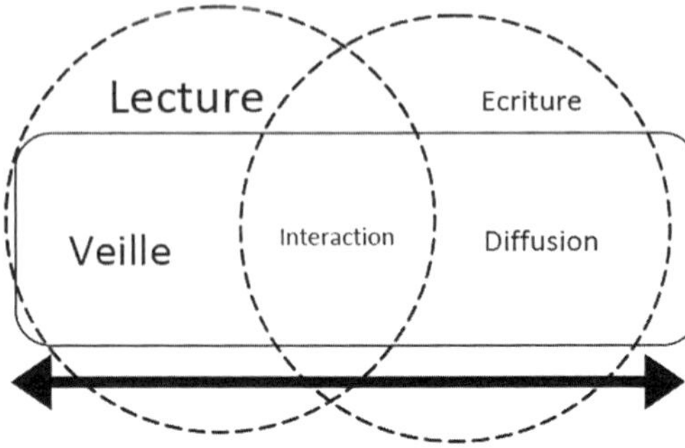

Il pourrait en être de même pour l'usage qui est fait du dispositif par les personnalités politiques, tout au moins c'est ce que nous avons tenté de mettre en évidence à travers nos analyses réalisées sur le corpus de tweets collectés et plus spécifiquement par le biais de la maîtrise de ce que nous avons choisi de nommer des indicateurs d'interactions (soit les codes propres au dispositif qui permettent d'entrer en relation avec d'autres utilisateurs). Ainsi, en observant l'utilisation des hashtags, mention et retweets, nous retrouvons ces mêmes mécanismes entre logiques d'écriture et de lecture, de veille et de diffusion (fig.3).

Figure 8.8 – Processus d'interaction au travers des fonctions principales du dispositif

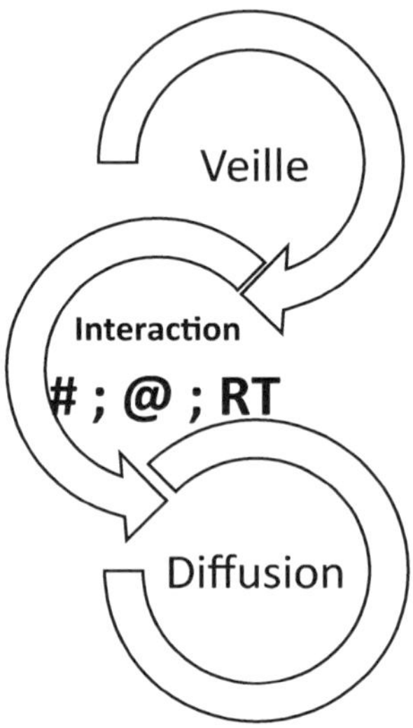

Parallèlement à cet usage des plateformes par les politiques, nous pouvons observer et constater que les échanges entre ces derniers et les individus se développent sur les réseaux socionumériques. De ce fait, la question se pose de savoir s'il existe des mécanismes, des formes courantes d'une « ritualité numérique » (Lardellier, 2013), qui régissent l'usage des réseaux sociaux, et donc de *Twitter*, par les politiques. Ces ritualités seraient identifiables par l'échange, le partage et l'appropriation de symboles autour de l'élaboration des tweets[107], et donc des interactions présentes dans le dispositif, dans un processus de co-construction et de coproduction de celui-ci par les utilisateurs (fig.4).

Figure 8.9 – Interactions et ritualités dans les échanges sur Twitter dans le cadre du projet TEE2014

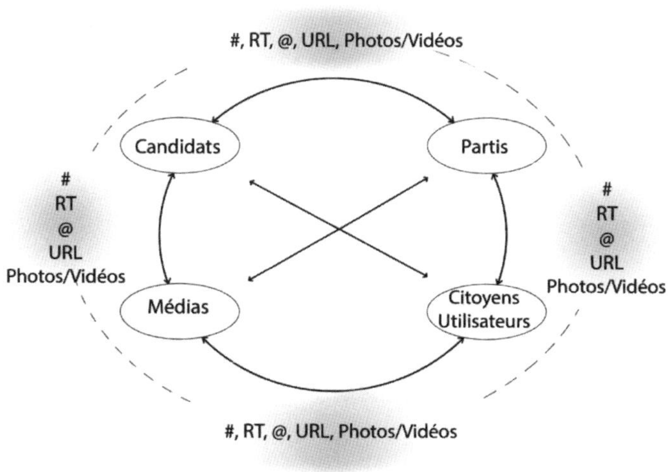

107 *Les tweets peuvent ainsi prendre différentes formes et renvoyer à d'autres médias présents sur le Web. Concernant les formes, on peut rapidement évoquer l'utilisation de mots ou expressions accolés à un hashtag (dont l'utilisation est indiquée par un « # » et qui permettent de se référer à un thème ou un sujet précis). Il est également possible de s'adresser à un autre utilisateur de la plateforme en inscrivant dans le message le symbole « @ », ce qui permet de rechercher l'interaction avec un autre utilisateur. De la même manière, le retweet (RT) est une façon de faire écho à une information que l'on souhaite partager. De plus, on peut insérer des liens de type adresse URL ou encore des images et/ou des vidéos. Enfin il est également possible de tweeter sans utiliser de marqueurs spécifiques (tels que #, @, etc.), en respectant la limite des 140 caractères en insérant une citation, posant une question ou juste en donnant son avis.*

Le rapprochement à la dimension rituelle du dispositif est lié au fait que, pour se propager, un message « tweet » est dépendant du nombre de retweets. De la même manière, pour qu'un sujet soit discuté, il faut qu'il soit inscrit sous un hashtag afin de que se fédère, sous ce hashtag, un nombre plus ou moins important d'utilisateurs qui s'interpellent entre eux au moyen d'une mention. Ainsi, l'analyse de ces différents types d'échanges, au travers de l'utilisation de symboles imposés par le dispositif dont les utilisateurs se sont appropriés les codes qui constituent des indicateurs d'interactions, permet de comprendre comment s'organise l'usage des partis et des candidats et comment les informations circulent. Enfin, ces analyses nous permettent de voir comment les candidats se sont organisés pour apparaître sur les réseaux sociaux, de voir quelles stratégies ont été adoptées pour mettre en scène leur vie quotidienne et aussi politique, et ainsi nous aide à découvrir leur choix en matière d'« identwité » (Mercier, 2013), choix qui s'effectue dans le cadre d'un usage normatif du dispositif lié à leur rôle d'acteurs politiques, mais aussi en fonction des possibilités d'expressivité individuelle qu'offre *Twitter*, où l'identité numérique qui est construite au travers de la présence dans un dispositif vient renforcer l'identité réelle au travers de jeux d'exposition de soi (Allard/Vandenberghe, 2003).

L'utilisation de ces symboles, partagés par la communauté des utilisateurs, permet de s'offrir une meilleure visibilité sur le réseau. En effet, dans le processus qui accompagne la construction de son identité en ligne, l'utilisateur est amené à partager différents marqueurs de la reconnaissance identitaire (Cardon, 2008). L'appropriation des règles et des codes du dispositif permet de compléter sa démarche d'intégration symbolique dans un dispositif. Ainsi, utiliser le hashtag ou le RT par exemple, participe d'une certaine manière à compléter le dispositif identitaire et à s'inscrire dans la communauté des utilisateurs « initiés ». Cette observation a joué un rôle important dans l'objectif d'analyser la construction des relations en ligne au sein du dispositif *Twitter* puisque nous nous sommes appuyés sur ces codes partagés pour extraire des données sur l'usage du dispositif par les politiques.

Cette recherche exploratoire nous a permis d'interroger le contenu des comptes des utilisateurs, candidats et partis lors de l'élection européenne de 2014. Les constats opérés nécessitent encore de larges analyses comparatives qui pourront confirmer ou infirmer notre propos. Toutefois, bien qu'il s'agisse d'une phase d'expérimentation, notre premier bilan nous indique qu'il est possible d'exploiter ces données afin de produire des bases quantitatives sur lesquelles peuvent se fonder nos analyses.

Ainsi, si les requêtes considérées individuellement proposent des résultats qui n'apparaissent pas forcément significatifs pour répondre aux différentes questions que nous avons posées au début de cet article, c'est par l'intermédiaire des opérations de croisements et d'interprétations que nous parvenons à mettre en lumière les pratiques et les usages des candidats. Par exemple, si l'on essaie de mesurer le degré d'intégration des pratiques liées à l'usage de *Twitter* au sein des différentes formations politiques, il est possible de croiser les données d'utilisation des différents moyens d'échanges du dispositif. Pour ce faire, on peut extraire les données relatives à l'utilisation globale de *Twitter* par un parti (nombre de tweets), et de les confronter à l'ensemble des tweets contenant un RT ou un hashtag. Le résultat de cette analyse permet de mettre en lumière l'usage qui est fait de *Twitter* par la formation politique. Par exemple, un niveau élevé des indicateurs d'interactions indiquera une appropriation importante du dispositif alors qu'un niveau faible pourra révéler une pratique balbutiante ou une méconnaissance de l'outil pouvant entraîner un mésusage.

De plus, les résultats mettent en évidence une participation inégale des partis (en nombre de tweets et de RT). Concernant les RT réalisés par les partis, ils ont principalement servis à soutenir les publications des candidats. De plus, sur les données observées à propos des candidats, on constate que les candidats à faible notoriété ont eu un usage de *Twitter* plus important que les candidats têtes de listes. Cela souligne la place de *Twitter* comme un outil servant à la prise de parole dans l'espace public élargi par les dispositifs socionumériques. Enfin, le croisement des données entre tweets et RT des candidats têtes de liste, nous indique que les usages sont différents, entre logique de production et de reproduction. Pour les partis, nous pouvons constater que le FN, qui a remporté cette élection en France, est largement en tête sur le dispositif. Cela peut apparaître comme un marqueur pertinent de la popularité. Cependant, cette popularité « virtuelle » ne se confirme pas si l'on regarde le second de ce classement qui est le Front de Gauche. Aussi, si nous constatons que la popularité sur *Twitter* peut refléter une tendance, elle n'est nullement représentative d'une probabilité de résultat et peut au mieux, se rapporter au résultat d'un sondage d'opinion. Toutefois, ce n'est pas dans cet objectif que nous réalisons cette étude qui vise davantage à comprendre les utilisations faites du dispositif *Twitter* et son rôle potentiel dans l'échange d'informations et donc, en conséquence dans les stratégies de communication mises en œuvre par les candidats et les partis.

Références bibliographiques

Allard, L., & Vandenberghe, F. (2003). « Express yourself ! Les pages perso ». *Réseaux, no 117*(1), 191–219, consulté le 19 juillet 2014, URL : http://www.cairn.info/revue-reseaux-2003-1-page-191.htm

Brachotte, G., Frame A., L'usage de *Twitter* par des journalistes politiques français : un outil de recomposition de la pratique professionnelle journalistique, *in* Liénard, F., & Zlitni, S. (Eds.). (2015). *La communication électronique: enjeux, stratégies, opportunités*. Limoges, France: Lambert-Lucas, DL 2015.

Breton P., « Interactivité, intériorité, et lien social démocratique », *Cliniques méditerranéennes*, 2007/1 n° 75, p. 27–45. DOI : 10.3917/cm.075.0027, p. 28

Breton P., *Le culte de l'Internet*, Paris, La Découverte « Sur le vif », 2000, 128 pages. ISBN : 9782707133021. Lien : http://www.cairn.info/le-culte-del-internet--9782707133021.htm

Cardon, D. (2009). Le design de la visibilité. *Réseaux, n° 152*(6), 93–137.

Cardon, D., & Granjon, F. (2013). *Médiactivistes*. Paris, France: Sciences Po, Les Presses, DL 2013.

Flichy, P. (2008). « Internet, un outil de la démocratie ? » – *La Vie des idées*. Consulté le 18 juillet 2015, URL : http://www.laviedesidees.fr/IMG/pdf/200801147_internet.pdf

Lardellier P., « Introduction. Ritualités numériques », *Les Cahiers du numérique* 2013/3 (Vol. 9), p. 9–14. DOI 10.3166/LCN.9.3–4.9–14ù

Licoppe, C., Cudicio, R., & Proulx, S. (2011). Présence connectée" au travail : les usages de la messagerie instantanée, le genre des "questions rapides" et l'économie morale de la "contribution. *ethnographiques.org*, (Numéro 23 – décembre 2011). Consulté le 25 octobre 2015, URL : http://www.ethnographiques.org/2011/Licoppe,Cudicio,Proulx

Mercier, A. (2013). « L'identité des journalistes. Étude des profils *Twitter* des journalistes français et anglophones ». Consulté le 3 aout 2015, URL : http://doi.org/10.13140/2.1.3639.0088

Caja Thimm, Jessica Einspänner-Pflock & Mario Anastasiadis,
University of Bonn

9. Twitter during the 2014 European Elections in Germany – Analyzing politicians' campaigning strategies

Abstract

This chapter examines the different tweeting strategies of the electoral candidates in Germany during the EU election 2014. Based on 8219 tweets, quantitative and qualitative analyses are carried out in order to find out about the ways EU candidates convey their messages on Twitter. Are classic forms of campaign communication still central to political advocates in the social media world or have these been extended or substituted by new digital forms of communicating?

9.1 Mediatized politics and the European elections

Since the advent of the internet questions of its potential impact on all levels (micro, meso, macro) and all actors have been at the very core of many studies in political and communication science (Kamps, 2007, Strömbäck, 2008, Schweitzer & Albrecht, 2011, Vowe, 2013). In this respect, the appropriation of the internet by political parties and politicians, especially as a tool for refining political campaigning strategies, is becoming more important. Even though "there is still a lively debate about whether e-campaigning replicates the patterns of offline campaigning or contributes to a fundamental change in the democratic discourse, there is little doubt that the internet is increasingly important as a tool for political parties and candidates to provide information and stimulate political engagement" (Vergeer, Hermans, Sams, 2011, 478).

Whereas in the pre-internet era, political campaigning clearly was unidirectional (Norris, 2000), social media can serve as a technical infrastructure in which the communicative gap between the political sphere and the voters can be diminished (Carpentier, 2011, Bürger and Dorn-Fellermann, 2014). Besides, social media enhance the political actors' possibilities to bypass traditional mass media gatekeepers and to address potential voters directly (Lilleker and Jackson, 2011). Also, social media like Facebook and Twitter play a crucial role for the ongoing personalization of politics and political campaigning (Enli and Skogerbø, 2013). More and more political actors utilize these digital tools as an enhanced possibility to address voters and to communicate key messages, especially during times of elections. Social media have become integrated parts of professionalized and strategic political campaigning communication.

Since the very first one in 1979, the EU elections have always attracted less voter participation and media attention than national elections (de Vreese et al., 2006, Giebler and Wüst, 2011). For many voters the EU election serves very much as a proxy for national issues (Marsh, 1998, Brunsbach et al. 2011). Reif and Schmitt (1980) even characterize the EU election as a second order election, because a lot of voters go to the polls with a view to national issues rather than European politics. This also refers to a periodically diagnosed lack of public legitimation of European politics, actors and institutions, not least reflected in low election turnouts in a lot of the EU member states. This deficit is also linked to the fact that more and more decision-making processes are being transferred from national parliaments to the European level, whereas the formation of political will is still closely linked to national issues in the respective EU member states. This also leads to widespread ignorance among voters regarding supranational party alliances as well as most politicians on the EU level, who remain almost unknown to a major part of the European public sphere. Against this backdrop, all political actors on the EU level require increased communication efforts to inform voters, to get in dialogue, and to justify itself.

The high fragmentation of the European public sphere in terms of language, cultural, or economic differences, means that political campaigning is challenging for political actors and institutions alike. Social media like Facebook or Twitter raise questions as to whether the digital public sphere online can bring forth a supranational European public, or if the digital public sphere should rather be described as an even more fragmented accumulation of several coexisting national publics.

The internet, and especially social media, provide political actors with communication tools, which can help to bridge the gap between EU politics and voters. The aim of this paper is to assess patterns of politicians' Twitter activity in terms of political campaigning by drawing on distinct qualitative results gained from the analysis of politicians' tweets.

9.2. Twitter and political campaigning

By keeping up with their responsibility to create public interest and to inform about political decision making processes, politicians using social media contribute to making EU politics more tangible (Bieber and Schwöbel, 2011). The micro blogging platform Twitter has become an increasingly relevant tool for political campaigning. Its use can be analysed as part of an ongoing process of modernization and mediatization of political communication in general and campaigning in particular, in which new communication technologies are being adopted by candidates, parties, political communication strategists and voters. As Bruns and Highfield (2013) state, the adoption of social media is a global trend for national, regional, local and international elections alike. Social media visibility nowadays is one key factor to electoral success.

Whereas in the US, Barack Obama already started using Twitter during his 2008 campaign, Europeans have taken more time to adopt Twitter for political communication activities. During the EU election 2009 for example, Twitter was only rarely used for political campaigning. Within five years, Twitter has gained more and more relevance as a tool for monitoring and participating in the public discourse among politicians and citizens alike. It is Twitter's affordance of rapid information distribution and the possibility it gives users to share news and arguments that are influencing the digital discourse. Drawing on existing research (Larrosa-Fuentes, 2015, Thimm et al., 2016) it can be assumed that especially during times of election politicians use Twitter as a "public stage" in order to advertise their campaign goals. They do this strategically, for example by uploading pictures from campaign events or tweeting personal status updates and thus appear to be approachable.

In Germany, about 56 million people (79,5 % of the population) use the internet (Frees and Koch, 2015) and 67 % of them (36 million) actively use social networks (Bitkom, 2013).

Compared to other EU countries, especially France or Spain, Twitter in Germany has not yet carved out its niche, even though public and media attention is growing and Twitter usage seems to increase continuously. Regarding Twitter usage statistics, however, it seems difficult to gain reliable numbers since different measurements and methods exist. Different studies lead to varying results ranging from 3.8 million users (Statista, 2013) to 10 million (b4p, 2014). Another study distinguishes active and passive users (ARD/ZDF 2014, n=1434). According to this, 9 % (5 million) of the German internet users connect to Twitter less than once a week and 5 % (2,8 million) use the micro blogging platform every week. The second method by which Twitter usage is measured is based upon the analysis of the Twitter users' account information and aggregates the given information about time zone, language and location. However, as it is not mandatory to specify such information when using Twitter, the respective data is fragmentary. This leads to significantly lower results regarding user statistics from these studies compared to the aforementioned ones. For example, calculations from PeerReach (2013) state a Twitter penetration rate for Germany of 1 %, which is only around half a million active Twitter users.

A closer look at the adoption of Twitter by German politicians with a mandate for the National Parliament in 2013 (around 10 months before the EU election) reveals that almost four fifths of Green Party members the parliament had a Twitter account (79,4 %), followed by The Left Party (65,3 %), the Free Democrats (61,3 %), the Social Democrats (50,7 %) and the Christian Democrats (39,7 %) (Fuchs, 2013) (Figure 1). This adds up to 328 politicians out of 620 members of the German Parliament in 2013 who use Twitter.

Figure 9.1: Twitter adoption in the German National Parliament in July 2013 in % (Fuchs, 2013, ©hamburger-wahlbeobachter.de)

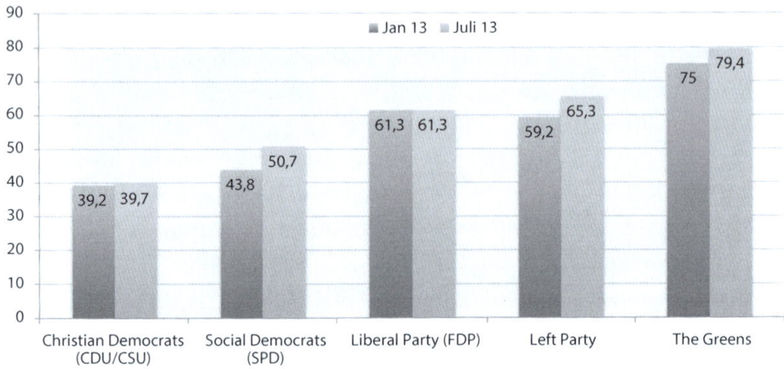

The numbers show that compared to the "average citizens" MEPs in Germany () can be regarded as more active Twitter users. Among German parliamentarians, the usage of the micro blogging platform as a tool for political campaigning seems common. Noticeable is that the EU Election, which took place in May 2014, only caused a marginal increase in the adoption of Twitter on the national level.

9.3 Analyzing campaign strategies of German EU-candidates on Twitter

The data of the present study consist of tweets sent by the German candidates during the 2014 European Election. They were collected three weeks before and one week after the EU election day (4th of May until 1st of June, 2014). This time frame was chosen in order to document not only tweets during the "hot" phase in the run-up to the election day but also during the following week when the election results are discussed on Twitter. Hence, the data do give some insights into the more general relation between Twitter as a communication tool and permanent campaigning.

The tweets were collected via Twitter's streaming and search APIs with the help of the open source solution SNFreezer (http://sourceforge.net/projects/snfreezer/). After the data collection, the tweets went through a process of data cleaning and were then analyzed using a combination of quantitative (SPSS) and qualitative tools (QDA Miner).

In the following section, we first give a quantitatively focused overview of the candidates' activity on Twitter during the election, before we finally turn to the qualitative analyses and assessment of their communication strategies.

9.3.1 German EU Politicians' Twitter activity

Altogether, 8.219 tweets were collected from a total of 106 German candidates, from which, however, only 68 were tweeting actively (see table 1 for an overview of the data obtained). Even though using Twitter nowadays is clearly more established among politicians than during the EU election 2009, there is still only a fraction of the German EU candidates who use it for campaigning purposes.

Tableau 9–1: Tweets collected during the EU Elections 2014 in Germany

Number of candidates in national corpus	1.103
Number of candidates on Twitter	108
% of candidates on Twitter	9,79 %
Number of candidates tweeting during period	68
% of candidates' accounts tweeting during period	62,96 %
Number of tweets sent by candidates	8.219
Average tweets per candidate tweeting	120,87

63 % of the German EU candidates owning a Twitter account were actively tweeting during the evaluation period. Candidates from the major parties were most active: The Christian Democrats (CDU) rank on top with 20 active candidates, the Social Democrats (SPD) and the Green Party both have 17 candidates tweeting actively, while the Free Democrats (FDP) have only four, the Left Party two and the extreme Right (NPD) only one candidate tweeting actively. This distribution of candidates' Twitter activity also reflected the parties' distribution of seats in the EU parliament, which was led by the CDU (29 seats), SPD (27 seats) and the Green Party (11 seats).

The results reveal that particularly the progressive and rather left-leaning parties, such as the Pirate Party, or the Green party, have been most active on Twitter during the EU campaign. However, in contrast to analyses of politicians' tweeting during the EU election 2009 in the Netherlands (Vergeer et al., 2011), our study shows that there is also a considerable number of politicians from the established or rather conservative parties, such as the Social or Christian Democrats, tweeting (see table 2).

Tableau 9–2: List of the top 10 German EU candidates based on the tweets sent during the election campaign.

Rank	Twitter account name	Candidate's name	Party affiliation	Total tweets sent
1	@anked	Anke Domscheit-Berg	Pirate Party	1.266
2	@JanAlbrecht	Jan Philipp Albrecht	The Greens	810
3	@DosOz42	Fotios Amanatides	Pirate Party	680
4	@kliehm	Martin Kliehm	Pirate Party	560
5	@Gilles_PPDE	Gilles Bordelais	Pirate Party	534
6	@EuropaJens	Jens Geier	Social Democrats (SPD)	385
7	@CarstenOvens	Carsten Ovens	Christian Democrats (CDU)	301
8	@RebHarms	Rebecca Harms	The Greens	274
9	@JuttaSteinruck	Jutta Steinbruck	Social Democrats (SPD)	227
10	@TerryReintke	Terry Reintke	The Greens	198

While all top candidates of the major parties were tweeting, namely David McAllister from the Christian Democrats (CDU), Martin Schulz from the Social Democrats (SPD), and Rebecca Harms from the Green Party, the top candidates of the smaller and more polarizing parties like the new (eurosceptic) party Alternative for Germany (AfD, Bernd Lucke) or the far right party NPD (Udo Voigt) did not tweet (although both of them had a Twitter account). Even though these parties were tweeting via their official party accounts (such as @ AfD_Bund) or had single candidates who tweeted (e.g. Jens Pühse from the NPD, also see below in section 3.2), these findings confirm the research of Vergeer et al. (2011) that fringe parties, especially the right wing, did not try to compensate their relatively low coverage in traditional mass media (airtime and newspapers) on Twitter. In this respect the smaller parties' top candidates still fail to use Twitter as an alternative way to bypass traditional gatekeeping mechanisms and to reach out for potential voters directly.

9.3.2 Patterns of politicians' Twitter usage during the European Election campaign 2014

The broader political context in which the EU election 2014 took place was marked by the financial crisis in parts of Europe and the general strengthening of Eurosceptic and anti-European sentiments. The election results in some countries reflected these tendencies by giving anti-European parties a majority of the votes: In France for example, the right-wing Front National came in first with 25 %, and in England, the anti-European party UKIP gained 27 % of the votes. In Germany, Eurosceptic and anti-European parties like the "Alternative for Germany" (AfD) and the right wing extremist National Party (NPD) stood for election but both failed in their goals, since only 7 % of the votes went to the AfD and 1 % to the NPD.

In the following paragraphs, we present findings from our qualitative analyses of the EU candidates' tweets, which point to consistent patterns of Twitter usage with respect to campaign communication. Hereby, we less focus on the candidates' topical contributions to EU politics but more on the strategies and mechanisms of their Twitter communication. Building on categorizations of traditional campaigning strategies but by taking into account the specifics of the micro blogging environment, the following categories of *Twitter campaigning* can be identified:

- Passive Twitter presence
- Informing & broadcasting
- On-the-scene and live-reportage
- Self-promotion
- Negative campaigning
- Creating mini-publics
- Interacting on the public Twitter stage
- Emphasizing and establishing supranational alliances

(1) Passive Twitter presence

A large number of the German EU candidates who had a Twitter profile were inactive and did not tweet at all during the evaluation period. Interestingly, the inactive or "alibi" accounts, often received tweets from other Twitter users nevertheless. One particularly interesting case is that of Alexander Graf Lambsdorff (@Lambsdorff), top candidate of the Free Democrats (FDP) and a well-known member of the European Parliament. Although this candidate has a Twitter profile he did not send a single tweet during the election campaign 2014, but received a lot of tweets in return: Within the four weeks evaluation period, 509 tweets were directly addressed to or mentioning @Lambsdorff. Apart from that, 114 tweets contain the hashtag #Lambsdorff and 712 tweets the keyword "Lambsdorff" (without #). The altogether 1335 tweets mentioning the politician's name (with or without the @- or #-operator) indicate that Lambsdorff is a key figure in German Euro-politics and hence a person of interest to the Twitter public. In fact, compared to the other 106 politicians in the data set, Lambsdorff is ranked amongst the top 10 German EU candidates receiving the most attention on Twitter although being the only one of them who did not send a single tweet during the corresponding period (see table 3).

Tableau 9–3: List of the top 10 German EU candidates based on tweets they received during the campaign

Rank	Twitter account name	Candidate's name	Party affiliation	Total tweets received
1	@MartinSchulz	Martin Schulz	Social Democrats (SPD)	15 923
2	@sven_giegold	Sven Giegold	The Greens	2 741
3	@SkaKeller	Ska Keller	The Greens	2 578
4	@JanAlbrecht	Jan Philipp Albrecht	The Greens	1 644
5	@TerryReintke	Terry Reintke	The Greens	1 404
6	@Lambsdorff	Alexander Lambsdorff	Free Democrats (FDP)	1 335
7	@davidmcallister	David McAllister	Christian Democrats (CDU)	1 238
8	@RebHarms	Rebecca Harms	The Greens	1 149
9	@bueti	Reinhard Bütikofer	The Greens	900
10	@MarkusFerber	Markus Ferber	Christian Democrats (CSU)	293

When looking at the tweets addressing Lambsdorff, it becomes evident that they often refer to the politician's offline campaigning activities. Media accounts or journalists report about Lambsdorff's statements in interviews or during campaign events, such as the party congress of the FDP (marked with #fdpbpt – "FDP party congress"). Affiliated party accounts or fellow politicians praise Lambsdorff in their tweets and often underline their arguments with multimedia content, e.g., @OlliLuksic and @FDP_Saar tweeted on May, 11th 2014:

> "Alexander Graf Lambsdorff at the Party Congress in Dresden, Germany: serious, competent, sympathetic [inserted link to a YouTube clip from the party congress]".

In addition, citizens comment on the politician's public appearance by using rhetorical devices such as polemic or sarcasm:

> "Populist #Lambsdorff warns against populists [inserted link to a news website]" (@pukki01, tweet sent 12 May, 2014)
> "This #FDP demonstrates every day that they quite rightly got thrown out of the Parliament! [inserted link to a news website] #TTIP #Lambsdorff" (@DerRotschopf, tweet sent 15 May, 2014)

These brief examples show that even if a politician does not use his or her Twitter account actively for tweeting, just having a Twitter profile appears to be an important aspect of a digital campaigning strategy. Even if a politician does not use Twitter to actively communicate or engage in discussion, a Twitter account allows for being virtually present and connected and therefore "networkable" within the political Twitter sphere. In this respect a Twitter account is at least a symbolic representation of a politician – which is particularly important during election times – and enhances the politician's visibility within the digital public sphere.

(2) Informing & Broadcasting

One of the candidates' most favorite Twitter activity patterns is the distribution of information relating to their campaign activities and events. This finding is in line with studies on politicians' Twitter usage in regional or national elections (Broersma and Graham, 2012, Thimm et al., 2014, 2016). Twitter is mainly used as a tool to distribute news and information. Politicians broadcast information to their followers in order to show that they are actively involved in the campaign and to stay visible in the digital public. Here is a typical example of a tweet sent by a politician of the Social Democrats (*@Groote, Matthias Groote).*

Figure 9.2: Tweet of Matthias Groote "Brief pit stop in the office. Refilling the material. After that to Dötlingen to the AfA regional conference north [inserted link to Foursquare]"

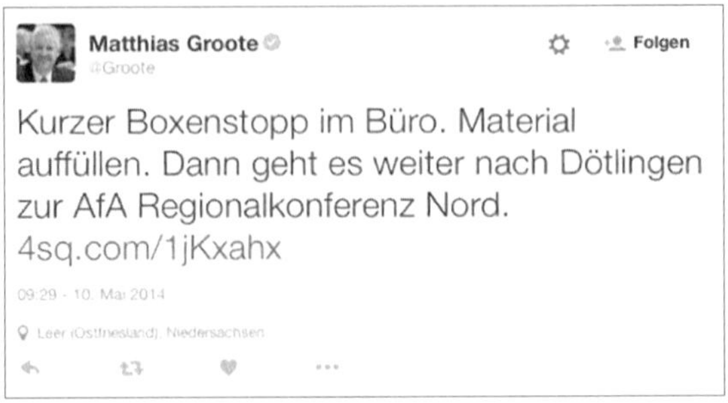

Overall, this pattern shows that some politicians use Twitter as a broadcasting medium, or as Vergeer et al. (2011, p. 469–497) put it, "the social medium devolves into a traditional uni-directional medium, not so much in its technical architecture but in its actual use". It seems that the candidates' Twitter accounts are predominantly used for "informing citizens, and not for being informed by citizens, or to communicate" (ibid.). As Thimm et al. (2012, 2016) show, this broadcasting strategy can also be described as the *topical-informative* tweeting style. This style refers to an activity pattern which is characterized by the intense usage of hyperlinks to external sources and a lack of mentioning or retweeting to others via the @- and RT operators. The information sharing and broadcasting style represents one of most frequently used patterns of political campaigning, as it is closely linked to self-presentation and self-staging as a politician. Consequently, the broadcasting style tends to come with a rather low proportion of interaction or dialogue with the voters.

(3) On-the-scene and live-reportage

Closely linked to the information broadcasting pattern, a lot of candidates employ a strategy of "live reporting" from campaign events or other occasions they choose to tweet about. This on-the-scene and live-reportage pattern reflects Twitter's relevance as a real time medium for instant communication. This strategy is characterized by the expansion of the limited text format of 140 signs by including links, videos or pictures from external sources. Due to these system options, politicians often illustrate their activities by adding photos to their tweets. One particular effect of this pattern is to allow backstage insights in real time. The tweet displayed below give a good example for this strategy. It was posted by Jean-Claude Juncker, leading candidate of the German conservative group, and shows himself and his counterpart from the socialist group, Martin Schultz, waiting for the TV duel to start:

Figure 9.3: Tweet of Jean-Claude Juncker before a TV duel

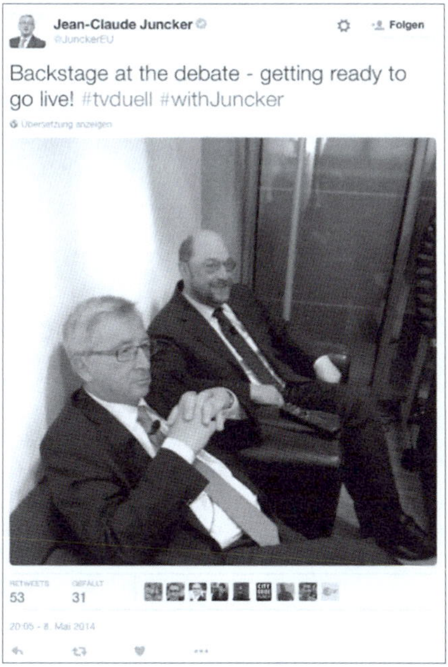

However, the pattern is not limited to live reporting. It also includes tweets, which suggest an almost-live participation in the politicians' actions, as another example of Jean Claude-Juncker visiting a construction site in Athens demonstrates:

Figure 9.4: Tweet of Jean-Claude Juncker from a construction site in Greece

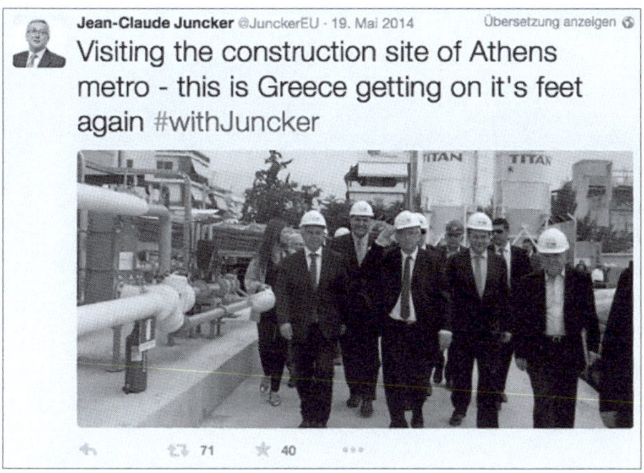

Although such insights are unquestionable elements of strategically planned communication, they reveal perspectives, which the traditional media usually do not offer, not least because of journalists deciding if such a piece of information is newsworthy. In this respect, the on-the-scene and live-reportage pattern very much represents the empowerment of political actors in terms of bypassing traditional journalistic gatekeepers.

(4) Self-promotion

Another Twitter campaigning strategy, directly connected to Twitter's functionality and the politicians' empowerment to bypass traditional media gatekeepers, can be described as politicians' self-promotion. A lot of research suggests that this pattern is among the most commonly used during election campaigns (Grant et al., 2010, Larsson & Kalsnes, 2014).

> "Now in Potsdam together with @schierack_cdu and Christian Ehler (MEP) at the opening event on the municipal- and #Europeanelection! Thank you for the invitation:) #CDU" *(@davidmcallister, David McAllister, Christian Democrats, tweet sent 5 May, 2014)*

Self-promotion via Twitter allows politicians to communicate political information as well as personal insights into their private lives in order to present themselves in a particularly attractive way, underlining their proximity with voters and, for example, trying to appear young and active:

Figure 9.5: Self-promotion strategy of a German EU candidate (Christian Democrat) showing his sport activity.

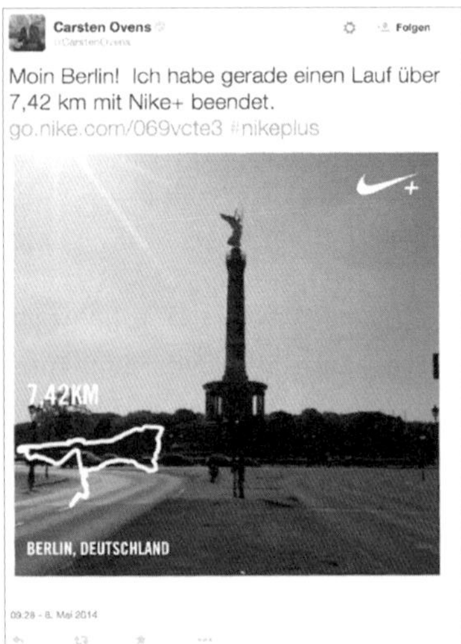

Additionally, their campaign teams use self-promotional tweets for retweeting, as an example from the Green politician Terry Reintke shows:

> "RT @RasmusAndresen: 2 end-fifties on the future of Europe. Good that there are young candidates like @SkaKeller @JanAlbrecht @TerryReintke"

Self-promotion on Twitter is an element of the increasing personalization of politics, which has been observed for more than a decade (Holtz-Bacha, 2006). Personalization, however, must not be mistaken for a higher amount of insights into the politicians' private lives. In fact, private tweets were rarely found in the dataset. On the one hand, this can be interpreted as an approach by the politicians to stick to the professional and 'factual' side of the campaign by mainly referring to political issues. On the other hand, this implies that insights into private events like for example family matters, are not part of the self-definition and self-presentational style of German politicians – at least in the Twitter public sphere.

(5) Negative Campaigning

Another strategy put forward by politicians as well as their parties' accounts on Twitter is that of negative campaigning. In some political cultures negative campaigning is a frequently used means of putting the political opponents to the test, but it is, particularly in the German political sphere, a two-sided sword: Many voters don't like offensive criticism during election times (Walter et al., 2013). In the present dataset two main strategies of negative campaigning can be identified: The first has a focus on political content and is strongly connected to political issues, while the second is a strategy to offend the political opponent more on a personal level.

Figure 6 shows an example of the first category, in which negative campaigning gets aligned with concrete issues and political positions. In this tweet sent by the account of the German Green Party, it is argued that Martin Schulz (Social Democrats) overtly acts as if he was against the Transatlantic Trade and Investment Partnership (TTIP), although his parliamentary group actually voted for it. The issue of the TTIP has been a very important and controversial discussion topic in Germany during the EU election. It was mainly the smaller and partially left-leaning parties who were against the trade partnership, while the bigger, conservative and liberal parties put arguments forward favoring TTIP. For the first mentioned, it thus became an important task to use their Twitter presence (which slightly exceeds that of the conservative parties in quantitative terms, see section 3.1 above) in order to argument against the politically more powerful.

Figure 9.6: Tweet of the Green Party criticizing Martin Schultz

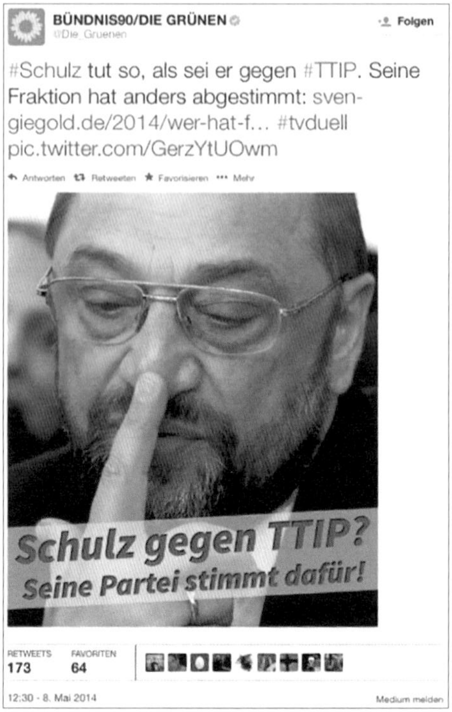

The second way of performing negative campaigning on Twitter can be seen as a strategy to subtly offend the political opponent on a more personal level (and less on the topical level): In a tweet sent by Daniel Caspary, EU candidate of the German conservatives (CDU) on May 14, 2014, a photo upload of a wilting green plant is hashtagged with the word "green" in different languages and spellings (including English and German). While the tweet content itself does not overtly relate to politics, however, seen in the context of 1) an EU candidate from an opposing party 2) tweeting this picture 3) during the election campaign it has to be interpreted as a political statement. In fact, subtle information in public communication is characterized by being deniable (Boyd and Marwick, 2011, 23), and the present example is definitely refutable.

Figure 9.7: Subtle negative campaigning on Twitter

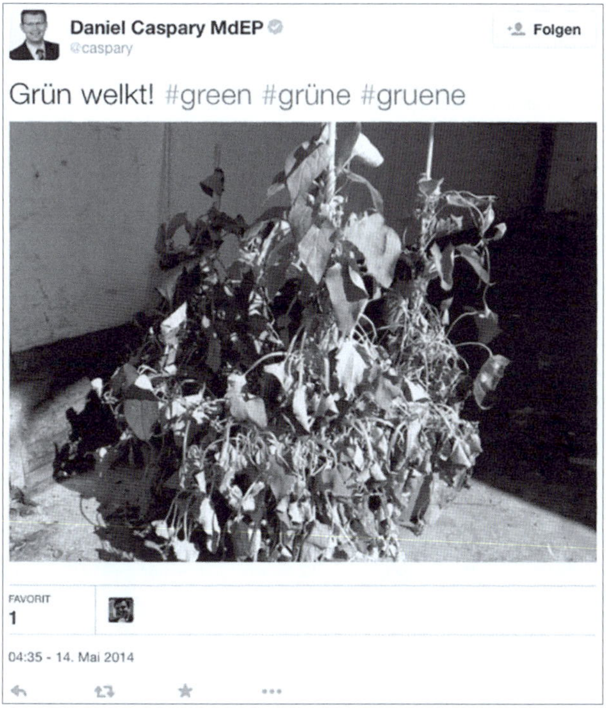

When we compare our findings from the EU campaign with the data collected in national or regional election campaigns in Germany (i.e., "Bundestagswahl 2013"), we find less negative campaigning in the EU data set. It seems that mutual polemic or sarcastic comments among politicians are given a more meaningful stage on the national level than on the "higher" – and maybe more anonymous European level, where factual political content seems to be more relevant than personal sensitivities. This, however, has to remain a speculation as the qualitative assessment of tweets categorized as negative campaigning cannot be outweighed with a mere quantitative argument.

(6) Creating Mini Publics

The many changes in political communication not only allow for optimistic perspectives on more political participation in all parts of the world (Tufekci and Wilson, 2012), they also point to a new challenge for politics and politicians: audiences are not easily reached anymore, as traditional mass media have lost their dominating role within public discourse. On the contrary, many claim there has been a fragmentation of the public sphere (Webster and Ksiazek, 2012). In more recent work, however, it is argued that any over-generalization might not grasp the real activities of participants in the digital public and argue for a more situated and contextualized approach (see contributions in Einspänner-Pflock et al., 2014). If we see opinion formation and debates as a central quality of political participation and political engagement, we have to regard smaller publics, such as a hashtag discussion thread, as a part of the public sphere and not as a second rate public, which has fallen victim to fragmentation (Thimm, 2016). Consequently, more and more media scholars call for a 'rethinking of the public sphere' (see contributions in Lunt and Livingstone 2013).

As Thimm (2016) suggests, the digital public sphere can best be conceptualized as a network of "online mini-publics" which must be understood as 'a group of online users referring to a shared topic in a publicly visible and publicly accessible online space over a period of time, by means of individual activities such as textual or visual contributions' (p. 227). These mini-publics can be differentiated from the perspective of initiation into (1) user-initiated mini-publics, (2) event-driven mini-publics, (3) commercially launched mini-publics and (4) institutionally/politically launched mini-publics. In terms of political campaigning the event-driven and institutionally launched mini publics are of higher relevance, because it is an integral part of politicians' Twitter usage to try to generate online mini publics, in which potential voters can discuss and interact. Such politically-driven mini publics are mostly hashtag based. The hashtag functions as the informative technical element, which leads to certain topics and discussions in the Twitter sphere. It is the main networking element that not only connects topics but also the people participating in the respective discussions, i.e. in hashtag-communities (Thimm et al., 2016, 179). Hashtag-based mini publics can serve as political echo chambers in which a certain argumentation or a certain political position is presented and discussed. Online mini publics are intended to have a persuasive effect on the potential voters, to advocate the party's issues and to drive the campaign. For this reason, forming hashtag-based mini publics is an integral part of the political campaigns issue management strategy, and in this respect another effort to set the agenda on Twitter.

As Martin Schulz was a endorsed by the German Social Democrats (SPD) during the EU elections 2014 with their party account @spdde, Twitter support was an expected consequence. Some hashtags were especially created for the campaign. The most prominent example is #nowschulz. This slogan was often put at the end of a tweet of Schulz (or his campaign team) and should motivate or active his Twitter followers for his campaign. This hashtag does not have a relevance for EU politics but is only used as a marker for Schulze's campaign.

> "RT @spdde: Germany is well off only when our European partners are well, too. #howareyou #nowschulz http://t.co/CWAbc9g3Ee" *(@MartinSchulz, Social Democrats tweet sent 22 May, 2014)*
> "RT @spdde: @MartinSchulz is right: Europe needs a perspective for the middle-class #nowschulz #howareyou. http://t.co/E6Ap9egLYN" *(@MartinSchulz, Social Democrats, tweet sent 22 May, 2014)*

Another case is the hashtagging strategy of the new party Alternative for Germany AfD. The party's main Twitter account @AfD_Bund served as their campaign organ on Twitter, with which they tried to make themselves part of the Twitter EU sphere. In the tweets sent from the party account the hashtag #AfD was often used together with the hashtag #EP2014 – one of the official hashtags related to the EU elections 2014 (acronym for "European Parliament 2014"). #EP2014 was also one of the most recognized hashtags during the EU election as it has been not only widely on Twitter but also in other online or offline contexts (e.g. in advertisements for the TV debate or in election posters). By linking this important hashtag with "their own" hashtag, the AfD tried to place their topics (mainly Eurosceptic arguments) in the Twitter sphere and to form a "hashtag family". The party thus formed a mini public within the broader context of the digital public created around #EP2014.

(7) Interacting on the public Twitter stage

Creating mini-publics on Twitter is also part of candidates' "public staging" strategy, which refers to their positive self-presentation in the digital public sphere. Two major forms of "Twitter staging" can be found, of which the first can be seen as a way of presenting oneself without an apparent substantive context, while the second is linked to political argumentation.

The following example, illustrating the first type of Twitter staging by candidates, shows a sequence of tweets referring to a TV interview with Alexandra Thein, EU candidate from the Free Democrats, sent and/or retweeted by the participating actors of the TV discussion.

Figure 9.8: A sequence of acknowledgements for participating in a political TV discussion, sent and retweeted by the presenter and the politician alike.

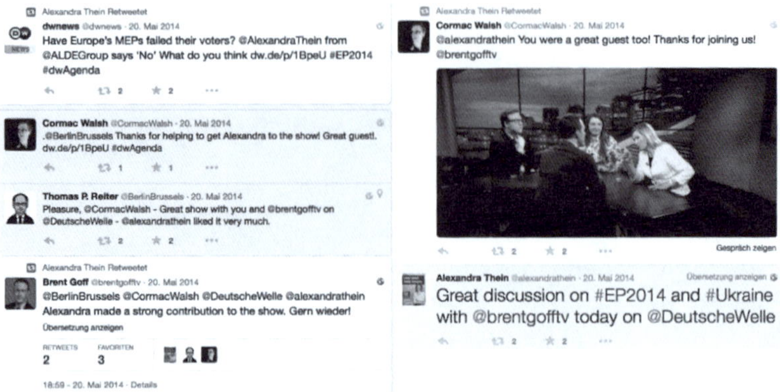

These kinds of allegedly 'empty conversations', which are full of self-praise and acknowledgements, are to be seen as part of the politicians' self-presentation strategy – formed between authorities (e.g., journalists or other politicians) within an exclusive mini-public but meant to be "followed and judged by their voters" (Einspänner-Pflock et al., 2016: 62). Thus, politicians emphasize their belonging to a certain "exclusive" group or network of people.

The second form of Twitter staging by politicians can be found in tweets that form conversations or discussions, which are settled around a certain politically relevant topic. They are mostly contextualized (and thus found by other users) by a hashtag or the @-operator, as can be seen in figure 9. In the depicted Twitter conversation, two opposing politicians discuss aspects of the European social system, i.e. youth unemployment. The discussion also refers to one of the TV debates during EU election between Juncker and Schulz (see above (4)) and is tagged with #tvduell. On the one hand, the @-operator serves as the 'conversational anchor' between the two discussants as the tweets thus become technically linked to their accounts and the two politicians become notified upon a reply. On the other hand, this conversation is opened up to the larger interested Twitter-community around the TV debate as it is tagged with #TVduell. The hashtag here serves as a contextual marker.

Figure 9.9: EU candidates Jens Geier (Social Democrats) and Ulrich Beul (Christian Democrats) discussing aspects of the European social system on Twitter

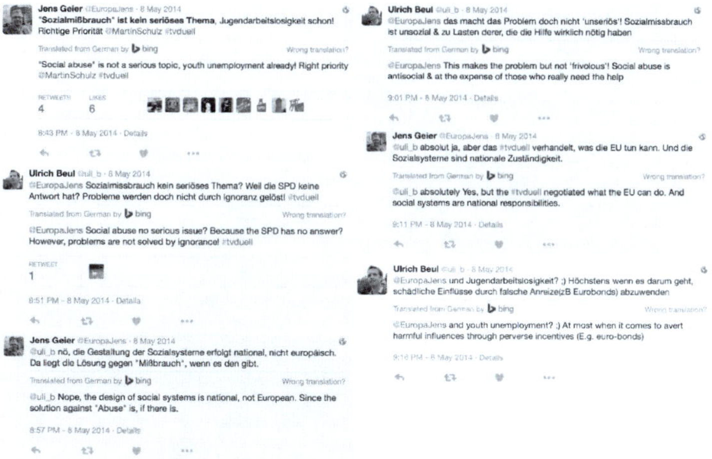

The politicians' strategy of connecting and presenting oneself within these kinds of content-rich discussions on Twitter does not have a mere networking function as in the exclusive mini-publics but is more focused on presenting arguments related to a certain political question. By keeping up the conversation, the politicians are also able to show their commitment and respect towards their discussants and simultaneously give insights into their own political positions.

(8) Emphasizing and establishing supranational political alliances

Political alliances between parties or parliamentary groups on the European level are not usually very well known to many voters since people feel more tied to their respective national parties and politicians. The desire to strengthen those alliances might be a reason why some politicians mark their supranational party alliance explicitly in their tweets. In the present dataset, we found candidates of the same supranational alliance who often relate and link to each other by using @-mentions, retweets, hashtags, linked multimedia content or even emoticons in order to emphasize their closeness. Rebecca Harms from the Green Party for example did a campaign event where she went from Berlin to Brussels on a boat, accompanied by other "green" politicians from the Czech Republic and from Finland.

Figure 9.10: Tweet of the Rebecca Harms, "This time it worked out again with the boat! From Brussels off to Berlin with @SkaKeller @odrejliska @HeidiHautala"

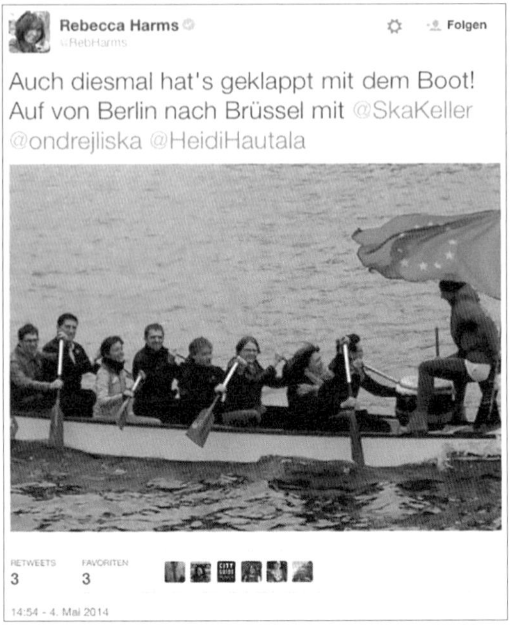

Also the top candidate of the left, Gabi Zimmer, who started her Twitter account just one month before the EU elections 2014, used Twitter in order to strengthen supranational "leftist" alliances by retweeting or directly addressing party members of other European leftist parties:

> "Strong message of @tsipras_eu Alexis Tsipras, candidate of European Left #TellEurope May 15, 2014" *(@Gabi_Zimmer, the left, tweet sent 15 May, 2014)*

The endorsement of like-minded parties is often mutual, as a tweet from the Greek leftist Alexis Tsipras shows:

Figure 9.11: Tweet of Alexis Tsipras, call to vote for the Left Party

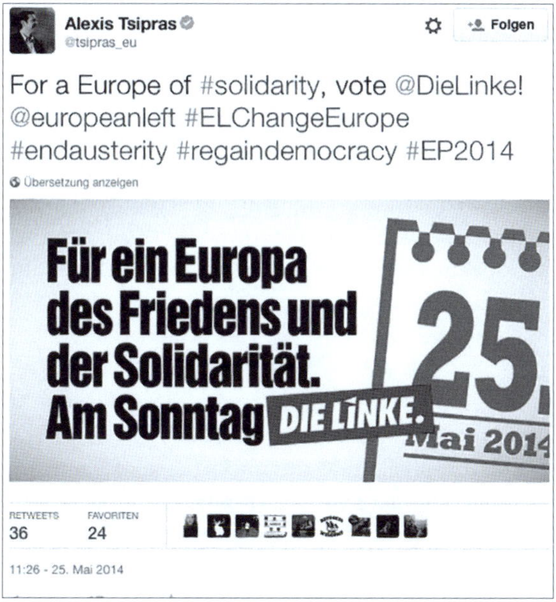

Politicians choose this strategy to strengthen their network and to appear highly engaged within their party's activities.

9.4 Conclusion and Outlook

As a part of the mediatization of political communication Twitter becomes more and more an established tool for strategic communicative purposes, especially during times of election campaigns. While Germany is still lagging behind other European countries regarding Twitter usage for political communication, it seems that the politicians' usage of the microblogging tool in this regard is becoming more differentiated. What is striking is that politicians do not seem to use Twitter much to get into dialogue with citizens and voters, but predominantly to broadcast their messages to their followers and for self presentation. This leads to one of the most important consequences of social media usage within the framework of political campaigning: to bypass traditional media and journalistic gatekeepers. Social media indeed do set political actors free from structural and time-consuming limitations associated with traditional distribution channels and help them to avoid journalistic framing, for better or worse. For this reason, Twitter has become an integrated part of a strategically-organized communication environment online, which almost every political actor tries to benefit from. The more online publics grow, the more important it becomes for political actors to establish themselves within a communication infrastructure of their own, outside traditional media. Looking at Twitter in particular, future research needs to focus on the question in how intensively the microblogging platform is used and which of the patterns of political campaigning still remain relevant. One pattern of special interest is the on-the-scene and live-reportage pattern. The Twitter affiliated new application "Periscope", a live-reporting video tool, makes it seem very likely that these patterns will be of growing importance.

In terms of European politics there is still a special demand for political communication in the European public sphere – online and offline. For these reasons, EU related Twitter communication should also be analyzed outside electoral periods, but during political day-to-day-business and EU-wide crisis situations, for example like the increasingly difficult question of how EU countries deal with the growing number of refugees from the Middle East.

It does not seem very likely that the importance of Twitter will decrease in the near future, at least not as a tool for political campaigning. More research is needed to better understand in how far Twitter can play a specific role in the European online public sphere. In this context one of the most important challenges for future research will be to focus on Twitter's fragmentation into myriads of different online mini-publics.

References

Anastasiadis, Mario and Caja Thimm. 2011. Soziale Medien – Wandelprozesse sozialer Kommunikation. In Mario Anastasiadis and Caja Thimm (eds.), *Soziale Medien: Theorie und Praxis digitaler Sozialität*, pp. 5–15. Frankfurt, New York: Lang.

Best 4 Planning (b4p). 2014. http://www.futurebiz.de/artikel/b4p-studie-facebook-googleplus-twitter/

Bieber, Christoph, Schwöbel, Christian. 2011. Politische Online-Kommunikation im Spannungsfeld zwischen Europa- und Bundestagswahl. In Jens Tenscher (ed.), Superwahljahr 2009. Vergleichende Analysen aus Anlass der Wahlen zum Deutschen Bundestag und zum Europäischen Parlament, pp. 223–244. Wiesbaden: VS Verlag.

Bitkom. 2013. Soziale Netzwerke 2013. Dritte, erweiterte Studie Eine repräsentative Untersuchung zur Nutzung sozialer Netzwerke im Internet. https://www.bitkom.org/Publikationen/ *2013/Studien/Soziale-Netzwerke-dritte-erweiterte-Studie/SozialeNetzwerke_2013.pdf*

Boyd, Danah and Marwick, Alice. 2011. Social Privacy in Networked Publics: Teens' Attitudes, Practices, and Strategies. Presentation "A Decade in Internet Time: Symposium of the Dynamics of the internet and Society", Oxford, September 22, 2011. http://papers.ssrn.com/sol3/papers.cfm?abstract_id=1925128.

Bürger, Tobias and Dorn-Fellermann, Esther. 2014. Interaktion oder Partizipation – wo beginnt politische Partizipation im Netz. In Jessica Einspänner-Pflock, Mark Dang-Anh and Caja Thimm (eds.), *Digitale Gesellschaft – Partizipationskulturen im Netz*, pp. 41–61. Berlin: Lit.

Bruns, Axel, Highfield, Tim. 2013. Political Networks on Twitter. Tweeting the Queensland State Election. *Information, Communication & Society* 16(5).

Brunsbach, Sandra, John, Stefanie, Volkens, Andrea, Werner, Annika. 2011. Wahlprogramme im Vergleich. In Jens Tenscher (ed.), *Superwahljahr 2009. Vergleichende Analysen aus Anlass der Wahlen zum Deutschen Bundestag und zum Europäischen Parlament*, pp. 41–64. Wiesbaden: VS Verlag.

Carpentier, Nico. 2011. The concept of participation. If they have access and interact, do they really participate? *Communication Management Quarterly* 21: S. 13–36. Online http://www.costtransforming-audiences.eu/system/files/pub/CM21-SE-Web.pdf.

Einspänner-Pflock, Jessica, Anastasiadis, Mario, and Thimm, Caja. 2016. Ad hoc mini-publics on Twitter: Citizen participation or political communication? Examples from the German National Election 2013. In Alex Frame and Gilles Brachotte (eds.), *Citizen Participation and Political Communication in a Digital World*, pp. 44–67. New York: Routledge.

Enli, Gunn Sara and Skogerbø, Eli. 2013. Personalized campaigns in party-centered politics. Twitter and Facebook as arenas for political communication. *Information, Communication & Society* 16(5), 757–774.

Frees, Beate and Koch, Wolfgang. 2015. Internetnutzung: Frequenz und Vielfalt nehmen in allen Altersgruppen zu. Ergebnisse der ARD/ZDF-Onlinestudie 2015, *Media Perspektiven* 9/2015, 366–377.

Fuchs, Martin. 2013. Social Media in der Politik: 90 Prozent der Bundestagsabgeordneten nutzen soziale Netzwerke. http://www.hamburger-wahlbeobachter.de/2013/07/social-media-in-der-politik-90-prozent.html

Giebler, H. and Wüst, A. 2011. Campaigning on an Upper Level? Individual Campaigning in the 2009 European Parliament Elections in its Determinants. *Electoral Studies* 30 (1), 53–66.

Holtz-Bacha, Chistina. 2006. Personalisiert und emotional: Strategien des modernen Wahlkampfes. *Aus Politik und Zeitgeschichte* (APuZ), 7/2006, 11–19.

Kamps, Klaus. 2007. *Politisches Kommunikationsmanagement. Grundlagen und Professionalisierung moderner Politikvermittlung.*Wiesbaden: VS Springer.

Larrosa-Fuentes, Juan S. 2015. Twitter's Messages During a Governor Election: Abundance of One-Way, Top-Down and Auto- Referential Communications and Scarcity of Public Dialogue. Paper presented at the 65th annual conference of the International Communication Association, San Juan, Purto Rico.

Lilleker, Darren G. and Jackson, Nigel A. 2011. Elections 2.0: Comparing E-Campaigns in France, Germany, Great Britain and the United States. In Schweitzer, Eva Johanna and Albrecht, Steffen (eds.), *Das Internet im Wahlkampf. Analysen zur Bundestagswahl 2009*, pp. 96–117. Wiesbaden: Springer VS.

Marsh, Michael. 1998. Testing the second-order election model after four European elections. *British Journal of Political Science* 28 (4), 591–607.

Norris, Pippa. 2000. *A Virtuous Circle. Political Communication in Postindustrial Societies.* Cam- bridge: University Press.

PeerReach. 2013. 4 ways how Twitter can keep growing. http://blog.peerreach.com/2013/11/4-ways-how-twitter-can-keep-growing/

Reif, Karlheinz, Schmitt, Hermann. 1980. Nine Second-Order National Elections – A Conceptual Framework for the Analysis of European Election Results. *European Journal of Political Research* 8(1), 3–44.

Schweitzer, Eva Johanna and Albrecht, Steffen (eds.). 2011. *Das Internet im Wahlkampf. Analysen zur Bundestagswahl 2009.* Wiesbaden: Springer VS.

Statista. 2013. Top 10 Soziale Netzwerke nach der Anzahl der Besucher im September 2013 (in Millionen). http://de.statista.com/statistik/daten/studie/170467/umfrage/besucherzahlen-sozialer-netzwerke-in-deutschland/

Strömbäck, Jesper. 2008. Four Phases of Mediatization: An Analysis of the Mediatization of Politics. *The International Journal of Press/Politics*, 13(3), 228–246.

Thimm, Caja .2016/in print. Partizipation und Soziale Medien. In Jan-Hinrik Schmidt and Monika Taddicken (eds.), *Handbuch Soziale Medien*. Frankfurt: Springer.

Thimm, Caja, Einspänner, Jessica, and Dang-Anh, Mark. 2012. Twitter als Wahlkampfmedium. Modellierung und Analyse politischer Social-Media-Nutzung. *Publizistik*, 57. Jg., Heft 3, 293–313.

Thimm, Caja, Mark Dang-Anh, and Jessica Einspänner. 2014. Mediatized Politics – Structures and Strategies of Discursive Participation and Online Deliberation on Twitter. In Friedrich Krotz und Andreas Hepp (eds.), *Mediatized Worlds: Culture and Society in a Media Age*, Hrsg., S. 253–269. Basingstoke: Palgrave Macmillian.

Thimm, Caja, Frame, Alex, Einspänner-Pflock, Jessica, Leclercq, Eric, Anastasiadis, Mario 2016. The EU-Election on Twitter: Comparison of German and French Candidates' Tweeting styles. In Christina Holtz-Bacha (ed.), *Europawahlkampf 2014: Internationale Studien zu Rolle der Medien*, pp. 175–203. Wiesbaden: VS Verlag.

Tufekci, Zeynep and Wilson, Christopher. 2012. Social Media and the Decision to Participate in Political Protest: Observations From Tahrir Square. *Journal of Communication,* 62(2): 363–379.

Vergeer, Maurice, Hermans, Liesbeth, and Sams, Steven. 2011. Online social networks and political campaigning: exploration of a new campaign tool and a new campaign style. *Party Politics* 19(3), 477–501.

Vowe, Gerd. 2013. Politische Kommunikation in der Online-Welt. In E. Czerwick (ed.), *Politische Kommunikation in der repräsentativen Demokratie der Bundesrepublik Deutschland. Festschrift für Ulrich Sarcinelli,* pp. S. 87–101. Wiesbaden: Springer VS.

De Vreese, Claes H., Susan A. Banducci, Holli A. Semetko and Hajo G. Boomgaarden. 2006. The News Coverage of the 2004 European Parliamentary Election Campaign in 25 Countries. *European Union Politics* 7, 477–504.

Vittorio Cobianchi, Maria Francesca Murru & Marina Villa,
UniCatt (Milan)[108]

10. Twitter and *double screen* in Italy during the 2014 European elections

Abstract

The chapter analyses the mutual hybridization between Twitter and television during European Elections 2014, paying attention to the ways in which the traditional role of gatekeeping played by television has been reframed by the networked connectivity made available by Twitter. A multi-method approach, consisting of content analysis (qualitative and lexical) and network analysis, has been applied to tweets published by political candidates and referred to television debates, and to tweets produced during the broadcasting of a popular Italian talk-show that hosted one of the main political actors of EP 2014.

10.1 Introduction

> *Hybridity offers a powerful way of thinking about politics and society, a means of seeing the world that highlights complexity, interdependence, and transition. (…) It eschews simple dichotomies and it alerts us to the unusual things that happen when the new has continuities with the old (Chadwick 2013, p. 8)*

In line with what has been argued by Chadwick, the present contribution considers the hybridization of the current system of political communication as a key and a matter of inescapable reality. The hybridization we are seeing is rooted in the process of media convergence that has affected the size of the economic and technological infrastructure. But what interests us more is the way it looks in the dimension of languages and expressive forms of political communication. More specifically, our attention will focus on the cross-fertilization between the flow of conversations taking place on Twitter and the television format of political talk shows. There are two main reasons why we are interested in this object of research. First of all, the linguistic and expressive contamination between Twitter and television is linked to the growing phenomenon of the practices of "second screen-communication" (Colombo, 2015). According to the recent *Global Survey of the Digital Landscape* by Nielsen (Nielsen, 2015), in Europe 44 % of the popu-

108 The chapter has been discussed jointly by the three authors. Vittorio Cobianchi has written section 4, Maria Francesca Murru sections 1 and 2, Marina Villa section 3. Section 5 has been written by the three authors.

lation goes online while watching television and 36 % follow live TV shows: By doing so, they have the chance to take part in conversations on social media. Data from Nielsen Italy (Nielsen Italy, 2015) say that the number of Twitter users who posted at least one comment on a television program has reached the number of 594,500 in 2015, increasing by 25 % over the previous year. The second reason is that both contexts of communication – the talk shows and the conversation on Twitter – host public debates that are extremely focused on – more or less – public characters or political issues. In the cases that we will consider as examples, the political talk shows – namely the TV debates in the European Elections in 2014 – have been the driving conversation on Twitter. Although it is difficult to evaluate the democratic quality of these conversations, we are confident that they represent an essential place for the formation of public opinion, on which civic cultures feed (Dahlgren, 2009). While it is now clear that the discussions that take place in the public spheres online are never or almost never approximate to the communicative inclusiveness and equality that are typical of deliberation (Habermas, 2006), it is equally undeniable that conversation in the media represents one of the most common communication patterns of the network society (van Dijk, 2005). As a matter of fact, this is an increasingly important site for public elaboration of symbols and meanings.

Social TV, which is the main subject of this chapter, highlights the mutual hybridization between two different conversational contexts: on the one hand, the talk show, the emblem of the traditional media which stages a political discussion usually limited to professional politicians, to presenters (often journalists) and to selected representatives of the public and civil society; on the other hand, the "networked" proscenium of Twitter, its conversational flows that combine public and private spheres (Papacharissi, 2010) and its relational variable geometry which is apparently scalable through the use of markers of speech as the hashtag (Bruns & Burgess, 2011). The analysis presented here explores the hybridization between television and Twitter starting from the dynamics of intersection between the two communication spaces. The first part of the study is focused on the tweets published by the candidates whose topics concerned TV shows. The second part of the analysis examines the tweets commenting on a popular Italian TV talk show, "Porta a Porta", that has played an important role in the national campaign for the European Elections. Content analysis is applied both to the text of the television program and to the tweets that comment on the program: this procedure makes it possible to explore the interdependencies and the reciprocal hybridization between the two discursive spaces.

10.2 Social Television

As the long tradition of *audience research* has amply demonstrated, the social dimension of television viewing is not an invention of social media. The television content has always triggered informal conversations, becoming an object of discussion and also a symbolic marker of cultures and tastes. However, if in the pre-digital era the "discursivization" of digital content was done in limited physical spaces, not necessarily domestic but definitely not mediated by other technologies, with the spread of social media, this social dimension has started to become visible in the half-public contexts of Twitter and Facebook, taking on new connotations and opening the way for new expressive styles. Often television programs invite the public to comment via Twitter on the show in progress; this practice is often encouraged through publication of comments in subtitles or as integration into the content of the program itself, for example by including interviews conducted in studio, adding questions or suggestions from the public. Although this is a relatively new phenomenon, there are already many studies that have examined the forms of using Twitter as a real-time back-channel for sharing comments and ratings on television programs.

Collecting the tweets produced during the airing of the final episode of five successful American TV series (Bones, Castle, Law & Order SVU, The Mentalist, NCIS), Hart and Taylor (2012) observe that 76 % of the profiles included in the sample (composed of 13000 tweets sent 30 minutes before the start, 30 minutes after the start and 30 minutes after the conclusion) had only produced one tweet, while 1.4 % tweeted more than 11 times. Although the sampling strategies may be considered less sophisticated than those applied by other research that will be presented soon, we can see emerge the presence of a leading group which produces most of the tweets collected. The study of the type of tweets highlights that interactive dynamics represent a minor part of the overall communication flow. Only 11 % of the sample consists of direct messages to others; the remainder is made up of 28 % other tweets and 61 % of retweets with no obvious interactive dynamics. Other research shows how the patterns of communication change with different types of television programs. Doughty et al. (2012) found that conversations on entertainment programs show a lower level of reciprocity than those in which current affairs programs are discussed. In the first case, tweets often consist of messages addressed to celebrities on the program and show a configuration of vertical and centralized communication patterns; on the contrary, the conversations on current affairs programs appear more transversal and often tend to coagulate around small groups of contacts mutually connected.

What motivates users to participate in live-tweeting has been carefully investigated by Schirra, Sun and Bentley (2014). Their empirical research made use of 11 semi-structured interviews conducted on a sample of spectators of Downton Abbey who were used to comment on Twitter during the broadcast. The results highlighted that live-tweeting is a complex social process which is gradually consolidating a set of social conventions and shared habits. In addition, the research investigated whether there is a link between social and personal feelings and what kind of label is gradually emerging in the audience of the known television series. For all participants, there are times when tweeting becomes a priority, which usually coincide with plot twists or arcs between two episodes. The reasons justifying the choice to participate in the live-tweeting can be grouped into three main categories:

From the interviews it emerged that participation in live-tweeting is motivated by three kinds of personal benefits. The first is about being part of a collective experience. Participating on Twitter is like the pleasure that you experience while going to the theatre or cinema with many other people who you don't know, but with whom you share the same interest. Many point out that this sense of belonging is strengthened by a constant presence on Twitter. Respondents perceive that the attention of others is not taken for granted or automatically received but must be won by personal participation and a timely experience of collective vision. For others, the involvement in live-tweeting is a substitute for the shared domestic habit of watching TV together, an experience they fail to have in real life for various reasons. Finally, for many respondents it is a way to assert their views and understand that they are shared by other spectators.

Although it does not relate exclusively to live-tweeting, the analysis of Macek (2013) on the reasons that lead the public to participate in a more or less active creation and redistribution of media content via web offers important insights for understanding the symbolic and cultural dynamics involved in social television. The specific practices on which his research is based are: the publication of user-generated-content, the consumption of products and content posted by others (both professional and amateur), the selection and redistribution of the content posted by others. While recognizing the importance of the size and power of its balance (or imbalance) in evaluating these textual practices of participatory nature, Macek emphasizes that not all cultural and symbolic dynamics can be explained by the logic of democratization. The decisive factor is rather the interest in the performance of themselves and their culture of taste and consumption. The object to share is not the content itself but rather a representation of their identity and their life worlds. So, if the author agrees with the Jenkins (2006) who says that these participatory practices are explained by the pleasure of consuming or challenging the discursive closure of a production, at the same time he suggests a broader perspective to seize two more orders of motivation. In light of his ethnographic research, Macek (2013) argues that the practices of selection, production and circulation of content can be attributed to three main logics: the desire for text, the desire for conformity, the desire to show off.

A large proportion of the current literature has focused on the communication patterns observed during live-tweeting. "Live-tweeting", or the publication of tweets during television programming, emerges as the majority declination of *Social TV*. Among the various intersections between Twitter and live broadcasting, Harrington et al. (2012) argue that the most relevant dimension corresponds to the possibility to have a space for a "live" discussion, relatively non-mediated, in relation with programs broadcast television. Users are able to offer their comments transmitted simultaneously, to interact with other viewers who are engaged in the same activity and, in some cases, to see their own comments becoming part of the program itself.

Although the exchange of comments on television programs is not limited to the time of broadcast, there is no doubt that the peak of conversations recorded during the transmission represents a highly significant phenomenon, showing that multiple dynamic enhancements converge. For spectators, connecting to Twitter during a program means sharing real-time experience and therefore recreating forms of collective sociability and synchronization of individual temporalities, similar to what existed in the pre-digital era. The multiplication of devices and distribution channels for television content is normally associated with a growing individualisation of television time; the ability to customize in an ever more consistent way their "media diet" means that the schedule no longer poses a collective calendar capable of tuning practices and routines of daily life. Against this backdrop of fragmentation and dispersion of television consumption, Twitter seems to offer an opportunity for a turnaround. In fact, the platform of microblogging promises to reassign to the synchronized TV consumption the added value of a social dimension where experience can be shared and content can be discursively enjoyed. On the other hand, this practice is strongly encouraged by the broadcasters that, in a period of highly dispersed TV usage, feel a strong need to create opportunities for convergence in order to make the public more easily monitored and immediately translatable into more profit. In their study on live-tweeting about the *Eurovision Song Contest*, Highfield et al (2012) point out the differences in the patterns of activity, interaction and interconnection between users that are members of the fan community and those that are attributable to a general audience. According to the authors, the strategies and television productions planning live-tweeting must take into account the fact that the greater internal cohesion seen in the fan community can potentially result in a different symbolic power to the detriment of the general public. The multiple connections between individual fans, combined with the determination to influence the production decisions, for example, can lead to a strategic and exclusive use of the hashtags by which the rest of the public is excluded from live-tweeting. Shamma et al. (2009) studied the use of Twitter during the presidential debates of 2008 and found that the structure of live-tweeting can be used to predict the structure of the program. However, the messages rarely summarize or discuss the content of the debate; rather they describe the emotional reactions or the personal feedback on the performance of the studio's guests. On the contrary, the quantitative research on live-tweeting about *X Factor* created by Lochrie and Coulton (2012) showed a stronger connection between the content of the program and the themes of the tweets. According to the research by McPherson et al (2012), the comments posted on Twitter by viewers of *Glee* offered live coverage of the storyline, and their comments were expressions of appreciation or condemnation of what was seen on the screen.

Research by Wohn and Na (2011) analyzed live-tweets associated with two big media events: The speech in which Obama announced that he accepted the Nobel Peace Prize, on October 9th, 2009 and an episode of the *ABC* talent show "So You Think You Can Dance", on air two days earlier. Inspired by the "uses and gratifications approach", the analysis classified the messages into two main categories: objectivity/subjectivity of the message (in the form of fact or opinion) and inbound/outbound (concerning something that happened to the author of the tweet or within the context of the program/live-tweeting). The intersections of these two categories are four types of messages: attention-seeking (an objective message through which the author of the tweet calls for public attention), information (an objective message on the program without any subjective reference), emotion (a subjective message about the author of the tweet) and opinion (a subjective message on the program).

In both the monitored live-tweeted events, the majority of messages collected were opinions, immediately followed by emotional ones. Differences emerge between the other two categories; within the live-tweeting that accompanied the broadcasting of Obama's speech, *informational* tweets took precedence over *attention-seeking*, while in the case of the talent show the proportion was reversed. This suggests that, in both cases, the prevailing frame is subjective and relates as much to the program as to the author of the tweet. When the tone becomes objective, the tendency is focused on research rather than on providing information: this is clearly seen in live-tweeting around the talent show.

Despite the diversity of practices, the research presented here registers a common line in the relationship between the observed spontaneous creativity on Twitter and the matrix of the text that is typical for a television program. We have seen how, in conversational dynamics, the content of comments reflects the structure of the television text; grassroots inventiveness still moves within the binary symbolic text dictated by the quality of the product broadcast. Although the lack of comparative analyses between different cultural contexts doesn't allow us to consider the results reviewed here as representative of a wider phenomenon. The data collected are sufficient to show that Twitter is emerging as a complementary platform to other media, and that its symbolic value arises in a relationship of interdependence with more consolidated media, like the television platform.

10.3 Television in the tweets of EU candidates

In order to explore the possibility of contamination between Twitter and television, following on from the previous discussion, this chapter looks at the tweets produced by all candidates of the six parties that elected members of the European Parliament: the Democratic Party (Democratic Party), Forza Italia, Lista Tsipras, NCD (New Centre-Right), M5S (5 Stars Movement), and Lega Nord. Content analysis will indicate how important the topic "television" is in the tweets of the candidates during the election campaign, and what kind of programs were being talked about. Furthermore, we will see how this issue is handled and which functions the tweets about TV have.

We catalogued all the tweets of candidates who: *invited people to follow* a program in which a politician talks (before or during the program); *participated in and invited others to participate in live-tweeting* during a political information program; *reported the words said by a politician* during a TV broadcasting (tweeting live or after the program); *commented the TV speech* of a politician: directly or through the retweet of another person; *spoke about a program of political information* in which candidates were featured; *commented on* themes, guests, presenter's style, performance of the actors; *cited and mentioned* a TV program (often using a retweet from the program account, sometimes with a hashtag or a quote).

10.3.1 The presence of the topic "television"

Many tweets about TV are related firstly to the activities of live-tweeting of the party and its members when their leader talks on television (the leader's most significant sentences are tweeted and retweeted); candidates comment on the issues, the performance of politicians, the presenter's attitude. In some cases, they support their leader against their opponents.

Some leaders frequently comment on TV programs in which they are involved (then they are retweeted). For example, Matteo Salvini (leader of Lega Nord) is very active: among the 699 tweets by candidates of Lega Nord about TV, 121 are written by him and 85 are retweets of his tweets. Even a leader who is not used to taking part in TV programs, such as Beppe Grillo, leader of M5S, often comments TV on Twitter: among his tweets, 196 are about TV out of a total of 435 by all the Movement.

Many candidates also anticipate, comment and retweet their TV speeches. They often retweet messages of supporters, especially tweets of encouragement/appreciation. Even M5S candidates like to comment TV speeches, but in this case dominant messages deal with critical views about the presenter and about the partiality of journalists (so called "newsagents"), sarcasm and attacks on opponents, according to the political style of movement. Finally, the habit of retweeting tweets of others – especially of the leaders and the party, but also of ordinary people –increases the number of total tweets.

Table 10.1: Number of tweets about television (and percentage of total tweets).

	Total tweets*	**Tweets about TV**	**% of tweets about TV (on total tweets)***
FORZA ITALIA	*19592*	*1401*	***7,15***
THE DEMOCRATIC PARTY	*14210*	*475*	***3,34***
M5S	8790	435	**4,95**
LEGA NORD	7907	699	**8,84**
NCD	5433	318	**5,85**
TSIPRAS	4680	256	**5,47**

* The total tweets and the percentage of the total tweets referred to all the tweets made by all candidates in the party list

Among the tweets that talk about television, the percentage of retweets is: 75.2 % for Forza Italia; 69.7 % for M5S; 49.9 % for Lega Nord; 40.6 % for Tsipras; 32.7 % for NDC; 27.8 % for the Democratic Party.

10.3.2 The content of the tweets about TV

To examine the contents of the TV related tweets, we can give an example of the two most productive on social media: Forza Italia and the Democratic Party. They differ in the importance given to television, because Forza Italia is the second party for the space dedicated to TV (7.15 %), while the Democratic Party is the one that publishes the least tweets about it (3.34 %). First of all, we distinguish the programs mentioned by typology:

Table 10.2: The typology of the programs mentioned in the tweets

Typology	Forza Italia	%	The Democratic Party	%
Talk shows	599	42,8	200	42,1
Political current affairs and debates	296	21,1	129	27,2
TV news, breaking news (and journalistic programs)	364	26,0	87	18,3
Official Political Broadcasts, with a debate	15	1,1	9	1,9
General information (not political)	109	7,8	40	8,4
Candidates debates in English language/programs by foreign broadcasters	18	1,3	10	2,1
Total	1401	100	475	100

Talk show programs are the most cited, with similar percentages for the two parties (around 42 %). Those programs are very popular and broadcast on national television in prime time ("Announo", "Ballarò", "Piazza Pulita ", " Virus", "La Gabbia") and the well-known talk show, "Porta a Porta", is broadcast in the late evening on RAI 1. All the shows talk about news and often host politicians. During the European campaign, the coverage about politics was extensive and the participation of the leaders wide, which inspired many tweets (in particular Silvio Berlusconi's appearances on TV).

Table 10.3: The contents of the tweets about TV

Contents of the tweets	**The Democratic Party**		**Forza Italia**	
Announcement of a TV speech of a politician, invitation to see it ("follow me on Rai 1 at 10pm")	149	31,4	292	20,8
Comment of the candidate on a TV program	39	8,2	71	5,1
Comment of the candidate on TV and on a network in general	27	5,7	5	0,4
Comment by a viewer of the program (RT)	33	6,9	257	18,3
Quotes of the text of a politician's intervention in a program – by the candidate	134	28,2	81	5,8
Quotes of the text of a politician's intervention in a program – by a viewer (RT)	20	4,2	67	4,8
Quotes of the text of a politician's intervention in a program – by the party or its leaders (RT)	0	0,0	446	31,8
Quotes of the text of a politician's intervention in a program – by the presenter or a TV account (RT)	25	5,3	93	6,6
Quote or comment about a foreign program (and about the TV duel)	6	1,3	17	1,2
Polls and statistics	3	0,6	9	0,6
Link to a video of a politician's intervention in a program	12	2,5	27	1,9
Parts of a current affairs program about the candidates	13	2,7	6	0,4
Parts of a TV information program about elections	0	0,0	4	0,3
Parts of a current affairs program commented by the candidate	5	1,1	7	0,5
Comments on the program "Porta a porta" with Beppe Grillo	9	1,9	19	1,4
Total tweets about TV	***475***	***100***	***1401***	***100***

If we consider the contents, most of the tweets of the Democratic Party on TV are about *the announcement of a TV speech of a politician* ("tomorrow at 21, follow me at *Ballarò*") and *the quote, by the candidate, of the text of a politician's intervention in a program* (the politician can be the candidate himself or a main personality of the same party or of another party). These tweets are quite often produced by the candidate. Also the third most present content, the *comment of the candidate on a TV program*, was due to him, without retweets.

The first two topics present in the tweets of Forza Italia on TV are the result of retweets: *comments by a viewer of the program* (example: "RT @coachjoetod: @comilara always polite in her speeches #SkyTG24") and *quotes of the text of a politician's intervention in a program – by the party or its leaders*. Also the third topic stated, *the announcement of a TV speech*, contains more than a half of the total number of retweets (134). Therefore the candidates of Forza Italia retweet frequently, especially the comments of the viewers: retweets of sympathizers, ordinary people, journalistic friends of politicians. The effect is "giving voice to the people" and promoting the image of the candidate (many of the tweets are accolades). When Forza Italia politicians pronounce speeches on TV, they are tweeted by official accounts of the party and Silvio Berlusconi, and retweeted a lot by the candidates, with an amplifying effect. There are candidates who do nothing more than this type of RT.

10.4 Case analysis: interview with Beppe Grillo, leader of the M5S

10.4.1 The argumentative plan

The second part of the analysis examined, in parallel, the discursive dynamics of the content of a TV current affairs program, and the content of the live-tweeting generated by the program itself. In particular, the episode of "Porta a Porta" broadcast on 19th May 2014, which hosted the leader of the M5S, Beppe Grillo, was analyzed. The content analysis took into account, on the one hand, the spectrum of the topics; on the other hand, the argumentative functions of each interaction between the anchorman and the politician. Content analysis was applied both to the text of the show, and to the tweets produced before, after and during the show: the tweets collected as part of the project (namely those with the hashtag #portaaporta) were integrated by tweets collected by the Osservatorio di Pavia using, as search keys, some specific hashtags from the interview (in particular, #vespachiedi and #grilloinvespa), and those addressing the Twitter account of Beppe Grillo (@BeppeGrillo). While not directly a candidate in the European Elections, Beppe Grillo was, in fact, the only member of the Movement who had national exposure during the election period, due to the lack of fame of the official candidates of M5S running for the European Elections. Despite a lack of national debates between the main political leaders on European issues, the television campaign in Italy featured individually-hosted interviews with the leaders of the main parties.

The content analysis and the argumentative flow of the interview highlighted the following dynamics:

- The functional, argumentative and teleological perspective of the interaction (in essence, the communicative purpose pursued by the political actor through his/her arguments).
- The thematic perspective of the argument: the subject of each interaction was detected, and a macro-theme was associated with each subject (in particular, the traditional distinction between *Policy, Political, and Personal Campaign*, applied by Patterson (1980), among others), in order to contextualize the data about the quality of the argumentative flow.

The coding form has been applied to each unit of classification, identified as a continuous flow of interaction characterized by uniformity in functions and thematics.

The content analysis of the program identified the ways in which the argumentative flow in television affects comments on Twitter, both from the point of view of the issues addressed, and from the point of view of quality and methods of argumentation.

Moreover, since the personal point of view of the Twitter users about Beppe Grillo and the M5S was coded for (*positive*, *negative* and *neutral*), we tried to understand how the opinion of those who tweeted about the TV program influenced the passage of the themes and the argumentative methods from the TV flow to the virtual agora.

Below, you will find some results of content analysis applied to the interview.

Table 10.4: Analysis of the content of the program "Porta a Porta" of May 19: functional analysis, and teleological argument (percentages on the total number of words)

Presentation of the program of the Movement	41.1 %
Presentation of values and principles of the Movement	20.9 %
Presentation of the strategies of alliance of the Movement	6.7 %
Opinion about political life (governmental or legislative) of an opponent	5.5 %
Presentation of the experience of civil commitment of Beppe Grillo	5.2 %
Opinion about the program of the opposite parties	4.7 %
Discussion about internal problems in the Movement	4.5 %

Presentation of the professional experience of Beppe Grillo	3.6 %
Presentation of the personality of Beppe Grillo	3.2 %
Discussion about the campaign run by Beppe Grillo	1.7 %
Discussion of the relation between Beppe Grillo and the media	1.4 %
Presentation of the personality of an opponent	1.1 %
Presentation of results of the political coalition at the national level	0.5 %
Total	***100.0 %***

The prevalence of a programmatic point of view is due to the presenter Bruno Vespa, who repeatedly brought the discussion onto the feasibility of policy and political proposals of the M5S. Vespa, therefore, put together an "aggressive" strategy, with topics less favourable to the Movement, such as *strategies of alliance* (the political struggle of M5S is founded on the rejection of any political or tactical agreement with all the other parties) and *relations within the Movement* (many expulsions from the Parliamentary group of M5S occurred in the first months of Legislature).

Nevertheless, Grillo was often able to bring the discursive focus into a more advantageous field: the illustration of the identity and of the values of M5S, particularly "honesty", "participation", and some proposals concerning the fight against corruption.

Table 10.5: Analysis of the content of the program "Porta a Porta" of May 19th: thematic analysis, micro-themes (percentages of the total number of words)

Euro, European Charts	18.9 %
Industrial policy, industrial development, production problems	12.8 %
Financing of the basic income for each citizens	10.5 %
Ideology, reference values of the party or of the alliance	8.4 %
Fight against corruption	7.1 %
Intra-party relations	4.5 %
Political history of somebody else	4.4 %
Privatizations	3.8 %
The cost of the policy	3.4 %
Tourism	3.3 %
Welfare (its importance, its defense, its reduction)	3.1 %

Immigration	3.0 %
Institutional Reforms	2.5 %
Quality of the campaign	2.4 %
The media's role in Italian politics	2.2 %
The values, ideals referred by the interviewee	1.9 %
Environment, energy policy	1.8 %
Other issues	6.0 %
Total	***100.0 %***

Concerning the macro-themes, we can see how *policies* have occupied almost three-quarters of the interview, followed by *political* issues. Strangely, for an interview with a popular character, with a rich TV past (Beppe Grillo was a famous standing comedian, before his political engagement), and for a face-to-face during European Elections campaign, *personal topics and topics of the campaign* have only been marginally addressed: a confirmation of how Bruno Vespa has tried to keep the interview in the terms of pure political practice: certainly, policies are not the easiest battlefield for the leader of M5S, who is much more comfortable with paradoxical monologues, and with using personal comic skills as polemical weapons against contenders.

Table 10.6: Analysis of the content of the program "Porta a Porta" of May 19th: thematic analysis, macro-themes (percentages on the total number of words)

Policy	71.3 %
Political	13.3 %
Personal	7.8 %
Campaign	7.6 %
Total	***100.0 %***

10.4.2 The flow of tweets

A content analysis was also applied to 1628 tweets randomly chosen from the total flow about the program. The tweet sample was examined on the basis of a coding table similar to the one used to analyze the program, identifying functional and thematic aspects of each tweet. Furthermore, we added an "appraisal variable" to the coding scheme, which collects the explicit position of the author of the tweet about Beppe Grillo or about the M5S.

Table 10.7: Content analysis of the tweets regarding the "Porta a Porta" talk show of May 19th: functional analysis (percentages of total tweets analyzed)

Comments on the program, performing analysis of Beppe Grillo	55.7 %
Presentation of the M5S program	19.8 %
Presentation of the personality of the guest	9.2 %
Promoting the values and ideals of M5S	6.4 %
Absent or undetectable	4.2 %
Comments about political life (governmental or legislative) of an opponent	1.7 %
Comments about the program of the opposite alliance	1.6 %
Other functions	1.4 %
Total	***100 %***

It may be noted that most of the tweets are designed to produce general opinions, sheer evaluations about Beppe Grillo's performance during the interview (judgments, therefore, not involving evaluations on the Movement and its leader, and not concerning single political proposals), about reviews of the show, about the choices of the questions, or about specific moments of the interview; "break your leg" tweets and mere tweets of encouragement are also massively present: M5S's militants were aware that their *leader* would be acting in a hostile communicative context. The first peak of tweets, before the start of the broadcast interview (which was not live but shortly deferred) was inspired by the publication on Twitter of the *selfie* that Bruno Vespa shot with Beppe Grillo before the-face-to face interview started.

When the show went ahead, however, the number of tweets grew expressing doubts about the ability of Beppe Grillo to communicate effectively in a format such as the face-to-face interview, posted by the opponents of the Movement. Supporters of M5S, however, noted how the host, for once, was playing the role of a "true" investigative journalist (Bruno Vespa is often accused of complicity with his political guests).

The first relevant result, then, is that most of the tweets are not directly linked to the content of the program. They are not tied to specific themes or arguments, but they are pure evaluations about the performance of Beppe Grillo, and simple notes about the program.

Nonetheless, we can find a correlation between the other functional aspects targeted by the tweets, and the functional aspects detected in the interview: a prevalence of tweets aimed to *highlight aspects of the program of M5S* addressed in the interview, followed by tweets commenting on *Grillo's personality,* and tweets about *political values* of the Movement.

Table 10.8: Content analysis of tweets related to the talk show "Porta a Porta" of May the 19th: functional analysis crossed with the explicit evaluation expressed on Beppe Grillo or M5S (percentages of total tweets analyzed)

Function	Neutral	Positive	Negative
Comments on the program, performing analysis of Beppe Grillo	29.2 %	38.1 %	32.6 %
Presentation of program *M5S*	9.9 %	18.0 %	72.1 %
Presentation of the personality of the guest	2.0 %	8.1 %	89.9 %
Promoting the values and ideals of M5S	9.6 %	62.5 %	27.9 %
Absent or undetectable	69.6 %	21.7 %	8.7 %
Comments about political life (governmental or legislative) of an opponent	3.6 %	78.6 %	17.9 %
Comments about the program of the opposite alliance	11.5 %	84.6 %	3.8 %
Other functions	0.0 %	45.5 %	54.5 %
Total	***22.2 %***	***33.8 %***	***44.0 %***

NOTE: The information highlighted indicates the percentages which are furthest away from the distribution of the evaluation, and that, therefore, indicate statistically significant concentrations of positive and negative feedbacks.

Crossing the functional aspect with the commentators' ratings about Beppe Grillo and about M5S and its political actions, highlights the following points of interest:

- Comments on performance and on the program are slightly over-represented among positive commentators.
- Tweets about *the policy proposals of M5S* and about *the personality* of Beppe Grillo, show a strong over-representation of negative feedback for Beppe Grillo and M5S: 72 % of the tweets that comment the political proposal of M5S bring negative opinions, against 44 % of the total negative opinions. Criticism of the political action of the Movement, therefore, is focused on programmatic aspects and on the personality of the leader. In particular, commenters criticized the political positions of Beppe Grillo about immigration, deemed too vague and ambiguous, especially by right-wing voters, and, in particular, those of the Lega Nord, or deemed too similar to those of the Right by liberal and progressive voters.

- Commenters also strongly criticized *European policy and industrial policy* of M5S: in particular, these issues, and the paradoxical way Grillo debated them, have massively attracted the sarcasm of detractors. Even tweets aimed to review the personality of Beppe Grillo were negative: mainly, tweets can be found which denounce the heaviness of Grillo's communication style out of his natural context (the stand-up comedian "one man show"), and tweets that denounce his vulgarity. Conversely, tweets that appreciated his personality underline its "authenticity" and forthrightness, which should be read as variations of his "honesty" and his moral rectitude.
- Among the tweets aimed to emphasize *the values of M5S*, and among those aimed at *criticizing the government's action* and the political programs of the opponents, the tweets by M5S supporters prevail. These data tend to confirm the substantial difference between M5S and other movements inspired by populism (as the Lega Nord in Italy): while the latter support their political action on a few specific policy proposals, especially related to immigration and tax system reform, the former bases its identity on the moral issue, claimed as foundational to every political proposal, and on deep criticism of "old politics", portrayed as being influenced by large lobbies against the interests of citizens. An "ontological difference" proudly claimed by the militants of the Movement, which justifies and dwarfs any possible uncertainty shown by the leader (and even recognized by some militants) about mere programmatic aspects of the policy proposed by M5S.

Table 10.9: Content analysis of tweets related to the talk show "Porta a Porta" of May 19th: thematic analysis (percentages of total tweets analyzed)

Findings on performance in the televised debate	59.6 %
Slogan, voting intentions	6.4 %
Jokes about political opponents	5.8 %
Fight against corruption	5.7 %
Industrial policy, industrial development, production problems	3.3 %
Euro, European Charts	2.8 %
Hypothesis of results	2.2 %
Quality of the campaign	1.5 %
Immigration	1.4 %
Consequences of the elections on institutional arrangements	1.3 %

Financing of basic income	1.3 %
Intra-party relations	0.9 %
Environment, energy policy	0.9 %
Institutional Reforms	0.9 %
Military spending	0.7 %
Other issues	4.4 %
Total	***100.0 %***

As for the specific issues faced by those who commented on the interview with Beppe Grillo via Twitter, in addition to tweets that contain only a judgment about the quality of the TV debate, we also detected a strong presence of *slogans* and *voting intentions* (with a prevalence of *endorsement* in favor of M5S and Beppe Grillo), and jokes about political opponents: in particular, jokes on Beppe Grillo by opponents of the Movement (the majority), and jokes on Prime Minister Matteo Renzi by militants of M5S.

Among the programmatic issues, some prevail, like *fighting corruption, industrial policy, and European policy.* The subjects and feedback cross-distribution confirms that some issues were mainly used to carry negative judgments on the proposed policy of M5S *(industrial policy, European policy, immigration and citizen's income:* the latter, in particular, because of the lack of clarity with which Grillo has exposed the covering of his costs).

Conversely, the most frequent topics by supporters of the Movement were *fighting corruption* and *the proposal to reduce military spending*, the latter being the key proposal to mobilize funding for the basic citizens' income. If you compare this distribution with the topics addressed during the TV interview, it is obvious that the agenda of the audience has proved slightly different from the agenda of the presenter: the main theme of the interview, *the relation of M5S with Europe*, with its Charts and its Institutions, was very scarcely taken into account by commentators on Twitter (the issue of Europe has been addressed by 2.8 % of the tweets of the sample, while occupied nearly one-fifth of the interview: a further proof of the little interest that European issues have for Italians); vice-versa, it has been virtually ignored by the militants and supporters of M5S.

The comments about the *proposals of M5S for the fight against* corruption, however, was over-represented on Twitter: recognized by the militants as the main theme of identity of their political proposal, it was the most commented policy subject on Twitter, while, during the interview, it occupied less than a tenth of the total space.

Table 10.10: Analysis of the content of tweets related to the talk show "Porta a Porta" of May 19th: thematic analysis crossed with explicit evaluation expressed on Beppe Grillo or M5S (percentages of total tweets analyzed)

Theme	Neutral	Positive	Negative
Findings on performance in face-to-face debate	29.1 %	27.3 %	43.6 %
Slogan, voting intentions	2.9 %	80.0 %	17.1 %
Jokes about political opponents	15.8 %	30.5 %	53.7 %
Fight against corruption	4.3 %	76.3 %	19.4 %
Industrial policy, industrial development, production problems	5.6 %	18.5 %	75.9 %
Euro, European Charts	24.4 %	24.4 %	51.1 %
Hypothesis of results	11.1 %	38.9 %	50.0 %
Quality of the campaign	25.0 %	29.2 %	45.8 %
Immigration	4.5 %	18.2 %	77.3 %
Consequences of the elections on institutional arrangements	19.0 %	14.3 %	66.7 %
Financing of basic income	0.0 %	4.8 %	95.2 %
Intra-party relations	0.0 %	33.3 %	66.7 %
Environment, energy policy	28.6 %	35.7 %	35.7 %
Institutional Reforms	8.3 %	25.0 %	66.7 %
Military spending	14.3 %	42.9 %	42.9 %
Other topics	11.1 %	47.2 %	41.7 %
Total	***22.2 %***	***33.8 %***	***44.0 %***

NOTE: The information highlighted indicates the percentages which are furthest away from the marginal distribution of the evaluation, and that, therefore, indicate statistically significant concentrations of positive and negative feedback.

Finally, the analysis of the macro-tweets gives us the following results:

- The low incidence of *personal issues* in the comments: also in this case, through the analysis of the tweets we have the confirmation of the fact that the M5S is an "atypical" charismatic movement, compared, for example, to the first steps of Forza Italia by Berlusconi; it is a movement in which the presence of the leader is secondary in the construction of the identity, which is based, above all, on ideals and values.

- The relevance of the *themes of the campaign* in contrast with the importance given to them during the interview; in particular, as mentioned, the analysis has detected a large presence of election slogans and forecast polls.
- The lack of importance given by commentators to *political relations*, however, seems natural, given the simplification imposed by the leadership of the movement to the internal relations of M5S itself, and to the relations between parties, which are virtually absent in the political action of the Movement.

Table 10.11: *Analysis of the content of tweets related to the program "Porta a Porta" of May 19th: thematic analysis, macro-themes (percentages of total of the tweets analyzed)*

Meta debate	60.5 %
Policy	19.1 %
Campaign	17.2 %
Political	3.1 %
Personal	0.1 %
Total	***100.0 %***

Crossing the distribution of macro-themes with the feedback of commentators on M5S, shows an over-representation of negative feedback in tweets about policy and political relations (related, mainly, to issues of dissent within M5S), and an over-representation of positive feedback on the *themes of the campaign*, because of the number of slogans and voting endorsements by militants present in the sample.

Table 10.12: *Analysis of the content of tweets related to the talk show "Porta a Porta" of May 19th: macro-themes analysis crossed with evaluate explicitly expressed on Beppe Grillo or M5S (percentages of total tweets analyzed)*

Theme	Neutral	Positive	Negative
Meta-debate	29.8 %	27.1 %	43.0 %
Policy	10.3 %	39.9 %	49.8 %
Campaign	10.7 %	51.1 %	38.2 %
Political	12.0 %	30.0 %	58.0 %
Personal	0.0 %	50.0 %	50.0 %
Total	***22.2 %***	***33.8 %***	***44.0 %***

NOTE: The information highlighted indicate the percentages which are furthest away from the marginal distribution of the evaluation, and, therefore, indicate statistically significant concentrations of positive and negative feedback.

10.4.3 Thematic trend

Chart 1: the time course of the space devoted to the various macro-themes within the TV-show

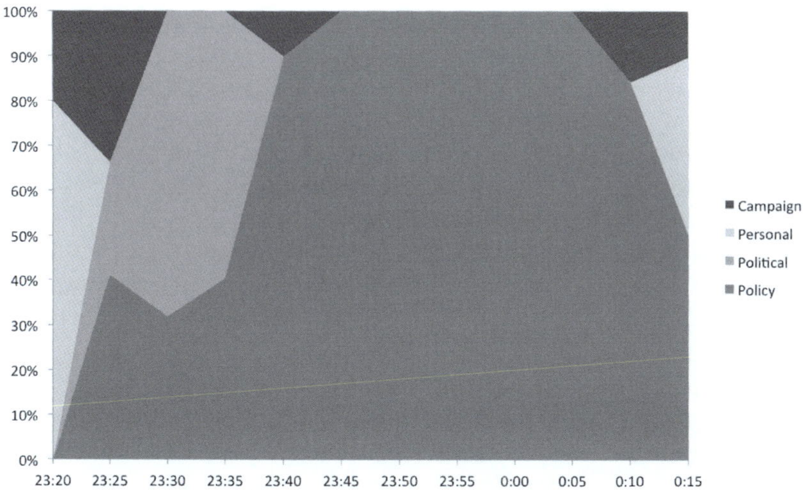

With this series of charts, we tried to investigate the relation between the time trend of macro-themes in the debate, and the time course of the same in the comment on Twitter. The *Chart 1*, in fact, describes diachronically the amount of space dedicated to each of the macro-themes in the course of the program. The initial phase devoted primarily *to personal issues and campaign issues* (build especially on questions about the possible political consequences at national level of a victory of M5S in the European Elections), has followed by a section mainly devoted to political relations (in particular, to some questions by Vespa on banishment by the parliamentary groups of some members of M5S, following positions or behaviours deemed inconsistent with the regulations of the Movement). Then, the whole central part of the program is dedicated to policy issues. Finally, the last section goes back to personal themes and the themes of the campaign.

Chart 2, on the other hand, describes the diachronic evolution of macro-themes in the debate on Twitter. Chart 3, finally, shows the same data as Chart 2, purified, however, by the "noise" made up of the tweets containing jokes or mere comments about the TV debate.

When comparing the different temporal trends, the following considerations become apparent:

- The argumentative trend in the show produced *an explosion of tweets dedicated to issues of policy* by commentators, virtually absent before the show started. The end of the interview resulted – as you can see by reading the charts 2 and 3 – in a visible decline of attention by commentators about economic issues and, more, about the management of public affairs. However, policy issues were significantly present in the tweets related to the program until the end of the survey. Therefore, it can be said that the interview, and, in particular, the care with which Bruno Vespa tried to maintain the focus on concrete proposals, have in part prompted the attention of commentators (especially commentators against M5S) on the policy proposals of the Movement.
- Before the show started, the themes of the campaign were prevailing, in particular *endorsements* and voting intentions; the number of this type of tweets declined sharply during the show, to return to a quite significant level after the end of the show.
- The tweets about the "meta-debate", about the whole discourse on the TV face-to-face debate and the type of media, reach a peak just before starting the show (tweets of "break your leg" to the leader), and always remain the most of the total tweets, but another peak appears just after the end, with the final assessments on the "final result" of the face-to-face.
- The *personal topics* in the program were almost entirely absent from the flow of the tweets: they emerge – in a very marginal percentage – only at the end of the interview, with a few comments about the supposed economic benefit that Grillo would gain from the management of the Movement's official blog, as a direct result of his political commitment.
- The tweets about *political relations* (in particular, as mentioned, those related to the management of internal relations in M5S) experienced a peak at the exact time of the question by the presenter during the interview. After that, the issue regained interest among commentators just after the conclusion of the debate, always accompanied with observations on the mode of administration of internal relations in M5S. Again, you can see a very clear correlation between the development of the topic in the program and the development of the organization of the comments on Twitter.

Chart 2: the time course of the space dedicated to different macro-themes in the show (number of tweets)

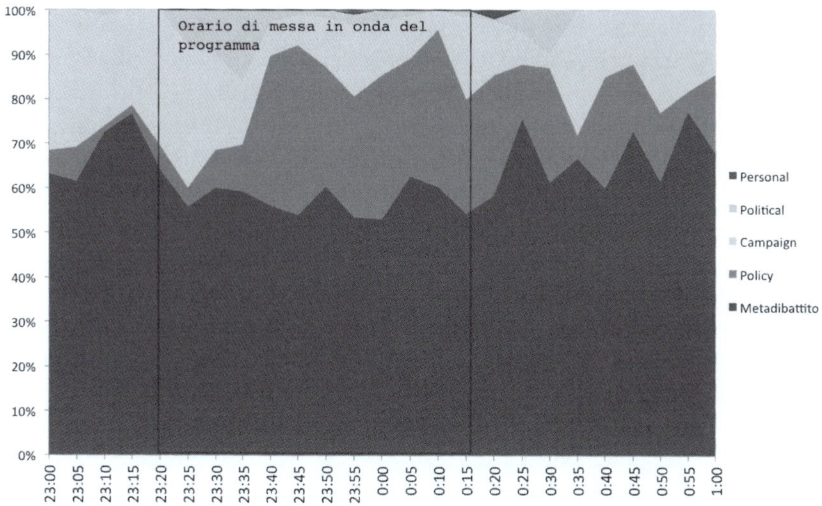

Chart 3: the time course of the space dedicated to different macro-themes in the show without the tweets related to the development of the face-to-face on TV.

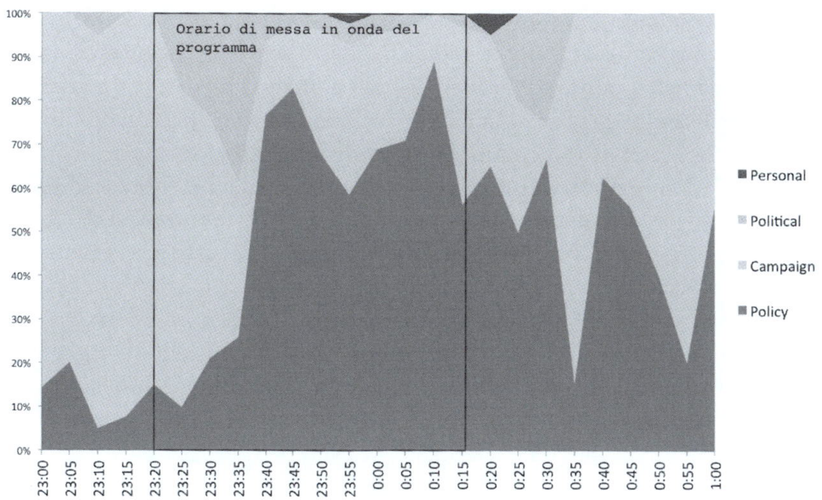

10.5 Conclusions

TV occupies an important place in the tweets of the candidates during the election campaign. As described in the content analysis of the tweets posted by the candidates of Forza Italia and the Democratic Party, the talk-show programs are among the most commented. When they speak about TV, all six parties examined often reproduce the content of the program (mainly, the statements of politicians) or announce its airing: Twitter therefore has a function of *amplification* and *multiplication* of the political message conveyed through the medium of television. This is particularly the case when the party leaders attend the TV show: the accounts of both candidates and the related parties are mobilized to spread the message already broadcast on TV. The television appearances of Silvio Berlusconi, during which we recorded the most significant cases of live-tweeting, are an example of this. The function of *propagation/multiplication* of the messages delivered on TV becomes clear when we focus on retweet rates: for three out of six parties, retweets represent the majority of the tweets produced (77.2 % for Forza Italia). In order to amplify and disseminate slogans and statements that leaders produce during TV shows, the candidates of the same party often re-tweet what was published during the airing from the broadcaster's account, from the Twitter profile of their own party and from the account of their leader. This is especially true in cases of leaders who are very present on social media and TV, such as Salvini and Berlusconi, or in the case of Grillo and the M5S. We can say that live-tweeting is linked to the functions of amplification, recovery and retransmission of the message delivered via TV, and of comments about it, rather than as discursive or dialogic enrichment of the contents conveyed through television. In this first part of the analysis, Twitter therefore emerges as a discursive space, complementary and subordinated to the television arena. The communication dynamics that take place here do not differ in some ways from the paradigm of mass media broadcasters; on the contrary, they work to enhance the diffusion capacity of the traditional electronic mass media, bringing each node in the "Twitter-sphere" to act as a megaphone of messages spread through television.

The second part of the analysis has enabled us to focus on the counterpoint of this phenomenon: if the communication strategies activated on Twitter by candidates remain firmly anchored in the mass media paradigm, what happens instead in large conversational flows, powered by spectators and citizens? Are there opposing forces that offset, mitigate, or even reverse the trend? Our data show that, even in this case, the television arena has a decisive dragging capacity of the discursive dynamics taking place on Twitter, in relation to both content and expressive forms. However, when the gaze is extended beyond the strategies of the candidates to capture the wider communication flows, the dependence of Twitter on television takes on specific features that are a direct result of the cultural conventions that are established on the micro-blogging platform. The flow of the content published and redistributed on Twitter finds an important filter in the needs of self-representation and self-positioning that arise from the increasingly widespread practice of "curation" and "management" of social profiles (Marwick & Boyd, 2010; p. 2012). In particular, the analysis has shown a correlation between the effectiveness with which the Guest has treated the themes proposed by the Host of the TV show, the resumption of the themes themselves by commentators on Twitter, and their political positioning. In fact, what happened was that the self-declared supporters of the M5S enhanced with their tweets the constitutive issues of the movement – as for political corruption – while abandoning the subject areas of policy and economy (the main issue in the program), with which the Guest had more difficulties. The latter area was on the contrary taken up, revived and highlighted almost exclusively by detractors of the movement, who turned the same weapons against Beppe Grillo that the leader of M5S pointed at political opponents: irony, sarcasm, and accusations of inadequacy and incompetence. At the same time, a large slice of tweets targeted the television performance of the leader, emphasizing some strong and weak points of his communicative effectiveness, instead of focusing on the content of the program or on the covered topics. Only on the ground of this performative assessment did opponents and supporters converge in a direct confrontation. Otherwise, if the thematic focus was prevalent, discursive flows were characterized by a strong polarization: the commentators on Twitter who dealing with the political content of the program, basically, occupied the most useful areas to argue and justify their positions against or in support of the political leader, while avoiding a real dialogue with opponents.

References

Bruns, A. & Burgess, J.E.: "The use of Twitter hashtags in the formation of ad hoc publics". In: *6th European Consortium for Political Research General Conference*, 25–27 August 2011, University of Iceland, Reykjavik.

Chadwick, A.: *The Hybrid Media System: Politics and Power*. Oxford University Press: New York, 2013.

Colombo, F.: *Social TV. Produzione, esperienza e valore nell'era digitale*. Egea: Milano, 2015.

Dahlgren, P.: *The Media and Political Engagement*. Cambridge University Press: Cambridge, 2009.

Doughty, M., Rowland, D. & Lawson, S.: *Who is on your sofa? TV audience communities and second screening social networks*. In: *Proc. EuroiTV '12*. ACM, New York, NY, 2012, pp. 79–86.

van Dijk, J.: *The Network Society, Social Aspects of New Media*, Second Edition. Sage: London, Thousand Oaks, New Delhi, 2005.

Habermas, J.: "Political Communication in Media Society: Does Democracy Still Enjoy an Epistemic Dimension? The Impact of Normative Theory on Empirical Research". In: *Communication theory*, 16 (4), 2006, pp. 411–426.

Harrington, S., Highfield, T. & Bruns, A.: "More than a backchannel : Twitter and television". In: Noguera, J. M. (ed): *Audience Interactivity and Participation*. COST Action ISO906 Transforming Audiences, Transforming Societies: Brussels, 2012, pp. 13–17.

Hart, W. & Taylor, E. "Social Media Use While Watching Prime-TimeTV". In: Langmia, K., O'Brien P., Sturgis, I. & Tyree, T. C. M.: *Social Media and Intersections between Politics, Culture and Law – Proceedings*, Howard University, Bowie State University, 2012, pp. 32–38.

Highfield, T., Harrington, S. & Bruns, A: "Twitter as a Technology for Audiencing and Fandom: The #Eurovision Phenomenon". *Information, Communication & Society*, 16(3), 2013, pp. 315–339.

Jenkins, H.: *Convergence Culture: Where Old and New Media Collide*. New York, NY: New York University Press, 2006.

Lochrie, M. & Coulton, P.: "*Sharing the viewing experience through second screens*". In: Proc. EuroiTV'12. ACM, New York, NY, 2012, pp. 199–202.

Macek, J.: "More than a desire for text: Online participation and the social curation of content". In: *Convergence. The Journal of Research into New Media Technology*, 19(3),2013, pp. 295–302.

Marwick, A. & Boyd, D. "To See and Be Seen: Celebrity Practice on Twitter". In: *Convergence*, 17(2),2011, pp. 139–158.

Nielsen Italy: *Nielsen Twitter TV Ratings for Italy*, 2015, retrieved 11.13.2015, from http://www.nielseninsights.eu/info-pages/marketing-effectiveness/nielsen-twitter-TV-ratings-for-italy?previewId=w2rroem

Nielsen: *The Battle for Eye Space in a TV-Everywhere World*, 2015. Global Survey of Digital Landscape by Nielsen, retrieved 11.13.2015 from http://www.nielsen.com/us/en/insights/reports/2015/screen-wars-the-battle-for-eye-space-in-a-TV-everywhere-world.html

Page, R.: "The Linguistics of Self Branding and Micro-celebrity in Twitter: The Role of Hashtags". In: *Discourse and Communication*, 6 (2), 2012, pp. 181–201.

Papacharissi, Z.: *A Private Sphere: Democracy in a Digital Age*, Polity Press: Cambridge, 2010.

Shamma, D., A., Kennedy, L. & Churchill, E. F.: "Tweet the debates: understanding community annotation of uncollected sources". In: *Proc. WSM '09*. ACM, New York, NY, 2009, pp. 3–10.

Schirra, S., Sun, H. & Bentley, F.: "Together alone: motivations for live-tweeting a television series". In: *Proceedings CHI*, 2014, pp: 2441–2450

Wohn, D. Y. & Na, E. K.: "Tweeting about TV: Sharing television viewing experiences via social media message streams", *First Monday*, 2011, 16 (3).

Fernando Bonete Vizcaino, Elena Cebrián Guinovart &
Tamara Vázquez Barrio (CEU Madrid)

11. Pablo Iglesias' Tweeting Style: Unsuccessfully Aspiring to Renew Spanish Political Discourse

Abstract
This chapter analyses Pablo Iglesias' tweeting style during the European campaign and the quality of his attempts to establish a dialogue with citizens, suggesting that Podemos' new message, based on being closer to citizens' concerns and the increase of participation, is not necessarily reflected in its leader's conduct on Twitter.

11.1 Introduction

The left-wing reformist party *Podemos* erupted on the Spanish political scene in January 2014 with a promise of renewal. The economic crisis and the strong laws passed by the government to tackle it, subsequent unemployment and the numerous corruption scandals affecting Spanish political parties have served these last few years as precursors for the birth of numerous social movements and political parties demanding deep change in the way politics is understood. The answers *Podemos* gave to these requests, based on a constitutional reform that suited the vast majority of them, linked the party with the new social and political spirit. Furthermore, since its arrival on the Spanish scene, the party has been associated with a young, fresh, dynamic form of doing politics. Its direct and aggressive discourse was initially reinforced by the massive success of the Coalition of the Radical Left *SYRIZA* in Greece (The Economist, 2014), which equally targeted people's wariness to the same old message from traditional Spanish parties and their inner corruption, and provided Podemos with an outstanding opportunity to portray itself as an emergent party in the context of the European Elections. That was understood days after the elections by The New York Times, which interpreted *Podemos*' success as follows: "Given the deep unpopularity of Spain's mainstream politicians, the endemic corruption exposed by the financial crisis and the pain felt by the 26 percent of the work force still unemployed despite hints of recovery, politicians and analysts are taking the threat posed by *Podemos* seriously" (Rapahel Minder, 2014).

Indeed, *Podemos* soon received strong media coverage. Over and after the campaign, the media placed great emphasis on the authenticity of *Podemos*' social networks activity, because it was supposedly a faithful reflection of its new-look proposals. Thus, for instance, Spanish and left-wing national newspaper Público stated "the main key of this social media whirlwind is to make citizens protagonists, not the other way around, like the rest of parties usually do, because they understand social networks as an eminently unidirectional tool" (David Bollero, 2014). This publication also considered *Podemos* as the most constant and participative political party in social networks, truly open when creating and establishing a dialogue with citizens. The degree to which some of these claims by the media are representative of reality is something that will be shown here, especially because the media hype was enhanced the day after the elections, when the hashtag "Pablo Iglesias" achieved the first position on the Spanish top ranking of Twitter's Trending Topic list (Trendinalia, 2014).

The category NGO reflects a will to debate social affairs. Finally, retweets categorized as Citizen imply a disposition for dialogue with the general public, the electors. A last category called Other includes any other type not covered by the above.

When talking about Intention, we have established the following categories for every tweet or retweet: "Visibility of the Politician", "Live Tweeting of a Political Act" and "Advertising Achievements", on one hand; "Ideological Discourse", "Proposal", "Critical Message" and "Defensive Message", on the other. Tweets categorized within the first three are considered as low quality messages in terms of participation. They are focused on @Pablo_Iglesias_' self-promotion. The last four appear to be considerably more promising as far as they set up an ideological bulwark that may propitiate political debates. Personalization of politics, a further category called "Human Side", has been also taken into consideration, being matched as a form of low quality participation. The category "Call for Action" represents @Pablo_Iglesias_' requests to his supporters, and the quality in terms of participation depends on his sollicitations, which could either be self-promoting petitions or requests for citizens' opinion. Moreover, every tweet with a specific aim not listed above has been classified as Other.

In order to note the theme, we followed the same procedure for all tweets and retweets, using the categories employed by the Spanish public opinion research organism Centro Superior de Investigaciones Sociológicas (CIS): 20 categories that we had previously split into two different macro-types based on political participation. The first group includes 16 themes related to political engagement that may represent valuable political interaction. It is the case of "National, International and Regional Politics", "Economy", "Employment", "Population", "Environment", "Housing", "Health", "Justice", "Science and Technology", "Education", "Social Problems", "Media", "Culture", "Sports" and "Ideology". The second group incorporates three topics, "Political Activity", "Political Leader" and "Electoral Campaign", all of them linked to political theatricals. By contrast, these three categories are likely to represent trivial political participation. The remaining category has been called "Other" to note any other theme not listed above.

The use of hashtags and mentions has been approached not only to quantify them, but to evaluate whether @Pablo_Iglesias_ is using these resources to create or maintain a dialogue (a new debate or a pre-existing one, mentioning users or topics placed outside his party), to call upon electors to take part in a certain action or to ask them for their support or, on the contrary, whether he uses hashtags and mentions as a repeated source of promotion (mentioning only what provides more visibility to his proposals). We have followed the same method when taking into account links. Apart from knowing their number, we evaluate which ones have enriched political discourse by considering their contribution to the debate.

Retweets, favourites and comments received by @Pablo_Iglesias_ in all of his tweets have been also considered, though they give us few clues about his interaction. The keys about real interaction have been obtained with the second part of the analysis: the 527 responses sent on 8th, 15th and 22nd of May. We have distinguished between conversations, when Pablo Iglesias replies to users, and comments, when users respond to @Pablo_Iglesias_ but they do not receive a reply from him. Both cases are evaluated and categorized: even when the politician does not reply to public opinion received, comments are still instances in which the public expresses its political concerns and aspirations.

The categories employed in this case are Authorship, Theme, Intention and Quality. Authorship and Theme follow the same parameters applied in the analysis of @Pablo_Iglesias_' tweets. Those comments in which we have found a clear intention have been categorized as "Favourable", "Unfavourable", "Neutral" or "Question", depending on the reaction showed when facing the politician tweets. Not only have we described the content of the tweets written by the users, but we have also measured their quality according to *consistency* with the theme of the original tweet posted by the politician, and *relevance*, when a comment raises or addresses a politically main issue.

11.2 Tweeting style: the account's activity

All 322 tweets registered during the campaign were published in a changing frequency, which we could define as irregular. The maximums coincided with the initial, half-way and last stages of the campaign: 31 tweets for the 9th, 26 for the

16th and again 31 for the 23rd. Before and after these peaks, ups and downs were registered in the number of tweets published, minima taking place on the 8th (12 tweets), the 18th (7 tweets) and the 24th (4 tweets).

However, not all messages were tweeted by @Pablo_Iglesias_. Leaving aside retweets, representing some 28 % of all published in his account, we counted that 77 % of tweets are written by the communication team, and only 23 % of them can be attributed to @Pablo_Iglesias_. Taking into account these data, we have plotted the following graph, showing the evolution of the account through the campaign, counting tweets published by the politician, tweets written by his team and retweets separately.

*Fig. 1 Amount and authorship of Tweets published by the account @Pablo_Iglesias_*

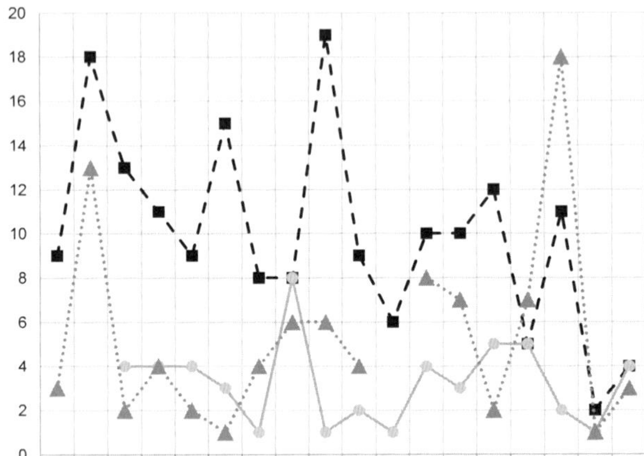

	8	9	10	11	12	13	14	15	16	17	18	19	20	21	22	23	24	25
TEAM	9	18	13	11	9	15	8	8	19	9	6	10	10	12	5	11	2	4
POLITICIAN			4	4	4	3	1	8	1	2	1	4	3	5	5	2	1	4
RETWEETS	3	13	2	4	2	1	4	6	6	4		8	7	2	7	18	1	3

As seen in the table, maximums are powered by retweets on 9th and especially on 23rd, in the final drive of the campaign. The most significant differences between authorship are placed on these three peaks, as well as the 13th and 21st. In these five cases, politicians published less tweets than their teams. Indeed, if Pablo Iglesias personally posted as many tweets as his team on 15th, 22nd and 25th, he posted none on 8th and 9th, the two very first days of the campaign. On the whole, *Podemos'* communication team posted 179 tweets, three times more than the politician, who posted 32 tweets. The retweets totalled 91, doubling the politician's ones.

As previously mentioned, retweets registered their maximum on 23rd, having another outstanding rise at the beginning of the campaign, on 9th. The lowest numbers were counted on the first and last day, and 10th and 13th. This last day Pablo Iglesias only retweeted once, while his publications were on the rise, above all those written by his team. Taking into account the information collected, it becomes clear that Pablo Iglesias' account gets its quantitative intensity thanks to his team's publications and not by his own tweets, which really appears to show that the importance the politician gave to Twitter, as a good monitoring tool for being in closer touch with the elector's worries, remained secondary. The same attitude seems to be shared by the politician's team, which at certain moments of the campaign left it to be filled by retweets, without maintaining about their own contributions to the account. The irregular rhythm of the account's publications could suggest the lack of a comprehensive plan or communication program specially designed for Twitter.

On the contrary, in relation to retweets, favourites and comments, as showed in the graphs placed below, the evolution is much more regular, as they follow a similar progression through the campaign:

*Fig. 2 Retweets, favourites and comments received by @Pablo_Iglesias_*

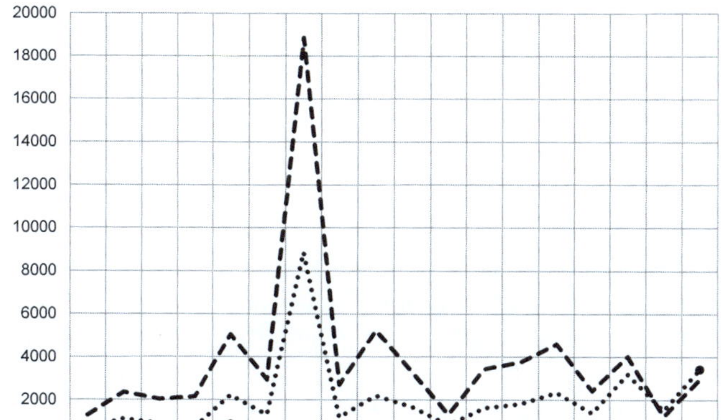

	8	9	10	11	12	13	14	15	16	17	18	19	20	21	22	23	24	25
RETWEETS	1294	2355	2039	2161	5053	2939	18851	2705	5239	3295	1322	3437	3763	4604	2428	4035	1259	2970
FAVOURITES	636	1127	890	739	2222	1311	8865	1188	2201	1678	837	1634	1819	2352	1399	3203	1515	3432
COMMENTS	180	370	382	169	970	317	290	269	584	323	171	540	291	319	224	260	38	191

Numbers of retweets are always greater than favourites and comments, while the latter, by contrast, is placed everyday below retweets and favourites. Nevertheless, the maximum was registered for the three of them on 14th making a huge difference when compared to the days before and after. Other peaks were registered on 12th and 16th, and at the final stage of the campaign, on 21st and 23rd. On the whole, we could say these peaks coincide with the amount of publications made each day: the more tweets are published, the more retweets, favourites and comments are gained by the politician. There is a noteworthy quantitative difference between these parameters on 14th, the day on which @Pablo_Iglesias_ received great attention when publishing a joke about the Popular Party: a witty comparison between the envelopes used by propaganda mailing and the ones used to bribe, which means the peak is not due to a participation with significant serious political content.

On the whole, this close and proportional relationship between the three variables mentioned could be a benchmark of the expectation created by @Pablo_Iglesias_' messages. The users are continuously waiting for his words in order to reply, to retweet or to give them a favourite, and the more tweets they read, the more they interact.

Considering all tweets published by @Pablo_Iglesias_, a total of 75 mentions have been counted, which means less than a quarter of all published: 23 % of tweets written included them. 29 turned out to be self-mentions, what means that @Pablo_Iglesias_ mentioned one of the accounts owned by his party or his party's leaders, 38,6 % of times he used the mention resource. Among the self-mentions, *Podemos*' account (@ahorapodemos) was the most significant consistently mentioned, followed by a varied range of mentions that included *Podemos*' local bases placed in different cities (@PodemosBerlin, @PodemosCordoba, @PodemosMalaga, @PodemosSa, @PODEMOS_LH) or Podemos' leaders such as Pablo Echenique (@pnique), Lola Sánchez Caldentey (@LolaPodemos), Tania González Peñas (@TaniaGonzalezPS) or Teresa Rodríguez (@TeresaRodr_). 46 tweets were mentioning accounts without any direct relation with the politician and his party, more than a half of times Pablo Iglesias' account used the mention resource. Among these, the accounts of the opposition candidates for the European Parliament were the most mentioned, Popular Party's Miguel Arias Cañete (@AriasCanete_, @Canete2014_) and Socialist Elena Valenciano (@ElenaValenciano). Mentions to both candidates always included a critical message and real debates with them or others and the ideological-political exchange that we would take as a given in a campaign are rarely achieved by the use of this resource.

However, there is an exception, which is not used too many times, but which we would like to highlight: @Pablo_Iglesias_ used a combination of the mentions @AriasCanete_ and @ElenaValenciano with #CaraACaraTVE, the hashtag used by Spanish national network RTVE for a debate between the candidates of the two Spanish majority parties. The appearance of the hashtag seemed aimed to criticise the absence of the rest of the parties and, in some way, @Pablo_Iglesias_ and *Podemos* used these Twitter resources to take part in the debate overcoming the setback.

These two recurring mentions are followed by the Spanish television morning magazine Mañanas Cuatro (@mananascuatro), where Pablo Iglesias eventually participated. This latter means a sort of self-mention, considering that the politician used it in order to inform people about his activity, his participation in the program, relaying some of his appearances. On the whole, mentions seem to be used to spread news of the politician's activity which, added to the extensive use of self-mentions, turns the use of Twitter mentions into trivial political participation.

Fig. 3 – The frequency of all mentions used (number of times each one appears during the campaign). The ones highlighted indicate self-mentions.

@ahorapodemos	11	@DcaValle	1
@mananascuatro	6	@ensanro	1
@ElenaValenciano	5	@espebuitrago	1
@publico_es	5	@FacuDiazT	1
@Canete2014_	4	@Grayfields	1
@pnique	4	@IsabelDuran_	1
@_Rubalcaba_	2	@juventudsin	1
@AriasCanete_	2	@la_informacion	1
@cuatro	2	@la_tuerka	1
@eldiario	2	@LaManoPeli	1
@Ierrejon	2	@LolaPodemos	1
@TaniaGonzalezPs	2	@marienkadner	1
@TeresaRodr_	2	@MonederoJC	1
@Ainhat	1	@PODEMOS_LH	1
@Armeteo	1	@PodemosBerlin	1
@berlunes	1	@PodemosCordoba	1
@Caminator	1	@PodemosMalaga	1
@CasaReal	1	@PodemosSa	1
@CSOALaMadrenha	1	@podemosuvieu	1
		@Zamora24horas	1

Pablo Iglesias used hashtags in four out of ten tweets, and all of the most significant ones present a clear attempt to spread and promote Podemos, with claims such as #DifundePodemos, #Podemos1000razones, #YoVotoPodemos and #Podemos25M. Only two of the hashtags registered covered public concerns, such as unemployment (#ParadosM4) and retirement (#Jubilados). #SinBancosPodemos was used to highlight *Podemos*' independence from banks financing and show its crowdfunding efforts. Nevertheless, the three hashtags mentioned were used only on one occasion. One more time, as said above about mentions, Pablo Iglesias is using Twitter hashtags for two main purposes: contributing to his party propaganda and criticising the opposition and the political establishment, which avoids political exchanges and closer dialogue with citizens.

Fig. 4 – The frequency of all hashtags used (number of times each one appears during the campaign).

#YoVotoPodemos	19	#Sevilla	2
#DifundePodemos	13	#Gracias	1
#SinBancosPodemos	11	#democracia	1
#VotandoPodemos	11	#España	1
#ClaroQuePodemos	10	#Europa	1
#Podemos1000Razones	10	#Jubílalos	1
#Podemos25M	9	#LaMadenaNunPieslla	1
#CartaPodemos	7	#LosSimpson	1
#QueTeneisQueEsconder	7	#Madrid	1
#Podemos	6	#Mafalda	1
#CaraACaraTVE	5	#Málaga	1
#25M	3	#Málaga	1
#Alicante	2	#NadaQueEsconder	1
#Almería	2	#ParadosM4	1
#Berlin	2	#Quino	1
#Cultura	2	#TomamosLesPlaces	1
#JuegoDeTronos	2	#VotandoPodemos	1
#literatura	2	#Zaragoza	1

Links counted present similar numbers: about half of the tweets (45 %) incorporated a link. Most of them (28 %) are photographs, which are employed to publicize political acts and show *Podemos*' propaganda. We have also found an extensive use of journalistic pieces linked (25 %), above all to the interviews made with @Pablo_Iglesias_ during the campaign, and a huge variety of videos (16 %), though the vast majority of them spread the official video made by *Podemos* for the campaign. Moreover, the large number of times *Podemos*' official video was repeatedly announced showed a lack of creativity and digital resources, and highlighted again that @Pablo_Iglesias_' main goal, in terms of hypertextuality, is to achieve the highest efficiency in promoting his party, even when political public concerns are left aside.

As noted in the methodological introduction, the appearance of hashtags as well as links has a significant meaning that goes beyond the interest of measuring: they show the politician's willingness to introduce into his account a new debate based on the concerns of the Spanish public or to participate in a pre-existing discussion. However, as predicted above, the cases observed during the European campaign do not support the idea that @Pablo_Iglesias_' uses these tools to introduce qualitatively relevant political debates. Hashtags and links were published in about half of the messages, but their intention is invariably related to either the candidate himself or the party, rather than towards significant political, ideological or public issues.

Moreover, @Pablo_Iglesias_' trend to include references to his own party is confirmed by the source of his retweets. As showed in the graph placed below, the 60,44 % of the publications retweeted came from *Podemos*, which added to the 5,48 % from Podemos politicians and the 2,20 % of *Podemos* base politics, means that the 68,12 % of all retweets are based on *Podemos* proposals and propaganda, leaving only a much lower 12,09 % to citizens. @Pablo_Iglesias_ did not make electors the main characters of his campaign. The account seemed to be setting them aside.

Fig. 5 – Sources of retweets

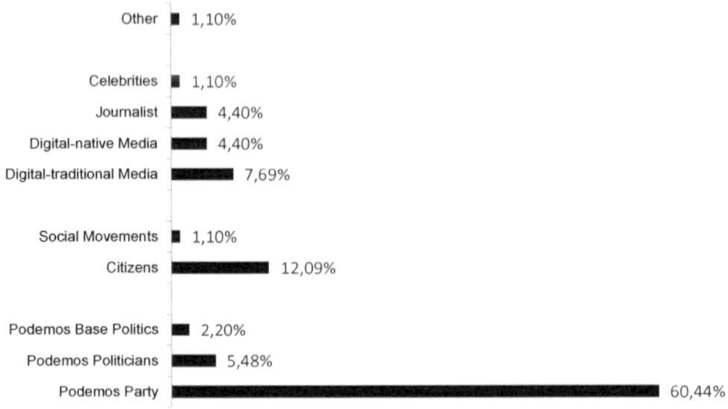

11.3 Account content: themes and intentions

As noted in the methodological introduction, the 20 categories used to classify tweets' and retweets' theme were divided into two different macro-types based on political participation. Two of the categories that belong to the group linked to political theatricals are placed in the top three. The topic *Electoral Campaign* represents 28.9 % of all published by @Pablo_Iglesias_, while *Political Activity* takes a 17.7 %, the first and the third positions in the ranking of themes considered, respectively.

Fig. 6 – Number of tweets published by themes

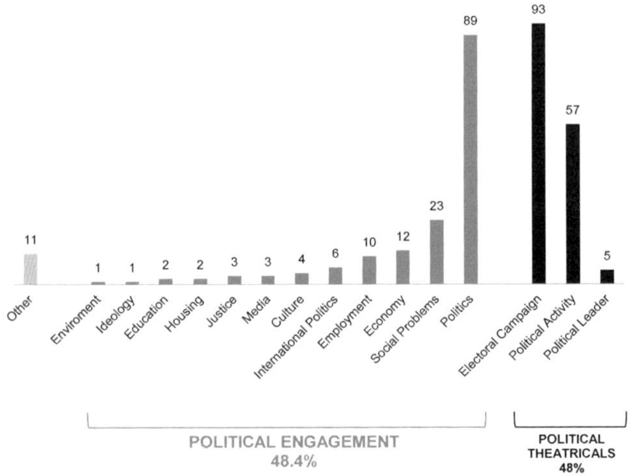

Indeed, if we put together by groups the numbers placed in the graph seen above, the one that represents political theatricals obtained a total of 48 %, while political engagement covered 48.4 % of tweets published. The remaining 3.4 % is referred to the category *Other*, where a huge and varied range of issues related to very specific conflicts were covered. Almost half of the total publications of the @Pablo_Iglesias_ account are thus likely to represent trivial political participation (political theatricals), while the other half may represent valuable political interaction (political engagement).

Furthermore, when talking about *Electoral Campaign*, Pablo Iglesias referred directly to elections, urging people to vote for *Podemos* and using some of the hashtags already mentioned, which were created explicitly for that goal, mainly #YoVotoPodemos, #VotandoPodemos, #Podemos25M and #Podemos1000Razones. Moreover, he used Twitter to promote campaign tactics and methods, such as encouraging Podemos' supporters to mailshot the party's propaganda (strengthening the traditional campaign), as well as calling on them to adopt the graphic avatar of the party as their profile photo to show their preference for *Podemos* (taking advantage of digital native resources). In both cases, the hashtag normally attached was #DifundePodemos, though in the ones specifically referring to mailshots, #CartaPodemos appeared occasionally. This last hashtag implies an interesting action, as it is the use of Twitter to create a closer and stronger relationship between the political campaign and *Podemos*' supporters. Though the hashtag was used by the politician on very few occasions, its appearance is important in order to highlight an original and unique use of Twitter: #CartaPodemos underscores Twitter's characteristic interaction and participation features, letting citizens become a part of the campaign and responsible for *Podemos*' triumph. It is a resource Jungherr (2010) proved to be a successful tool in creating strong communities during the German elections on 2009 and a strategy the two main Spanish political leaders did not use on Twitter during the 2011 legislative campaign (Cebrián and Vázquez, 2013).

Political Activity referred the vast majority of times to announcements or dissemination of news about political rallies and @Pablo_Iglesias_' appearances in the media. These tweets were often published linked to a photo, showing the rally poster or the politician surrounded by his supporters where the rally took place, or a streaming video link, where users could find the live program.

As opposed to this, the top two themes raised from the group related to political engagement are *Politics* (27,6 %) and *Social Problems* (7,1 %), which ranked, respectively, second and fourth in the general ranking. Among the specific issues covered by both themes, we concluded after the content evaluation that @Pablo_Iglesias_ focused his messages mainly on political parties and political leaders, followed by the ones about political institutions, demonstrations and social movements, this latter because 15th May was the anniversary of the protests that took place on 2011, and which gave their name to the 15-M Movement.

Following the Spanish research institute Centro de Investigaciones Sociológicas, we adopted the ranking of public political concerns which featured in the barometer that this institution produced for May 2014. The aim of this is to compare the ten national issues that Spaniards were most concerned about with the ones with national importance covered by Pablo Iglesias' tweets, in order to establish whether *Podemos'* leader was tweeting about the electors' worries or not during the campaign.

Among the top ten worries collected by the CIS, half of them were covered by Pablo Iglesias' publications: *Unemployment, Corruption and Fraud, Economic Problems, Political Parties and Leaders and Treasury and Fiscal Policies,* which summed up a total of 99 tweets. The rest of them, excluding the undefined *Other*, were not covered at all by *Podemos'* leader: Health, *Education, Social Conflicts and Immigration.* Indeed, 1 out of 3 tweets published by the politician's account dealt with any one of the CIS' issues, though, as can be seen in the table below, the level of importance changes when comparing one to another. Thus, *Unemployment*, the topic that concerns most Spanish citizens, occupies the third position on @Pablo_Iglesias_' priorities. On the contrary, the politician dedicates most of his messages to talk about *Political parties and leaders*, a theme that only worries electors in fourth place.

Fig. 7 – Top 10 ranking of Spanish public concerns covered by the CIS' barometer and Pablo Iglesias' account

	CIS' barometer	**Pablo Iglesias**
1	Unemployment (80,80 %)	Political parties and leaders (12,42 % / 40 tweets)
2	Corruption and Fraud (35,70 %)	Corruption and Fraud (7,14 % / 23 tweets)
3	Economic Problems (28,60 %)	Unemployment (3,11 % / 10 tweets)
4	Political parties and leaders (25,60 %)	Economic Problems (2,80 %, 9 tweets)
5	Health (10,40 %)	Social Movements (1,86 % / 6 tweets)
6	Education (8,7 %)	National Establishment (1,24 % / 4 tweets)
7	Social Conflicts (7,9 %)	International Affaires (0, 93 % / 3 tweets)
8	Other (5,3 %)	Other (0,93 % / 3 tweets)
9	Treasury and fiscal policies (4,8 %)	Treasury and fiscal policies (0,62 % / 2 tweets)
10	Immigration (4,3 %)	International Institutions (0,62 % / 2 tweets)

A quick glimpse of the percentages of *Intentions* achieved by @Pablo_Iglesias_ gives us the key to complete and to understand data provided by *Themes* covered: self-promotion and the spread of Podemos rallies was the most significant intention of @Pablo_Iglesias_' campaign, thus "Visibility of the Politician" and "Achievements Advertising" (33.2 %), followed by his critical messages (26.7 %) and calls for action (13.4 %). Thus, the intentions registered totally suit the top themes covered.

When talking about "Electoral Campaign" and "Political Activity" the intentions falls on urging his supporters to help and to vote *Podemos* and the announcements of his presence in political rallies and the media. This preference for self-promotion, propaganda and continuous and repetitive requests for assistance to supporters sidestep the political arena, making half of the campaign a showcase where the electors could find accurate personal information about Pablo Iglesias, but not necessarily as much information corresponding to dominant subjects of public interest.

Furthermore, the tweets focused on "Politics" and "Social Problems" generally criticize the opposition parties and leaders as well as the actions taken by them to solve the problems that concern Spaniards. The intention "Critical Message" was at the methodological introduction considered to be promising as far as it could set up an ideological bulwark that might propitiate political debates. However, that relationship with critics led Pablo Iglesias to avoid *Unemployment* as the first and most significant topic. During the second quarter of 2014, considering data provided by the Spanish National Statistics Institute (INE, 2014), unemployment was recovering, showing for the first time in the last six years positive figures. That recovery prevented @Pablo_Iglesias_ from focussing his critics on unemployment. On the whole, because of @Pablo_Iglesias_' determination to focus his discourse on a critical view, he even obviates the opportunity to build constructive dialogue and engagement, wasting again the chance to propose new solutions to issues which were causing considerable concern to the electors.

11.4 Interaction: from citizens to Pablo Iglesias

As anticipated in the introduction, we learn more about @Pablo_Iglesias_' interaction through the comments he received and the conversations he established with electors. As set out in the methodology, we have chosen three significant dates running through the campaign that represent three different stages of it (*supra*).

First of all, interaction around the account @Pablo_Iglesias_' is primarily due to the 527 comments/answers received by users. Thus, the research about interaction had to be influenced and framed since the very beginning by the claim that @Pablo_Iglesias_ did not really interact with the users, because he did not establish a conversation with the voters, missing out opportunities to set up a dialogue that could either answer people's concerns or criticism. Noteworthy is this absence of any kind of real interaction, if we keep in mind that *Podemos* claims have been focused on the effort to increase civic participation, and indeed Pablo Iglesias himself tended to put this forward when participating on media shows and newspaper interviews, presenting himself as a leader sensitive to citizens' concerns. The reality of his usage seems to be in stark contrast to this: @Pablo_Iglesias_ only used the "reply" option once.

Therefore, it is not @Pablo_Iglesias_ but the electors' attempts at interaction that were measured. Because the candidate is not carrying out the effort to be linked with citizen's concerns, the voters were the only ones attempting to establish a dialogue with the candidate and be closer to him, and hence the only source of data to analyze.

If we have talked so far about "citizens" and "electors", it is because percentages are very clear when showing the source of comments: 92 % of the total comes from citizens with no direct political affiliations indicated on their Twitter profiles. From the political scene, 6 % correspond to *Podemos*' own politicians, while 1 % is related to a range of *Podemos*' local political bases from different Spanish cities. These two groups involved themselves in dialogue to interact with citizens, answering the requests made, resolving some concerns already posed and, in conclusion, trying to accomplish some of the interaction eluded by @Pablo_Iglesias_. The remaining 1 % corresponds to journalists. This last 1 % rate may highlight the low interest showed by journalists to ask the candidate questions via Twitter, and the inconsistent media hype generated around Podemos and his leader.

Turning now to Themes evoked by citizens those three days, *Politics* is the most significant one, 40 % of the total, with concerns ranging from political parties and leaders to social movements. *Social Problems* such as fraud and corruption registered 14 %, occupying the third place right after *Other* (19 %), a huge range of topics whose variety made a specific analysis impossible, though many of them could be explained when getting a glimpse to the quality of the comments: 29 % of the total are irrelevant and incoherent, which means that 153 comments do not have any consistency with the theme of the original tweet posted by the politician and do not raise or address a political main issue. 68 % of comments are relevant and coherent, while the remaining 3 % is incoherent, not related to the topic posted by @Pablo_Iglesias_, but relevant in terms of politics.

*Fig. 8 – Percentages of the themes covered by the user's comments, and compared to the ones post by @Pablo_Iglesias_*

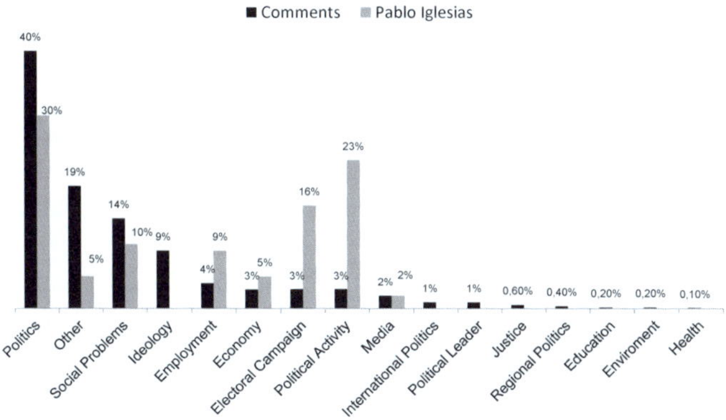

When talking about the citizens' *Intention*, the graph placed below shows us that half of them are *Favourable* to @Pablo_Iglesias_:

Fig. 9 – Comments' intention

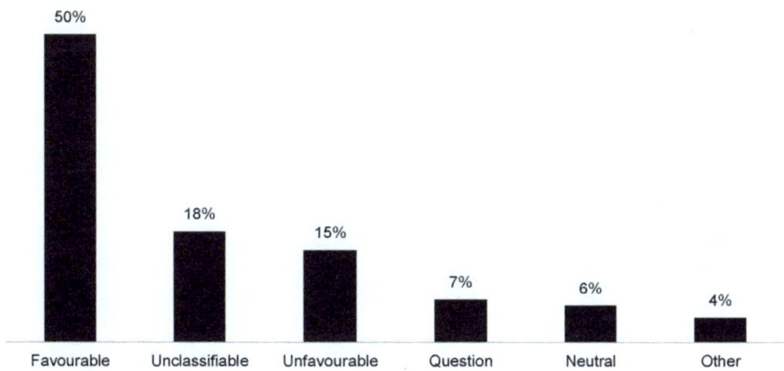

The high numbers presented by *Unclassifiable* comments can be explained, again, through the large portion of incoherent and irrelevant ones. The data collected by *Question*, combined by the total absence of @Pablo_Iglesias_dialogue, shows that at least 37 citizens' requests have not been directly replied to / dealt with.

11.5 Conclusions

The analysis developed throughout this chapter confirms a significant difference between the "new politics style" attributed to *Podemos* by the media, and the political communication strategy materialized in the Twitter account @Pablo_Iglesias_ during the European Election campaign.

First, the emphasis placed by the media on Pablo Iglesias as representing a renewed style of leadership was not materialized in the account's contents during the campaign:

1. Most of the tweets posted in @Pablo_Iglesias_ were written by his team (77 %), which reflects that the politician's attention was not focused on tweeting, throwing away the opportunity to address directly the citizens, without the mediatisation of other conventional channels.
2. The Twitter account even seems to have been considered as a minor channel during the European campaign: the intensity achieved by @Pablo_Iglesias_ at certain significant moments of the campaign, such as the final stage, is due to retweets, which means these moments are not followed by an extra effort by the team to manage Twitter and post its own original material on it.
3. @Pablo_Iglesias_ used Twitter operators and functions such as mentions, hashtags, links and retweets in order to promote Podemos' political acts and to inform people about his own participation in them as well as criticizing the opposition's procedures. As a general rule, very few attempts were made during the campaign to use these tools as a means to encourage political exchange between candidates, to discuss Spanish public concerns or to establish a real dialogue in order to be aware of citizens' opinions.
4. Self-promotion and propaganda for Podemos were the main goals achieved by Pablo Iglesias' account. The continuous and repetitive requests for assistance and support brought the absence of a real and interesting campaign based on the main goal of establishing a dialogue founded on citizens' concerns.
5. The themes covered by Pablo Iglesias' account highlight once more the importance the politician gave to self-promotion and propaganda, above all when considering that political engagement's top theme (*Politics*) was destined to criticize the opposition, avoiding the opportunity to achieve a political exchange between candidates and enrich the Spanish political scene by covering citizens' concerns with it. Moreover, differences between the CIS barometer and @Pablo_Iglesias_ thematic showed again the lack of attention when evaluating Spaniards' real worries and interests.

Second, the dialogical style proposed by Podemos as a sign of his renewed politics is not materialized in the @Pablo_Iglesias_ account during the European campaign.

6. Although the bidirectional expectations are confirmed by the figures of retweets, favourites and comments obtained, Pablo Iglesias' profile answers just once during all the campaign misusing the opportunity for personalized contact and dialogue with voters.
7. Contact and dialogue were presumably comfortable considering that most of the comments were favourable. The close and proportional relation between the retweets, favourites and comments obtained by Pablo Iglesias' tweets confirms the users' interest in Pablo Iglesias' publications: the more the politician tweets, the more his supporters interact.
8. On comparing the themes achieved by Pablo Iglesias and those posted by the citizens through their comments, significant differences were found: while citizens' concerns appear to be *Social Problems* and *Ideology*, Pablo Iglesias chose to engage in political theatricals and political parties and leaders.

Globally considered, the exposed results clearly suggest that Podemos' aspiration to renew Spanish political discourse on Twitter has not been achieved, on the whole, by its leader's account. The actions performed are not understood as opportunities to foster political dialogue with the public or as a chance to allow citizens to employ their Twitter accounts as a means to invigorate political interaction.

References

Bollero, David: "Podemos se consolida como la primera fuerza política en redes sociales". *Público*, 16.8.2014, from http://www.publico.es/politica/consolida-primera-fuerza-politica-redes.html

Cebrián, Elena / Vázquez, Tamara / Sarias, David: "Is Twitter Invigorating Spanish Democracy? A Study of Political Interaction Through The Accounts of The Prime Minister and The Leader of the Main Opposition Party". In: Frame, Alex / Brachotte, Gilles (eds.): *Citizen Participation and Political Communication*. Routledge: London, 2015, pp. 60–80.

Cebrián, Elena / Vázquez, Tamara / Olabarrieta, Ane: "¿Participación y democracia en los medios sociales?: El caso de Twitter en las elecciones vascas de 2012". *adComunica* (6), 2013, pp. 39–63, from http://www.adcomunicarevista.com/ojs/index.php/adcomunica/article/download/132/155

Cebrián, Elena / Vázquez, Tamara: "@marianorajoy VS @conRubalcaba: La campaña electoral de 2011 en las cuentas oficiales de Twitter de los candidatos del PP y del PSOE". In: Römer, Max (ed.): *Miradas a las pantallas en el bolsillo*. Universidad Camilo José Cela: Madrid, 2013, pp. 93–108.

Centro de Investigaciones Sociológicas (CIS): *Barómetro de mayo 2014 (3024)*, retrieved 6.6.2015 from http://www.cis.es/cis/export/sites/default/-Archivos/Marginales/3020_3039/3024/es3024mar.pdf

Instituto Nacional de Estadística (INE): *Encuesta de Población Activa (EPA). Segundo trimestre de 2014*, retrieved 7.8.2015 from http://www.ine.es/daco/daco42/daco4211/epa0214.pdf

Jungherr, Andreas: *Twitter in politics: Lessons Learned during the German Superwahljahr 2009*, retrieved 32.8.2015 from http://cs.unc.edu/~julia/accepted-papers/Superwahljahr.pdf

Minder, Raphael: "Spanish Upstart Party Said It Could, and Did. Now the Hard Part Begins". *The New York Times*, 29.5.2014, from http://www.nytimes.com/2014/05/29/world/europe/spanish-upstart-party-said-it-could-and-did-now-the-hard-part-begins.html?_r=1

Parmelee, John H. / Bichard, Shannon L.: Politics and the twitter revolution: How tweets influence the relationship between political leaders and the public. Lexington Books: Maryland, 2011.

Pérez, Pedro L. / Berná, Celia / Arroyas, Enrique: "La interpretación simbólica de los deshaucios en España a través del frame: un análisis semántico de la conversación en Twitter". In: Lloves, Beatriz / Segado, Francisco (eds.): *Actas del I Congreso Internacional de Comunicación y Sociedad Digital*. Universidad Internacional de La Rioja: Logroño, 2013, retrieved 6.6.2015 from http://dialnet.unirioja.es/descarga/articulo/4247767.pdf

The Economist. "Exit Rubalcaba. The Socialist leader quits after a humiliating election defeat". 29.5.2014, from http://www.economist.com/news/europe/21603040-socialist-leader-quits-after-humiliating-election-defeat-exit-rubalcaba

Trendinalia: *Trending topics en Twitter en España el 26 de mayo de 2014*, retrieved 13.8.2015 from http://www.trendinalia.com/twitter-trending-topics/spain/spain-140526.html

Zurutuza, Cristina: "¿De qué habla Rubalcaba cuando tweetea? La campaña del candidato socialista en Twitter para las elecciones del 20N". In: Mora, Alberto (ed.): *Actas del I Congreso Internacional en Comunicación Política y Estrategias de Campaña*. Universidad de Murcia: Murcia, 2012, retrieved 6.5.2015 from http://www.alice-comunicacionpolitica.com/abrir-ponencia.php?f=249-F50000aa32491342180003-ponencia-1.pdf

List of Contributors

Dr Elena Albu is a Swiss Government Excellence Scholarship holder at the University of Geneva. She completed her PhD dissertation "The Pragmatics of Negative Structures in Political Discourse: A Relevance Theoretic Approach" in September 2012. She conducts empirical research into various aspects of language structure and her research interests are found at the interface between pragmatics, discourse analysis, corpus linguistics and computer-mediated communication.

Mario Anastasiadis, M.A. is research assistant at the University of Bonn/Germany, Department for Media Studies. His research interests are social media and political communication, media and popular culture, popular music in the media, extremism on the internet and qualitative methods (online and offline). In the research project *Deliberation on the Net,* which is part of the DFG priority programme *Mediatized Worlds* (funded by the German Science Foundation) he is dealing with questions of online media logics and media change within the framework of political discourses on Twitter. E-mail: anastasiadis@medienwissenschaft.uni-bonn.de, Twitter: @M_Anastasiadis

Ian Basaille-Gahitte is a PhD student in Computer Science at the the Electronics, Informatics and Image Laboratory (LE2I) UMR CNRS 6306, at the University of Burgundy (Dijon, France). He is also a research engineer at a French company, where he works on client relationship management and social media.

Fernando Bonete Vizcaino is PhD student and assistant professor at CEU San Pablo University (Madrid, Spain), where he graduated in Humanities and Journalism in 2013. He is also running his professional career as internal communication manager at CEU Educational Group, Spain's main university corporation. He is a member of the INCIR TV ("Internet, Radio and Television Convergence") research group, where he specialises in information and communications technology and media convergence. E-mail: fernando.bonetevizcaino@ceu.es

Dr Gilles Brachotte is associate professor in Communication Science at the University of Burgundy, member of the CIMEOS/3S research team (EA 4177) and teaches at the web design department of Dijon-Auxerre Technological Institute (IUT Dijon-Auxerre). After started his career as an IT / networks teacher, his research has taken him into the field of communication science and more specifically ICT usage. He focuses on the way ICT is used in practice and more generally on social change resulting from adoption and integration of ICT in society, notably among young people and in the political sphere. His research focuses on the discursive, social, ergonomic and technical dimensions which are sources of meaning and contribute to complexify the communication processes involved. E-mail: Gilles.brachotte@u-bourgogne.fr.

Dr Elena Cebrián Guinovart is a lecturer at CEU San Pablo University, in Madrid (Spain), where she teaches Communication and Information Theory. Her research interests include Political Infotainment, Political Communication in Social Media and Religion in the Media. Current research focuses on the implications of social media on political participation. She was a visiting researcher at Pontificia Università della Santa Croche (Rome, Italy) in 2007 and 2009. E-mail: ecebrian@ceu.es

Vittorio Cobianchi is researcher for Cares-Osservatorio di Pavia; his main areas of research interest are textual analysis and textual data mining, and social network data mining. He is adjunct professor at Università di Milano-Bicocca. Among other publications, he contributed to the writing of the books *Lo spettacolo della politica. Protagonismo e servizio nel talk-show* (The Show of Politics), Rai-Eri, Roma 1998, and *Il caso Di Bella nella televisione e nella stampa italiana* (The Di Bella affaire as portrayed by Italian media), Rai-Eri, Roma 1999. E-mail: vcobianchisservatorio.it.

Dr Dario Compagno is Assistant Professor at the New Sorbonne University in Paris, where he teaches Semiotics and Social Network Analysis to undergraduate Communication students. Graduated in Italy from the University of Bologna and the University of Siena, his research focuses on digital objects (websites, social media, computer games) and their meaning, from a semiotic perspective. He is a member of the MCPN (EA 1484 – CIM) and the CREM (EA 3476) research groups.

Dr. Jessica Einspänner-Pflock is research assistant at the University of Bonn/ Germany, Department for Media Studies. She studied new media and communications in Bonn and Singapore, finishing her PhD in Bonn in 2015. Her research interests are social media and political communication, social interaction online, online privacy, public relations, digital methods. She is a member of the DFG priority programme *Mediatized* Worlds, where she deals with questions of online media logics and media change within the framework of political discourses on Twitter. E-mail: jep@uni-bonn.de, Twitter: @einpflock

Dr Alex Frame is associate professor in Communication Science at the Languages and Communication Faculty of the University of Burgundy (Dijon, France), where he runs the MA course in Intercultural Management. Born in Britain, he graduated from the University of Oxford in 1998, before settling in France and completing his PhD in Communication Science at the University of Burgundy, in 2008. He is a member of the TIL ("Texte, Image, Langage") research group (EA 4182), where he specialises in intercultural communication and comparative cross-cultural communication studies. He led the TEE2014 research project. E-mail: alexander.frame@u-bourgogne.fr.

Dr Thierry Grison received a Ph.D in 1994 in Computer Science. He is associate professor in Computer Science at the University of Burgundy, and member of the Electronics, Informatics and Image Laboratory (LE2I) UMR CNRS 6306. His research focuses on information systems, databases and data sciences.

Frédéric Junger is a PhD candidate at the University of Burgundy (Dijon, France). His thesis focuses on the staging of political personalities and more broadly on the ways in which political representation is reconfigured by the interactions that take place on digital social networks.

Dr Sergey Kirgizov is a lecturer in Computer Science at the Science and Technology Faculty of the University of Burgundy (Dijon, France). Born in Russia, he graduated from the Altai State University, before settling in France and completing his PhD in Computer Science at the Pierre and Marie Curie University (University of Paris VI), in 2014. In Paris he studied the Internet topology dynamics from network (graph) theoretical and statistical points of view. Now, he is a member of the team SISI of the research laboratory LE2I (UMR CNRS 6306), where he applies the complex networks methods in order to analyse analyse massive amounts of rich connected data.

Tatiana Kondrashova M.A. is PhD student in Communication Science at the Languages and Communication Faculty of the University of Burgundy (Dijon, France). Born in Saint-Petersburg, she graduated firstly as M.A. in linguistics and language teaching from the Herzen State University of Saint-Petersburg, and then received her M.A. in Communication Studies at the University of Burgundy. She is a member of the CIMEOS research group (EA 4177), where she works on political discourse on Twitter through contrastive and semiotic analysis. E-mail: tatiana.kondrashova@u-bourgogne.fr.

Dr Eric Leclercq received his Ph.D. in computer science from the University of Burgundy in 2000. Since 2000, he has been Associate Professor of Computer Science at the University of Burgundy, France, and member of the Electronics, Informatics and Image Laboratory (LE2I) UMR CNRS 6306. His research focuses on semantics aware data integration, semantic annotations, data models for complex networks and large scale data analytics.

Arnaud Mercier (PhD) is professor of information and communication science, at the University Panthéon-Assas (Paris), member of the CARISM research centre. Since 2014, he has been running a research program funded by the French National Research Agency, entitled, "Flow of information through social media". The purpose of this project is to study the upstream journalistic writing practices and innovative forms of action and self-presentation of editors and journalists on social networks, as well as new social practices and behaviors of Internet users, made of reappropriation, comments and (re) circulated information, via social networks & media.

Dr Maria Francesca Murru is a lecturer in Sociology of Media and Communication at the Università Cattolica di Milano, Faculty of Political and Social Sciences. Her research interests are focused on online public spheres and mediated civic participation and she is currently engaged in research projects dealing with mediated civic literacy and emergent publics. She has published in the field of media and audience research. E-mail: maria.murru@unicatt.it

Dr Nanta Novello Paglianti is associate professor in Communication Sciences at the University of Burgundy/Franche-Comte, France. She teaches semiotics and communication science. She is a member of the CIMEOS research group (EA 4177), where she specialises in mass-media communication and digital communication tools. E-mail: nanta.novello-paglianti@u-bourgogne.fr

Dr Marinette Savonnet received a Ph.D in computer science in 1996. She is associate professor in Computer Science at the University of Burgundy, and member of the Electronics, Informatics and Image Laboratory (LE2I) UMR CNRS 6306. Her research focuses on scientific information systems, semantic annotations and data models for large-scale data analytics. She is involved in several contractualized research projects, often in interdisciplinary collaborations.

Tamara Vázquez Barrio is Lecturer in Public Opinion at San Pablo CEU University (Spain). She holds a master`s degree in audio-visual production from the Complutense University of Madrid, and a further MA in needs and rights of children and youths from the Autonomous University of Madrid. She also holds a degree expert in design and statistical treatment of market research from UNED. Her research interest includes political communication, with a special attention to digital politics and politainment, and on the effects of the mass media in childhood and young people. In the latter field her particular interests are digital literacy, parental mediation and social responsibility of the mass media.

Caja Thimm, PhD, is a professor of "Media Studies and Intermediality" at the University of Bonn and head of the Institute for Language, Media and Music. She studied in Heidelberg, San Francisco and Berkeley and held positions at the Universities of Saarbrücken, Essen, and Darmstadt. She was visiting professor at UC Santa Barbara (USA), and at the Universities of Wales/Cardiff and Liverpool, (UK), and Dijon (France). She served as a member of various Enquete-Commissions, such as "Responsibility in the medatized world" and currently heads a German Foundation project on "Deliberaton online". Her main research interests are on digital cultures, social media, and political and organizational communication online. E-mail: thimm@uni-bonn.de; Twitter: @CThimm.

Dr Marina Villa is researcher in Sociology of Communication and Cultural processes at Università Cattolica of Milan/Brescia, where she teaches Theory and techniques of information. She completed her PhD in Sociology at Milan and Nanterre University (co-director: J. Mouchon). She worked in the Italian Audiovisual Regulatory Authority (AGCOM) and she collaborated with the Political Communication Observatories in Perugia and Torino. She is member of the Scientific Committee of Cares-Observatory of Communication in Pavia. Her research interests and publications are focused on political communication, journalism and public communication. E-mail: marina.villa@unicatt.it